FORGOTTEN SOLDIERS

Ordinary men whose extraordinary

deeds changed history

BRIAN MOYNAHAN

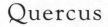

Quercus

First published in Great Britain in 2007

This paperback edition published in 2008 by
Quercus
21 Bloomsbury Square, London WC1A 2NS

Copyright © Brian Moynahan 2007

A CIP catalogue record for this book is available from the British Library

ISBN 1 84724 387 8
ISBN-13 978 1 84724 387 4

Printed and bound in Great Britain by Clays Ltd, St Ives plc

10 9 8 7 6 5 4 3 2 1

Contents

List of Maps

Picture Acknowledgements

FIRST SECTION *p.1* Private collection (upper), Corbis (middle), Keystone-France/Camera Press, London (lower); *p.2* Bundesarchiv Koblenz; *p.3* Topfoto (upper), Bundesarchiv Koblenz (lower); *p.4* National Portrait Gallery, London; *p.5* RIA Novosti (upper), Getty Images/Archive Photos (lower); *p.6* Imperial War Museum; *p.7* Imperial War Museum (upper), Private collection (left), Rex Features (right); *p.8* Corbis/ Bettmann (upper), Getty Images/Dick Swanson/Time Life Pictures (middle), Private collection (lower)

SECOND SECTION *p.1* Imperial War Museum; *p.2* Israeli Defense Forces Archive (top), *The Sunday Times* (lower); *p.3* Corbis/Bettmann (upper), Department of Defense Photo/USMC; *p.4* Courtesy Andrew Higgins Family (upper), Corbis/Bettmann (lower); *p.5* Corbis/Bettmann; *p.6* Airborne Forces Museum (upper), Private collection (lower); *p.7* Private collection (upper left), AKG/Ullstein Bild (upper right), PA Photos/Andy Butterton (lower); *p.8* Getty Images/Rischgitz (upper), Government of Japan (lower)

Introduction

"THE SOLDIER," CLAUSEWITZ WROTE, "is levied, clothed, armed, exercised, he sleeps, eats, drinks and marches, all merely to fight at the right place and at the right time."

This book relates how lowly soldiers and sailors – the most common rank is sergeant – fulfilled Carl von Clausewitz's dictum with an impact that swayed the course of a war, a campaign or a battle.

It details who they were, the war in which they were caught up, where they were and the situation they faced, and what they did. It looks at the effects of their deeds on the outcome of conflicts in which they served as part of the rank and file. It shows how their actions illuminate the different aspects of war, as classified by the great Prussian in his book, *Vom Kriege* (*On War*, first published in 1832, the year after his death).

We reverse, as it were, the old mantra. Here, one man becomes the nail that saves the shoe that saves the horse that saves the rider that saves the regiment that saves ... We might call it the Horatius Effect, after the Roman footsoldier who held the Sublican Bridge over the Tiber long enough for it to be destroyed behind him, and so single-handedly saved Rome from being overrun by Lars Porsena and the Etruscans.

Preventing defeat can be as important as creating a victory, and gathering intelligence as crucial as fighting in combat. The effort in one case here involves a single shot, in another the firing of thousands of rounds over 58 days. Unusual courage is a part of most of these stories, but it is by no means a prerequisite. In one instance, we look at a once obscure boatbuilder who never visited a theatre of war.

In time, we range from antiquity to the present. In place, from a ruined house in Stalingrad and the heights above the Sea of Galilee to the banks of the Meuse and the deeps of the North Atlantic. In people, from an American gunnery sergeant and a Roman standard bearer to a British naval pilot.

MY PERSONAL INTEREST IN THE ROLE OF the individual soldier in war dates from September 1964. As a young foreign correspondent, I spent a night in a C-123 aircraft on a flare-dropping mission over the Mekong Delta region of South Vietnam. A small outpost with an American adviser was being overrun by a large force of Viet Cong guerrillas. We could see the muzzle flashes of the two sides getting closer as the Viet Cong worked their way through the wire. Every few minutes, a Vietnamese in civilian clothes and winkle-pickers kicked a flare out of the aircraft. The two elderly American pilots, in dark glasses and baseball caps, chewing on cigars, kept the aircraft circling.

They didn't give a prayer for the outpost's survival, they said, or for the adviser. He came on the radio, very calm, and said the Viet Cong were through the wire and he needed an air strike. The pilots said they couldn't get VNAF, the Vietnamese air force, to fly at night: they put their aircraft to bed at sunset. Everyone knew that. Period. The adviser said: Well, he would light his fire arrow anyhow – a wooden arrow lit by burning kerosene lamps pointing to where he wanted ordnance dropped – and perhaps we could see what we could do to raise VNAF. If they couldn't, he thanked us for the flares anyway, and said it would be good if we could keep with him to the end.

He then got out of his bunker and lit the fire arrow, in itself an act of great courage. He came briefly back on the radio, to say that the tip of the arrow itself was the target, because the enemy were almost up to his position now. And, thanks again.

He would have melted hearts of stone. The two grizzled flare pilots began working their radio to the big airfield at Tan Son Nhut, the language fizzing blue across the dark cockpit, with pleadings and threats. They pointed out that a rogue flare ship could create a lot of very visible embarrassment if it began circling and illuminating, say, the presidential palace in Saigon. A grunt of satisfaction passed between them. It worked. Three Skyraiders came in, the napalm canisters tumbling by the fire arrow, and then they circled and strafed. The incoming muzzle flashes stopped. The adviser said the Viet Cong had broken off. Thanks again. We stayed with him till dawn, the outpost still smouldering.

It was the sense of the individual soldier that was so powerful – the person in the impersonal business of war. The American adviser had saved his own life, and those of the Vietnamese with him, by using all his qualities: courage, calmness, yes, but also psychological brilliance, the ability to perform in crisis, to touch two grumpy old men circling in the sky 2000 feet above him.

Had he been the nail in the shoe – had the saving of the outpost saved the district, which saved the province ... then he would have a place in this book. But this was a minor skirmish in a long war, and in the brutal way of things, he made little difference.

History abounds with heroes. But *our* touchstone is different. It is the *scale* of the effect created by the humble, unknown warrior: the way in which a single man of insignificant rank can, in exceptional cases, tip the balance of history itself.

1 · THE STURMPIONIER

The sergeant who ensured the Fall of France

In very rare cases, as here, a single soldier has acted as the "crack" in the enemy army in Clausewitz's warning on panic: "As with glass too quickly cooled, a single crack breaks the whole mass ... [and] changes into a kind of rodomontade of alarm, the French *sauve qui peut*" (BOOK III, CHAPTER V). The consequences were on a historic scale.

SEDAN, EASTERN FRANCE * 16:00 – 19:00 HOURS * 13 MAY 1940

IN THE LAST FEW MOMENTS OF THE *drôle de guerre*, the Phoney War, the day dawned in Paris like a "bath of the sun". The air was "sweet with the sound of unstartled birds" singing in the gardens, and the chestnuts were in bloom, shading the cobblestones where waiters would soon be setting up tables and chairs on the pavements. It was a Friday, 10 May 1940, and the city was plump with the promise of the Whitsun weekend.

Uniforms abounded. Men, as many as one in seven in some units, were on leave from the front. Fashionable women were wearing military-style outfits, Schiaparelli's "Camouflage" silk dresses, or Lanvin's "Spahi" suits, the lines taken from cavalry tunics. Horseracing had been cancelled when the war had started eight months before. Since then, so little had happened at the front that pleasures like the spring meeting at Auteil had been reprieved. The stands above the shimmering grass course would be filling with race goers in a few hours.

Further to the east, though, little tell-tale movements – by Adolf Hitler, by his tank commanders, by an assault-engineer sergeant called Walter Rubarth – hinted that this idyll was about to end.

Hitler had left Berlin aboard his personal train the evening before. The propaganda services said that he was visiting Schleswig-Holstein on the Danish border, and the train at first went north. Then it turned west and passed through Cologne before halting at Euskirchen, in the Eifel hills and forests close to the Belgian border. He transferred to a Mercedes here and was driven through villages, whose names and signposts had been removed, deep into woods of pine and birch.

The final part of his journey was along a dirt track to a group of low concrete buildings and bunkers, set beneath trees to be invisible from the air. This was the *Felsennest*, the Nest in the Rocks, one of Hitler's specially prepared field headquarters. His personal bunker had his bedroom, an office, rooms for his aides and a kitchen. It faced west, towards the Ardennes, the rocky and densely wooded hills and steep river valleys that block easy passage from Germany through Belgium and on to the plains of north-eastern France. Other bunkers held his bodyguards' quarters, a mess hall, and a conference room with a big map easel. Senior officers from OKW, the supreme command, were quartered a few hundred metres away in the Jagdhaus, an old hunting lodge lying amid meadows.

The Führer arrived a little before 04:00 German time on 10 May. French time was an hour behind. He brought with him secretaries, press aides, doctor, chef, pharmacist, photographer.

He had come to direct the biggest gamble of his life so far, and he planned to stay for some time.

That he would be done with his business – the conquest of France – so much more quickly than the world or he himself believed possible was due to others who were stirring with nervous anticipation in the chilly early hours. The commanders of the Panzer tank units, upon which all depended, had clambered aboard their armoured command vehicles, wedged tight with radios and cipher machines.

They included a still obscure brigadier general, Erwin Rommel, and, in particular, the brilliant strategist Heinz Guderian. Guderian had arrived at his corps headquarters near Bitburg in the evening. His troops and tanks were drawn up a few kilometres from the Luxembourg border. Sturmpionier Rubarth and his assault engineers were among them.

The staff of the French 2nd Army, holding a strong defensive line along the River Meuse at the western exit of the Ardennes, had spent the evening at the theatre in Sedan. They had only got back to their headquarters at 02:00, and now they were "sleeping the sleep of the just", suspecting nothing. The Belgian commander, though, whose forces lay between the French and Guderian's troops, General Keyaerts, was wide awake. His men had been listening to unusual activity over the border since midnight: engines, boots on cobblestones, muffled voices, the clatter of tank tracks. He put them on alert and prepared to blow rail and road bridges.

FALL GELB, PLAN YELLOW, THE GERMAN invasion of the West, was a wild, go-for-broke affair.

It was to use armour and mobility – "the tank engine," Guderian said, "is as much a weapon as its gun" – to cross the Ardennes forests and break through the French line at Sedan. Here the Panzers would slash across the rear of the Allied armies fighting in Belgium and Holland, to trap them against the Channel coast in a gigantic pocket.

No such penetration had been made by either side in four years of offensives on the Western Front in the First World War, despite the sacrifice of 5 million lives. The Germans were now entrusting this task to a mere three armoured corps. They were outnumbered in everything but aircraft.

The French had 104 divisions along the front, and the British 13, with an armoured division and a Highland division on their way across the Channel. Fall Gelb violated the neutrality of both Belgium and the Netherlands. Their 32 divisions were thus added to the Anglo-French forces to give an Allied strength of 149 divisions, with 14,000 artillery pieces. The Germans had 135 divisions available in the West, and only 7,378 guns.

In tanks – and Fall Gelb was an exercise in armour – the Wehrmacht was sharply inferior in quality and numbers. Its 2,439 battle tanks faced 4,204 on the Allied side. Only 278 of these were modern Panzer IVs, mounting a powerful 75mm gun, with 349 Panzer IIIs, with less effective 37mm guns. The 1,500 Panzer Is and IIs were old and poorly armoured. The under-gunned II was better than the I, which, with two machine-guns and no main gun, did not even classify as a tank by some definitions. Half the tanks in Rommel's 7th Panzer Division were not German, but seized from the Czechs.

The French and British had improved tank design continuously since 1918. It was only in 1934, after Hitler had come to power, that the Germans began development. The technology gap showed in armour and gunnery. The French Somua S-35 was the best medium tank of 1940, fast, well-armoured and with greater firepower than the Panzer III. The French heavy B-1 and B-1 bis tanks, which were armed with both turret and hull-mounted guns, had armour 60mm thick. The British Matildas had 80mm. The crews of Panzer IIIs and IVs had only 30mm of protection, and the Is and IIs less than 15mm. The French 47mm gun, too, was reckoned the best in the world.

Tank for tank, the French were more than a match for the Germans. In one action, near Sedan, a single B-1 knocked out 13 Panzers and two anti-tank guns, taking 140 hits without its hull being penetrated. By astute manoeuvre, and reconnaissance and communications, though, the Germans were usually able to avoid such debacles.

It was in the handling and the use of their tanks that they excelled. It was in fact a French general, Jean-Baptiste Estienne, who had created the world's first armoured division, the DLM, two years before the Germans. The French had three DLMs in 1940, with four DCRs, reserve armoured divisions. But they accounted for only 960 tanks, and the DCRs remained under corps or army command, locked into larger infantry outfits. They operated without air cover – no joint armour – air force manoeuvres were held – and they played little part in a strategy still wedded to the continuous front line held by infantry and fortresses. The French had 2,200 other tanks. They were tied to infantry in penny packets.

The *bataille conduite*, the closely controlled and systematic engagement, was at the heart of their thinking. French strategists held that the weight of modern firepower had doomed the *attaque à l'outrance*, the old hell-for-leather attack where local commanders seized the initiative. Defence was all. If the enemy did break through, they responded with *colmatage*, plugging the gaps with reserves in the same way as a road-mender filled in potholes with fresh gravel.

German doctrine was wholly different. The Panzers were massed into tank divisions, roaming across country like fleets of landships. They used momentum and concentrated firepower to drive their spearheads clean through defence systems, then wheeled in the enemy rear to entrap his armies. Above them, squadrons of Stuka divebombers acted as mobile artillery, blasting enemy strongpoints, and breaking his morale with the shrill sirens that accompanied their swoops on their earth-bound victims.

The invasion plan, all attack and armour, was extraordinarily bold. In effect, it hived off the elite armoured forces, and hurled them forwards scores of kilometres beyond the point at which the rest of the army could come to their aid.

The Wehrmacht of 1940 was split into ancient and modern. Only 16 of the 135 available divisions were fully motorized. Ten were Panzer divisions, and six were motorized infantry, capable of 40mph bursts. The rest moved at the pace of a horse, or of the men chanting an old mantra to the rhythm of their boots as they marched:

> *Zicke-Zacke*
> *Juppheidi*
> *das ist Deutsche*
> *Infanterie*

The Wehrmacht had only 120,000 trucks in May 1940 – the French had 300,000 – and its outdated supply wagons and gun limbers were drawn by horses.

The best-equipped, best-manned and best-trained units were gathered into Army Group A, the left wing, drawn up pointing at Luxembourg and southern Belgium. Its three motorized corps were assigned 1,900 tanks, more than three-quarters of the available strength. Guderian's XIX was the most powerful corps, with the 1st, 2nd and 10th Panzer Divisions, and the elite Gross Deutschland Regiment of motorized infantry. Army Group B on the right wing, opposite northern Belgium and Holland, was predominantly composed of infantry and horse-drawn artillery.

Fall Gelb was compared by its architect, General Erich von Manstein, to a revolving door. The campaign was to open with well-advertised assaults by Army Group B, to tempt the Allied armies to move northeast from France into Belgium and Holland, in the belief that this was where the main German thrust was developing. The fortuitous crash-landing of a Luftwaffe aircraft in Belgium in January, with documents showing this line of attack, had already predisposed the Allies to expect this.

As the French and British were sucked northwards, the true *Schwerpunkt* (focal point of attack) would be the Panzer corps of Army Group A, swinging southwest through the Ardennes for the Meuse. Once Guderian's men had crossed the river, and smashed through the French front at Sedan, the Panzers were to wheel north for the Channel, trapping the main Allied forces in a vast pocket along the coast.

This "sickle cut" depended entirely on speed. As soon as the Allies realized where the real blow was coming, they would move reserves up to block it. Guderian, who had worked on the plan with Manstein, dinned a slogan into his men: "In three days to the Meuse, on the fourth day across the Meuse." The river had to be crossed by midnight on 13 May at the latest.

If the timetable was not kept, the offensive would fail.

A PEA WHISTLE SOUNDED AT 05:25 on 10 May, startling the two Luxembourg gendarmes on duty at the Wormelange Bridge, on the border of the tiny principality. A German lieutenant came across the bridge with a drawn pistol and 20 men. One of them fired a white flare as the gendarmes put their hands up and the frontier barrier was lifted. The race to the Meuse had begun.

In three hours, the vanguard of Guderian's divisions had swept clean across Luxembourg and had reached the Belgian border at Martelange. The bridge over the River Sauer had been blown. The first armoured reconnaissance cars and a company of motorcycle troops were halted by a Belgian tank. They were also drawing heavy fire from a company of the 1st Chasseurs Ardennais infantry.

The Belgians were in prepared positions on high ground above the town, with pillboxes and fieldworks protected by minefields and barbed wire. Hermann Balck, commanding the motorized 1st Rifle Regiment, was with the lead motorcyclists. It was remarkable to find a staff officer so far forward, but the Panzers were advancing more by instinct than by the manual.

Balck ordered the men to attack straight off their motorcycles, without preparation and without support. They waded across the river and moved through the streets lining the riverbank. To close in on the defenders – each side numbered about a hundred men – they had to attack for 200 metres across open and steeply rising land. The Belgians were so startled by this suicidal approach that they hesitated, checked, and began to pull back. From early on, the campaign had a character.

The attack in the south was deliberately concealed, though, so that little news escaped from the steep-sided valleys and darkly shaded forests of the Ardennes. The Germans wanted the world to look at Army Group B and its progress in the Belgian and Dutch flatlands to the north.

The assault there began with the spectacular arrival of glider troops on top of the Belgian fort at Eben Emael. It was the world's most powerful fortress, manned by 780 men, whose heavy guns covered the canals, roads and bridges that the Germans had to cross to advance into Belgium. The gliders took off from airfields around Cologne and were released at 2,100 metres with 32 kilometres to run to their target, landing at 05:20, five minutes before Fall Gelb's ground troops moved forward.

The attack gave warning that some German NCOs had battle-winning qualities of dash and determination. The tow line on the glider carrying the commanding officer, Lieutenant Rudolf Witzig, parted early and it failed to arrive. A sergeant, Feldwebel Helmut Wenzel, realized that Witzig was missing as he scrambled out of his own glider. Wenzel found himself with 70 men and no officer on top of a catacomb of steel and concrete, whose defenders outnumbered him by ten to one.

He took command. The bunkers and retractable cupolas protecting the guns were attacked with flamethrowers and shaped charges, which directed a high-velocity jet of molten steel that penetrated the bunkers and distorted the barrels of the fortress guns. Exit passages were also destroyed, to seal the garrison below. Witzig commandeered another tow aircraft, and arrived two hours later. By then, Wenzel had silenced all the guns, and the fortress commander was directing artillery fire from other batteries on top of his own position, in a vain attempt to dislodge the Germans.

The glider troops expected to be relieved by ground troops within four or five hours. In the event, they did not link up until the following day. Eben Emael had served its purpose by then. German press and radio reporters revelled in the drama, and the bombing of Antwerp, and the other airborne raids, on bridges at Rotterdam, Dordrecht and Maastricht. "The fighting beginning today," Hitler broadcast, "decides the fate of the German nation for the next thousand years." It was surely here, the world thought, with Army Group B, that his main axis of effort lay.

NO JOURNALISTS OR NEWSREEL cameramen reported Guderian's progress, so nothing disturbed the French high command's conviction that the Ardennes were "impenetrable". No bombers hinted at the importance of the advancing columns by bombing targets along their route. The Luftwaffe, deliberately, was elsewhere.

Men had fought in the Ardennes forest since the Roman legions had battled the Germanic tribes two thousand years before. "A place full of terrors", Julius Caesar had said after a ten-day march beneath its gloomy canopy. Latterly, the Ardennes had become studded with tourist hotels, a place where people went motoring to enjoy its landscapes, hunted for deer and boar, and skied cross-country in winter. A British military analyst who visited in 1928 thought it a dangerous delusion to think that it would defend itself. He found it "well-roaded and most of it rolling rather than mountainous country".

Yet no mention was made of the Ardennes in the "Plan of War" that Maurice Gamelin, the French supreme commander, had drawn up just two months earlier. He assumed that it would take the Germans a minimum of ten days to cross the Ardennes to the Meuse, the river that bordered it to the west and south, partly in Belgium and partly in France, giving ample time to draw up reserves. He assigned the weakest of all his armies, the 9th under André Corap, to defend the Meuse front between Namur and the old fortress city of Sedan. South of Sedan, the line was held by the 2nd Army, commanded by Charles Huntziger. The ever-present risk of weakness at the junction of the two armies at Sedan was made worse by both generals stationing their flimsiest divisions at the boundary.

The approaching firestorm was to fall on divisions largely made up of light cavalry, fortress troops and units made up of B-series reservists, men in their thirties and above, some of whom had done their military service 20 years before. Corap was unhappy with his men and their equipment. He fretted at a "slackening of discipline in certain billets ... soldiers insulting and sometimes attacking locals ... not saluting". He wanted more regular troops to stiffen his reservists, but his sector was low priority. A British general, Alan Brooke (later chief of the imperial general staff), shared his misgivings. He found unshaven men and ungroomed horses at a 9th Army parade. He was shaken by the men's faces, and their "disgruntled and insubordinate looks".

Huntziger was 60 – Guderian was 42 – and famous for the swirl of his moustaches. He was tipped as a future commander-in-chief. He was a great bunker-builder, with five to the kilometre in some parts of his defence lines. He had doubled the number in the Sedan sector over the winter to 103 "completed" bunkers, with others being built. "Completed", however, referred only to the concrete structure. Many had weaknesses that a determined attacker could seize on. They lacked the steel shutters used to close gun ports against enemy shells and infantry. Some had no doors, so that grenades could be thrown into the bunkers from the rear.

He had convinced himself that the enemy would not come this way. On 7 May, just three days before Guderian's men set off towards him, he had said: "I do not believe the Germans will ever consider attacking in the region of Sedan." One of the very few who did was Pierre Taittinger, founder of the great champagne house, and a member of the French parliament's army committee. He knew Sedan to be "a place of misfortunes" for French arms: it was on the historic route for invaders moving westward into France, and it was at Sedan that the Prussians had routed Napoleon III's army in 1870. Taittinger feared a repeat. He toured the region in March, and his report stressed that a determined enemy would not be stopped by the Ardennes and the Meuse. The Germans had shown themselves masters of using woods for cover in 1914, he said, and the Meuse was neither wide nor fast-flowing enough for safety. He said he "trembled at the results of a German attack in this sector". Huntziger retorted that Taittinger was no soldier, and that there was "no urgency" for reinforcements.

The positions across the river from Sedan were held by General Lafontaine's 55th DI, an infantry division. The Meuse was a natural tank barrier here. The ground on its left bank rose steeply to the Marfée heights and woods. It was well covered with bunkers and fieldworks. But Lafontaine had compounded his men's inexperience – most were B-reservists – by spending much more time on building bunkers than on training. The French rotated their units, too, so that men did not become familiar with a particular part of the line. Companies were moved between battalions, and battalions between regiments, so that the men were not used to one another or to their officers.

Along the riverbank and water meadows, the defence lines were manned by the 147th RIF, a fortress infantry regiment. Captain Carribou, commanding its 2nd Battalion, had been happy at starting the war with men from the Sedan region. It made for a coherent unit. It was soon shuffled. As Guderian approached, Carribou had three companies from three different regiments under his command. One of them was the 6th Company from the 331st RI infantry regiment, stationed in the Marfée woods. Carribou knew almost nothing about them. He was to have no chance to find out.

GUDERIAN'S *SCHNELLE TRUPPEN*, his fast units, were attacking with extreme impetuosity. They had to. "If we were not across the Meuse in the evening of 13 May, then the whole thing would fail," said Graf von Kielmansegg, a captain with 1st Panzer. "The French would realize that this was the main effort, and not in the north, at Eban Emael, where it was simulated."

The strains on men and machines were enormous. The tank crews had to negotiate unfamiliar ground at speed, and manoeuvre to give one another mutual protection, and all the while remain on the look-out for a concealed pillbox or anti-tank gun. They refuelled on the move. Trucks loaded with petrol cans advanced with the spearheads. The cans were passed to the crews as the trucks went by. After they had refuelled, they threw out the cans at designated points on the road, to be picked up and refilled at the next fuel dump.

It was the momentum of uninterrupted attack – the advance detachments constantly pushing on, motorcyclists with stick grenades in their belts, a sub-machine-gunner riding pillion and another in the sidecar – that provided success. In front ranged the *Aufklärungsabteilungen*, the reconnaissance units. Above were

Henschel spotter planes, a dozen to each division, one for each battalion, with an observer guiding the tanks with the intimate embrace of a sheepdog: "Cut across the fields here ... you're clear to the crossroads ... avoid the copse ..." There were 135 radio-equipped command tanks to ensure communications.

On the operations maps, the Panzer divisions snapped forward like lizard tongues, narrow, black penetrations, long and vulnerable but for their speed. To make sure that tired men did not slow them down, relief tank crews were carried on trucks behind the spearheads, and rotated constantly. 1st Panzer had a supply of 20,000 tablets of Pervitin, the methamphetamine given to drivers to keep them awake.

Where they stood and fought, the Belgians slowed the torrent. At Bodange, where the River Sauer and the Basseille join, a village of solid farmhouses stood at some height above the protecting rivers. It was defended by a single company of Chasseurs Ardennais, their command post in the village watermill. They were expecting Guderian's men. A light spotter plane had circled them at noon on 10 May, a sure sign of what was coming. They had a quick meal of excellent Ardennes ham, given to them by a local *charcutier*, and waited. A *Kradschützen-Batallion*, motorcycle troops in the vanguard of 1st Panzer, ran into them at 12:50. They held. Anti-tank guns and light field pieces failed to budge them from their positions in the thick-walled houses. In mid-afternoon, cattle came back to the farms from the pastures. The machine-gunners on both sides held their fire, and the Chasseurs enjoyed draughts of warm milk. Four field howitzers were brought up, again without effect. It was only when 88mm guns began smashing the houses that an assault by a rifle regiment could go in. After hand-to-hand fighting, the Belgian light infantrymen finally gave way. By then it was 19:00. A company of Chasseurs had held up a Panzer division for six hours.

But the Belgians, and the French who moved up into the

Ardennes, were a lightly armed screen, not a defence line. The Panzers brushed them easily aside on 11 May. The French were centred on the village of Petitvoir, west of Neufchâteau. They were a mixture of motorized machine-gunners, mounted dragoons, and the reconnaissance unit of a light cavalry division. A battery of 105mm guns was drawn up south of the village. Cavalry began pouring back down the road from Neufchâteau at 12:00, with riderless horses and running men among them, hurling away their helmets. A few moments later, Panzer IVs burst out of woods onto the gunners, who ran in panic. The tanks lined up on the heights above the village and shelled it, terrified horses galloping wildly through the streets. The French fought on for some time, since they would be cut off from the main road of retreat to the west if they abandoned the village. Other Panzers bypassed Petitvoir, on a giddy cross-country steeplechase. When the French realized that they now had German tanks in their rear, they panicked and fled into the woods.

On 11 May, the first sounds of distant gunfire were heard in the Meuse valley. The Germans were at Bouillon. Less than 40 hours after starting out in Luxembourg, Guderian was only 18 kilometres from Sedan. A French captain got through by telephone from the pretty waterside town on the River Semois to the command post of a heavy artillery regiment. "It's Perruche," he said. "We can't hold at Bouillon." After a long silence, the artillery lieutenant colonel replied: "Take cover then. We'll open fire on your position."

Guderian set up his headquarters in the Hotel Panorama at Bouillon. It had splendid views over the valley of the Semois. The alcove where he set up his desk was lined with hunting trophies. When a truck loaded with grenades and mines caught fire, the explosion rocked the hotel, sent shards of glass flying through the air and brought a boar's head crashing down. "It missed me by a hair's breadth," the general said. He changed hotels. Bouillon, loved by ramblers and hunters, had several to choose from. The bridges were blown, but motorcyclists discovered a ford with only 50 centimetres of water. The Panzers could pass.

A SPECTACULAR AND FATAL SNARL-UP was still a real prospect. What was thought to be Europe's biggest ever traffic jam formed on 12 May. The convoys stretched for 250 kilometres, all the way back to the Rhine.

It was a fraught business to squeeze the gigantic stream of 41,400 vehicles onto a few narrow roads. At the very start, the lead elements of the second echelon had run into the tail end of the first, backing up for tens of kilometres. On the second day, traffic jams many kilometres long built up in the narrow river gorges as engineers struggled to clear the road of burnt-out vehicles, and filled in the huge craters – some of them 15 or 20 metres wide – blown by the retreating Allies. Though XIX Corps had largely kept to its schedule, getting to Bouillon by the evening on the second day, some of General Reinhardt's XXXXI Corps's supposed spearhead units were still on German soil. Panzer divisions became hideously entangled with one another, and with motorized infantry. "The division was torn apart during the advance by elements of 2nd Panzer as well as ... infantry divisions that slipped in between," 6th Panzer's war diary reported. "In the afternoon and the evening there was no longer any clear picture of where march movement groups and their individual formations were located." Radio communications were poor, with much static. Attempts were made to sort out the chaos from an aircraft. In the confusion, friend was not always distinguishable from foe: 6th Panzer's flak battalion were about to open fire on "enemy armoured vehicles" when they were found to be the scout cars of a German reconnaissance battalion.

"The whole plan was a house of cards," said Reinhardt. The jams were "*unbeschreiblich*", indescribable. Drivers swore and threatened each other, and the Luftwaffe flak units refused to bow to army discipline, while officers and military police struggled to keep order.

At times on 12 May, the only movement in the columns was in the middle. Had Allied air forces attacked, they would have had a turkey shoot. "Again and again, I cast a worried look up at the bright blue sky," a German officer wrote. "My division now presents an ideal attack target because it is not deployed and is forced to move slowly forward on a single road. But we could not spot a single French reconnaissance aircraft."

Guderian, whose corps was part of Panzer Group Kleist, flew to General von Kleist's headquarters during the afternoon. One of his three Panzer divisions, the 2nd, had been held up along the River Semois. Despite this, and the weakness of his force, Guderian was ordered to attack across the Meuse the next day, 13 May, at 16:00. He agreed that it was probably better to "thrust forward immediately without waiting for all our troops to be ready", but it made the assault a yet chancier affair. On his return, the young pilot of his Storch aircraft got lost in the fading light. "The next thing I knew we were on the other side of the Meuse, flying in a slow and unarmed plane over the French position," Guderian wrote. "An unpleasant moment. I gave my pilot emphatic orders to turn north and find my landing strip. We just made it."

His 1st and 10th Panzer Divisions were making much swifter progress than the 2nd. As they closed in, the French at Sedan began blowing the bridges. The Pont Neuf went first, at 20:30, the ancient stones that belied its name disappearing into the waters, or crashing in fragments onto the surrounding buildings. It was joined a few minutes later by the Pont Turenne and the others over the river and the canal that cut across the great U-bend the river made here. As the last French light cavalry got back to the left bank, bridges were blown all along the Meuse.

A staff officer, Lieutenant Colonel Cachou, was sent from corps headquarters to verify their destruction. As those that crossed into the sector held by the 147th RIF splashed into the river, 60 metres wide here and between 2 and 3 metres deep, he turned to Captain Carribou: "You can relax now." "*Mon colonel*," Carribou replied, "I'd be much happier if I had my old machine-gunners back, instead of these incoherent units ..."

Across the river, the first German columns began lapping into Sedan on the evening of 12 May. Guderian had, just, kept to his slogan. Three days to the Meuse.

"It's today we'll know if this operation works or not," General Busch, commanding 16th Army, wrote at dawn on 13 May. "If Guderian crosses the Meuse near Sedan, the *Unwahrscheinlichkeit*, the improbable, will become reality!"

The plan was taken from a war game Guderian had played in Koblenz, and it fitted perfectly. The attack order covered only three pages. Guderian concentrated his forces – he had 60,000 men, and 22,000 vehicles in his corps – at Sedan. The point of main effort, where the breakthrough attempts would be made, covered the bend of the river at Sedan, from Wadelincourt, just downstream from the city, to Glaire and Donchery upstream. The Germans were on the right bank of the river. The left bank gave on to meadows, with no natural defences beyond a railway line and embankment, and then to the Marfée woods, which rolled up to an arc of wooded heights. Once taken, these gave a protective screen from a counterattack from the south, enabling Guderian to wheel back northwestward for the Channel.

He was grossly short of artillery. The French had a 3:1 superiority in the number of guns. Given that the Germans were the attacking force, the ratio should have been the reverse. It was made worse by a shortage of shells, held up in the Ardennes traffic jams, with only a dozen or so rounds per gun. To compensate for this, the crossing by *Stosstruppen*, the assault teams of pioneers

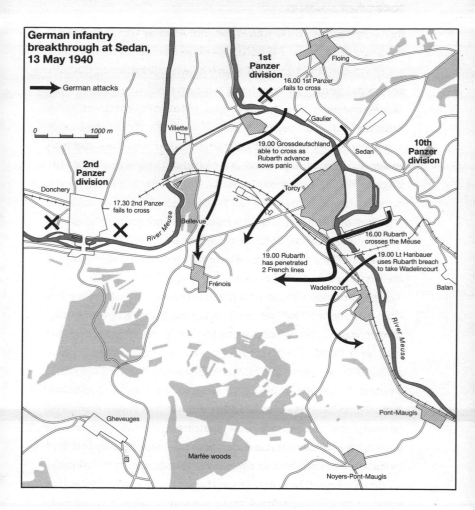

German infantry breakthrough at Sedan, 13 May 1940

→ German attacks

0   1000 m

1st Panzer division

16.00 1st Panzer fails to cross

Floing

Gaulier

Villette

19.00 Grossdeutschland able to cross as Rubarth advance sows panic

Sedan

10th Panzer division

2nd Panzer division

Donchery

17.30 2nd Panzer fails to cross

Torcy

River Meuse

Bellevue

16.00 Rubarth crosses the Meuse

19.00 Rubarth has penetrated 2 French lines

19.00 Lt Hanbauer uses Rubarth breach to take Wadelincourt

Frénois

Wadelincourt

Balan

River Meuse

Pont-Maugis

Gheveuges

Marfée woods

Noyers-Pont-Maugis

and infantry, at 16:00 was to be preceded by a massive aerial bombardment.

German units began taking up their positions along the river in the morning, putting down suppressive fire on the French across the river. Lieutenant Michard of the 147th Infantry Regiment was in an observation post on the heights of the Marfée woods. It was made from the turret of an old Renault tank mounted above a trench. He heard heavy firing from across the river to the west of Sedan after 10:00. A little later, automatic weapons stuttered harshly from Wadelincourt, a built-up village to the east of the town. He saw vehicles and motorcycles and engineering equipment come down to the right bank.

The first aircraft from the Third Air Fleet arrived at 08:00. The ferocity intensified when they were joined by the Stukas of VIII Air Corps at 12:00. The 55th DI had almost no anti-aircraft guns. The divisional staff had sent out hastily copied sheets overnight on how to use machine-guns against aircraft. Lieutenant Philipponat had got his at 07:30 that morning. It had crude drawings on how to "lead" a low-flying strafing aircraft, aiming ahead of it to compensate for its speed. But the Heinkel and Dornier medium bombers he was waiting for in his pillbox flew high, well above machine-gun range, and the Stuka divebombers came down in a near vertical dive before pulling out sharply as they dropped their bombs, a wholly different profile to a strafing run.

It seemed nothing could survive the first wave. The explosions rolled towards the French positions until they were on them, the ground shaking, the men pressing their faces into the ground, jaws working, eyes wide. "When it stopped, we breathed again, we looked at each other almost joyfully – they'd gone," said Michard, now at the company command post at Marfée. "I got out to see what the damage was, and they were back, and I flattened myself again. A second wave, a third. We had six hours of it ..."

This was the heaviest bombing yet recorded anywhere on earth. It absorbed two air corps, Bruno Loerzer's IInd Fliegerkorps, and the VIIIth of Wolfram von Richthofen, the nephew of the famous Red Baron, for whose Stukas Sedan was a mere ten-minute hop from their advanced airfield at Bastogne. Their orders were laconic: "Targets: all visible defensive positions." The 310 medium bombers came wave after wave, and the 200 Stukas formed a carousel in the sky, circling and diving in an endless dance of destruction.

Kleist had ordered a single, conventional mass bombing raid to deliver a massive blow on the Meuse bend, a 20-minute attack to be followed immediately by the *Stosstruppen*. Guderian had a new notion, of a "rolling raid", where smaller formations made attack after attack to wear down enemy nerves. To his delight, Guderian found the Luftwaffe had ignored Kleist, saying his order had come too late, and was flying to his method.

The Stuka pilots switched on their sirens, the "trumpets of Jericho", as they started their near-vertical dives, reaching 700kph before pulling out as they dropped their bombs, sometimes circling and diving again after their ordnance was gone, for there was no ground-fire to speak of, and the Stuka and its siren performed its mission of intimidating the enemy even when unarmed. The bombs, too, shrieked, the hideous noise coming from the "organ-pipes" fitted to their fins. Most of the pilots had flown in the Polish campaign. They knew that those exposed to a bombardment by medium-altitude bombers or artillery felt that their survival was a matter of fate. If the bomb or shell had your name on it, you were gone. It was impersonal. The Stuka, though, seemed like a bird of prey, circling in the brilliant spring sky, and then swooping down on a selected victim, so each man cowering beneath it was certain that the individual aircraft was out to get him, and even if the bomb landed a hundred metres away, until the last second the man was convinced that it was aiming at him.

Noise drummed out every other sensation, Michard found, as the Stuka siren got louder, and got closer, until it penetrated the skull. "The explosion was a deliverance, but then came another, two others, six others ..." The whistling and the engines and bombs made a maze of sound and concussion from which there was no escape. He crouched, silent, inert, hunched, his mouth open so his eardrums would not burst. "The noise drilled into the ears and stripped the nerves. It made you howl," he said. When the Dorniers came, it was like the growing thunder of an approaching train. "Twice I hallucinated ... I was in a railway station, a train was drawing in ... then the explosion brought me back."

Michard tried to eat a fillet of herring. He couldn't swallow it. He couldn't even smoke. The company commander's dog, Rex, was snoring peacefully at his feet. A sergeant lay inert, too, and quiet. But the cipher clerk was haggard, eyes unblinking, half on his knees, his body trembling with every explosion, repeating himself endlessly in a jerky monotone: "This one's for us. This time. This one's for us ..."

The field-telephone lines were cut by the bombs. The feeling of isolation was made worse by the dust thrown up by the bombing. It hung like morning mist, penetrating dry nostrils and throats, obscuring other positions, so that the men felt cut off and alone. Captain Carribou wanted to use the radio to contact his units. Permission was refused. Radio silence was to be maintained until contact was made with enemy ground forces.

In his concrete command post south of Bulson, General Lafontaine waited for the ground attack to start. He asked Gransard, the corps commander, for air support. The request was passed on to Huntziger, who said there was none available. Then he added: "It's a good thing the 55th DI has had its baptism of fire."

It was a brutal remark. The main-effort sector on the Meuse loop absorbed 1,215 bomber and Stuka sorties, and these attacks were continuous, reaching a crescendo between 15:40 and 16:00, but continuing in the French rear areas until the onset of darkness. It was true that the physical damage was minimal. Few if any bunkers were destroyed. Only 56 French soldiers were casualties.

But no air assault remotely on this scale had ever taken place before, and it fell upon a B-series division, in which only 1 officer in 25 was a regular, and, more particularly, on the 147th RI. A third of its reservists had been conscripted between 1918 and 1925. The average age of the rank and file was 31, and of captains 42. Its command was paralysed by the cut telephone lines, and many of its men by shock. "The gunners stopped firing and went to ground, and the infantry dived into the trenches and lay there motionless," wrote General Edmond Ruby, deputy chief of staff of 2nd Army. "They were deafened by the crashing of bombs and screech of the Stuka sirens ... Five hours of this nightmare was enough to shatter their nerve. They were no longer able to react to the approaching infantry."

The bombing invigorated the German infantry. They watched the Stuka squadrons screaming down, diving 12 in a line with one purpose, to "bust the Sedan invasion gateway wide open". They saw a sulphurous, yellow-grey wall of dust rise across the river. The pressure waves made the houses around them sway, and the window panes rattled and cracked. What must it be like, they thought, for the French who were undergoing it? "The imposing air bombardment, and the almost complete cessation of enemy artillery fire, had an extraordinary effect on our troops," said Lieutenant Colonel Balck. "Up to now, they'd taken cover in great haste at the slightest hint of incoming fire. Now they got out of their foxholes and trenches. The truck drivers didn't hesitate any more. They came right up to the banks of the Meuse to drop off the engineering equipment, sometimes unloading 50 metres from the river."

Tanks came out of the cover of woods and buildings and took

up positions close to the river, next to where the infantry and the assault pioneers were assembling; 88mm flak guns, intended for protection against non-existent Allied air strikes, were brought up for use against pillboxes and bunkers. Captain Leflon of the 147th RI reported heavy tanks, Panzer IVs, opposite the regiment's 6th Machine-Gun Company in bunkers at Wadelincourt. Lieutenant Nonat opened fire at them with his 75mm guns, but he was given strict orders to fire a maximum of 60 shells. The French could see at least 300 vehicles on the far bank. They made out strange black and red bands behind the tank turrets. They were *Blutfahne*, blood-red flags with swastikas, to identify them to Luftwaffe pilots.

TIME, THOUGH, NOW BEGAN slipping through Guderian's fingers. His three Panzer divisions, 10th, 1st and 2nd, were trying to cross at different points. All were failing. The motorized infantry were in position on the banks well before the trucks with the boats arrived. Sturmpionier Walter Rubarth's 49th Panzer Engineer Battalion was trucked for 5 kilometres round Sedan until craters barred the road and they dismounted. They marched on whilst occasional shells fell around them and halted upstream from the city in parkland at Wadelincourt to wait for the boats.

Oberst Wolfgang Fischer, the infantry commander at 10th Panzer's Wadelincourt crossing sector, was frantic to get the attack in on time, so as not to squander the terror effect of the Stuka raids, vowing "if necessary to swim across". He put himself at the head of an attack group, and was about to move forward when the trucks appeared.

Rubarth looked at the situation. He didn't like it. "In front of us was open ground," he said in his after-action report. "To the left were fields that ran 400 or 500 metres down to the Meuse. Immediately the other side of the river, and at the foot of the Marfée heights, we could see several bunkers. The city was behind us, still partly occupied by the enemy. The ground didn't look very favourable for attack. I brought up a gun to give us fire support. I told the gunners to concentrate on the bunkers that looked most menacing." The way to the bank was across wet and near-swampy water meadows. As well as their own kit and weapons, the men had to drag heavy rubber boats filled with hand and smoke grenades, flares, ammunition and specialist pioneer equipment – wire cutters, satchel charges, explosives, detonators and fuses.

The French defence line on both sides of Wadelincourt was solidly reinforced by bunkers and fieldworks. The Stukas and bombers had attacked the positions directly opposite Sedan. The gunners from the heavy batteries of X Corps on the heights to the south of Wadelincourt had escaped the bombing. They had a perfect view of the river. So did the machine-gunners and light artillery crews on the high ground behind the 10th Panzer's attempted crossing points.

Flanking fire from the heavy guns crashed into the engineers as they prepared the boats. Gas alarms sounded when a strange thin white smoke drifted across the meadows from exploding French shells. The Germans pulled on their gas masks and panted with exhaustion as they laboured. It was some time before it was found to be a false alarm, caused by shells that had been stored for too long.

A barrage of artillery fire hit the village of Bazeilles as Rubarth's fellow engineers unloaded boats from the trucks. The inflatables were, of course, hugely vulnerable – the slightest hole from a shell splinter made them useless – and 81 out of 96 boats were destroyed. At first, it was impossible to get even one boat to the river's edge. The boats, the unit's war diary reported, were shot to pieces or their crews got stuck in the swamp.

At Sedan, 1st Panzer was blocked. Its first assault boats dashed forward at 16:00. "French fire comes down and the engineers are unable to reach the river," its war diary recorded. "Nearly all enemy bunkers were still operational after the massive bombardment ... more assault boats are prepared for launch ... the *Pioniere* try again to cross the river and fail. Lieutenant Graf von Medem and two engineers are killed ..."

Downstream from Sedan, attacking into the bend of the Meuse at Donchery, 2nd Panzer was also foiled by French gunners. They were well sited on the heights that rose steeply to 150 metres on the south bank of the river, looking down on the Germans dragging their boats to the north bank. The concentrated fire of the 55th DI's 174 artillery pieces crashed into them. All attempts at a crossing failed. Most of the time it was impossible to get the boats anywhere near the bank. In desperation, eight boats were launched at 17:30. Only one reached the far bank, and the soldiers quickly swam back. A little later, a lieutenant and some volunteers swam across the river. They found they could do nothing.

The attack was in desperate trouble. It was not moving, and that was fatal. The art of Guderian's Blitzkrieg, the military theorist Major General J.F.C. Fuller wrote, was to "employ mobility as a psychological weapon"; not mobility to kill but to move, not to move to kill but to move to "terrify, to bewilder, to perplex, to cause consternation, doubt and confusion" in the rear of the enemy, which rumour would magnify "until panic became monstrous".

A stalled Panzer group, its momentum gone, presented a long and thin flank of huge vulnerability to the enemy. Allied commanders were at last having second thoughts about the significance of the Ardennes penetration. Guderian had to be across the river before nightfall, or the Allied air forces would catch him at dawn on 14 May and pound him all day. He had only enough flak guns to defend a bridge, a single target, not the mass of his 850 tanks and 20,000 vehicles.

And he was stalled on the Meuse.

IT WAS NOW THAT WALTER RUBARTH became the *Schwerpunkt* of the German invasion of the West, the flesh-and-blood speartip of an enterprise in which 3 million men on both sides were engaged. The platoon sergeant, a veteran of the Polish campaign, was 27, though he looked younger in his photograph, chubby and boyish with an open face, and a humorous set to his mouth.

The attempt by the 69th Rifle Regiment to cross, the war diary recorded, "is stopped by heavy French artillery fire sinking 48 or 50 rubber dinghies ..." With five of his pioneers, and six infantrymen, Rubarth began carrying one of the surviving boats down to the river just below a destroyed railway bridge. "At once we came under violent machine-gun fire," he said. "We had losses. I got to the bank in the shelter of a stand of trees. The machine-guns were hitting the slope of the bank. We collected all our energy. We put the rubber boats into the water and somehow we started across.

"During the crossing, our own forces kept the enemy under constant fire from automatic weapons and light guns. We didn't have too many casualties. We scrambled ashore near a strong earthen bunker. Corporal Podszus put it out of action with a satchel charge. French artillery hit our crossing point. I cut through barbed wire. We attacked another bunker from the rear. I used an explosive charge on it. The violence of the explosion blew out part of the walls. Then I threw grenades. After a brief fight, we put the bunker out of action. They showed the white flag.

"A few moments later, we put up a swastika flag on the bunker. We could hear whoops of joy from our comrades on the other bank. That encouraged us and we rushed two other half-hidden posts 100 metres to our left. We had to cross a stream up to our knees to get at one of them.

"Corporal Bräutigam attacked one of them on his own, with crazy fearlessness, and threw grenades and the occupants surrendered. I assaulted a second blockhouse with Sergeant Theophel and Corporals Podszus and Monk. This meant that we had taken out the first defence line of bunkers right behind the Meuse for a distance of about 300 metres. We pushed on to a railway line. The incoming fire was so heavy we had to take cover."

It was only now, Rubarth said, that he realized how isolated he was. No one else had got across the river. The French were hitting the boats as they were put into the water. He and his little group were alone on the left bank, and they had taken casualties. "I had just a warrant officer and four men," he said. "Our ammunition was exhausted, to the extent we couldn't go on. I went back to our crossing point, to ask for reinforcements and ammunition. I found that violent enemy fire had made passage across the river impossible. The rubber boats were damaged or destroyed. Four of our assault pioneers were dead on the bank."

His company commander on the other bank could see what was going on. He brought up new boats. One of them, with four members of Rubarth's platoon on board, managed to paddle across to join him.

"I went back to where I had left Theophel and the others, close to a railway embankment. I found both corporals lying badly wounded," he said. "Braütigan was dead. Theophels told me that the enemy had taken advantage of us having stopped, and had recovered their nerve and opened fire, putting the little group *hors de combat*.

"The enemy concentrated his fire on the railway embankment. In spite of that, we rushed towards what we thought was the next line of resistance. We had to cover 150 metres of open ground. Then there was higher ground in front of us with barbed wire. The enemy artillery seemed to be following us."

They came on a concrete bunker with two embrasures. It was not completed, and Rubarth was helped by the absence of steel plates on the embrasures and the lack of a door.

"We surrounded it," he said. "A Frenchman came out at the

moment we left our cover. He was put out of action with a grenade. We got into the trenches on both sides of the bunker. Corporal Hose threw an explosive charge into one of the entrances. The occupants recognized it was useless to continue and they surrendered. We got a French machine-gun into the bargain, which was very useful for us ... Enemy artillery was pounding our position, and we took cover in a trench. Then the fire died away and we continued the attack on the heights in front of us."

Rubarth had now taken out the second defence line that lay between Wadelincourt and Bellevue on the other side of the Meuse loop. As position after position fell, the French assumed that Rubarth and his handful of men were a major force. They began to abandon the fight. Captain Carribou tried to set up a centre of resistance in a forester's house in the Marfée woods. He gathered a ragbag of soldiers from those falling back. He could tell Rubarth's advance from the red flares the Germans fired to show their position to their artillery and tanks on the far bank.

Rubarth found it easier now to push on through trenches and fieldworks to take a key concrete bunker below the loop of the Meuse. Its defenders surrendered to him without a fight at around 19:00. Heavy machine-gun fire continued from the La Prayelle hill, and forced him and his little squad to take cover in a French trench for 15 minutes. Other infantry now began to join him.

The consequences of his action, carried out entirely of his own initiative and tactics, were colossal. "Rubarth," the war diary recorded, "conquers the only bridgehead on the west bank." He had made the decisive breach, smashing seven bunkers, and overrunning the two defence lines. He created a bridgehead and held it for almost three hours.

It turned 10th Panzer's fortunes, as a second assault team under a lieutenant, Heinrich Hanbauer, used the Rubarth breach to take Wadelincourt. It also opened the way for 1st Panzer, enabling two battalions of Grossdeutschland infantry to break through after house-to-house fighting in Torcy, the southern suburb of Sedan. As they began to clear the French positions that had been firing on Donchery, it became possible for 2nd Panzer to get boats over the river.

The rout was confirmed. Lieutenant von Courbière of Gross-deutschland, following on from the assault pioneers, said : "It was like a field exercise. Sections moved forward, shouting hurrahs of encouragement, and hurling grenades into the bunkers. The enemy came out, hands in the air, and were led to the rear. They ran like ferrets, throwing away their arms and equipment, happy just to escape ..."

A big bunker with six gun embrasures blocked the German line of advance. The attackers approached it under cover of an orchard. "A brief exchange of fire, and the enemy was smoked out with hand grenades," von Courbière reported. "It was beyond our wildest hopes. A big concrete position taken by an NCO and two men. The enemy were completely dispirited. Their faces showed the loss of morale. They bunched together in defeat."

As they reached the parkland of the château at Fresnois, they came under fire from machine-guns and an anti-tank gun. They took their first casualty – "a comrade asked his squad leader to pass on his dying regards to his mother and closed his eyes for ever" – but the advance did not falter. "The enemy must not be allowed any respite," von Courbière said. "We kept driving on." They found the French positions concealed by a barn at the edge of the castle park. The assault squad stormed them under covering fire. The lieutenant could not believe his luck. "We found twenty bottles of mineral water to slake our thirst. Providence was with us ..."

The lieutenant whose two assault engineer platoons extended the bridgehead at Gaulier, Günther Korthals, was astonished at his men's survival. They destroyed 11 concrete bunkers, and swept through numerous fieldworks, in taking the ground on the left bank of the Meuse where the first bridge was soon being built. They achieved this without taking a single casualty.

IT WAS CLEAR SHORTLY AFTER 19:00 that the panic Rubarth and the Stukas had engendered in the the 147th RIF was spreading through the 55th Division as a whole. A lieutenant left General Lafontaine's divisional command post on an errand, to return almost immediately with the chilling news that he could not make his way against a tide of fleeing soldiers. Discipline had gone, and the division was cascading to disaster. "A wave of terrified refugees, gunners and infantry, in cars, on foot, many without weapons but dragging kitbags, was hurtling down the road screaming 'The Panzers are at Bulson!'" General Ruby later recalled. He noted that officers were mixed in with the men, and that they all swore that they had seen tanks at Bulson, a village 4.5 kilometres south of Sedan and the Meuse. The Germans had not got a bridge across the river yet. The first tank was not to cross for 12 hours.

This, General Ruby said, was an "obvious case of mass hysteria". That night, some 20,000 soldiers fled in the "Bulson panic". They seemed so eaten up by fear, Ruby thought, that they told each other ever more fantastic and terrifying stories, as if they "wanted to forbid themselves any hope of return ..." Captain Carribou could find no trace of his 6th Company. It had dissolved in the woods.

Lieutenant Michard, his bombing trauma behind him, set up a machine-gun post in the Marfée woods. A sergeant came through the trees, without weapon or pack, "shaking like a child", begging to be allowed to the rear to "fetch ammunition". He got on his knees and swore he would return. Michard ordered him to stay, but knew the moment he turned his back, the man would be off. He had two characters who wanted to stay, though, and he ordered them to man the machine-gun. They were told a counterattack was coming, by an infantry regiment and two tank battalions …

In places, officers parked trucks across roads and paths to try to stem the flow, or stood with pistols drawn, but the men simply flowed around them, some of them firing blindly into the air. The woods broke them up into an incoherent swill of regiments, battalions, companies. Officers of all ranks among them claimed to have been given orders to retreat, though they could not say from whom. "*On ne peut plus tenir,*" said an NCO. They could no longer hold.

A report from an artillery officer seems to have been the spark that set off the conflagration. Captain Fouques had two batteries of guns in woods near Chaumont. Shells exploded a few hundred metres away, and he reported this over a field telephone at 19:30, adding that they "might be Panzer shells". By that, he meant that they could come from the Panzers that were firing on French positions from the other side of the Meuse.

When Fouques's report got onto the grapevine, however, it did so with a critical difference. The Panzer shell *hits* he reported became Panzer *muzzle flashes* – and that meant that the tanks had crossed the river and were advancing on the left bank. And so the rumours gathered pace and swept onward: "*Les Panzers passent la Meuse … Les chars sont à Bulson … Les boches arrivent, on se replie, vite … tout le monde se replie …* The tanks are across the Meuse … at Bulson … the Germans are coming, we are withdrawing, hurry, hurry …"

A lieutenant ignored the crazed men running back. He put together an ad hoc anti-tank unit. They waited, and waited. No Panzers came.

There was no bridge yet, and no tank was to cross for another 11 hours. Lieutenant Colonel Balck, who had come across with infantry by boat, was on the slopes of the Marfée woods without artillery or anti-tank guns. He felt so vulnerable to a French counterattack that he ordered his men to keep moving with night infiltration into French positions. It was highly dangerous. "Colonel, it'll destroy the regiment!" his adjutant warned him. "No. French regiments," he replied with a bravado he did not feel. It was only by keeping on expanding the bridgehead that he thought he could conceal his true weakness from the French.

Huntziger played into his hands. At 20:30 he ordered the heavy 155mm guns at Bulson to withdraw. He also moved 3rd DINA, a first-rate North African infantry division, further away from Sedan. Both these moves suggested that the Germans had made a big breakthrough, and helped spread the panic.

As the news came in to the French high command at 04:00 on 14 May, General Beaufre said, the "atmosphere was of a family which has had a death … Gamelin's deputy got up quickly. He was terribly pale. 'Our front has been broken at Sedan! There has been a collapse …' He flung himself in a chair and burst into tears."

THE MILITARY BRIDGE AT SEDAN, which Rubarth had made possible, assumed an operational-level significance seldom met in any war. Guderian had hundreds of tanks to get across it once its swaying pontoons were in position. It was the eye of the storm.

It was sited at Gaulier, a suburb a little downstream from Sedan. On the right bank, it abutted onto a large red-brick factory, the Espérance textile works, whose buildings offered some cover to men and equipment waiting to cross. The other side was meadowland. The bridge was made up of 40 metal pontoons, floating in pairs and attached to the banks by steel cables. The central planking, supported by small girders, was capable of taking tanks. A passage of duckboards ran on each side for infantry and motorcycles.

The bridge was driven out across the river whilst firing continued. French shells were landing within 50 metres of the engineers. A French artillery spotter plane was driven off by German fighters, as light scout cars were ferried across on pontoon rafts with outboard motors. The commander of a *Kradschützen-*

Battalion was seriously wounded by French shellfire close by. German trucks were driven behind a railway embankment for cover. The Panzers themselves, though, joined with the artillery in shelling the bunkers across the river that remained in French hands, with great accuracy. As darkness fell, Lieutenant Aubry in a 147th observation post heard a desperate voice from one of them: "They are firing into our *créneaux*, our observation slits. We can't stay inside any longer ..."

Major Knoppf and his pontoniers had the bridge finished at midnight. The first echelons over were anti-tank guns, light assault guns, and reconnaissance vehicles. The traffic was so dense that the pontoon rafts kept running back and forth across the river. Knoppf warned that he had come within a couple of pontoons of not reaching the far bank. No spares remained. If a pair of pontoons were badly damaged, the bridge would be out of action, and there would be nothing he and his men could do about it. Guderian's umbilical cord could be cut at any moment. Such was the gambling nature of the campaign.

The French and British realized the huge implications of the bridge. Cut it, and Rubarth's bridgehead could be crushed. General Billotte, commander of the 1st Army Group, appealed to the air commanders for every light bomber they had, with the famous cry: "*La victoire ou la défaite passent par ces ponts.*" It was a matter of life and death, a throwback in French minds to the earlier stunning defeat at Sedan, which had lost them the war against the Prussians in 1870. Then the French cavalry had ridden frontally into massed German artillery in a last-ditch *mission de sacrifice*. A huge monument to the cavalry had been erected on the hill from which the doomed horsemen had charged, and the pilots who came to emulate them saw it just a kilometre or two beyond the bridge, fire spitting at them from the German flak batteries that had hastily positioned themselves on its flanks.

A total of 303 flak guns of all calibres defended the bridge. It was the biggest concentration of anti-aircraft fire around a single target in history. It was backed by 814 sorties flown by Luftwaffe fighters, which started attacking the bombers long before they got near Sedan.

The first of those that got through arrived at 05:30. They went on all day and through into the flare and tracer-lit darkness until midnight. The effort was scattered into 27 separate raids, so that the German gunners found themselves confronting small packets of aircraft, 10 or 20 at a time, allowing batteries to select individual aircraft as targets. The one mass strike, by 71 RAF Fairey Battles and Blenheims shortly after 16:00, was a disaster. Forty were shot down in this raid alone, other crews perishing later after rearming and returning to the fray. "In no comparable operation had the RAF ever been forced to accept a higher loss rate," the official history stated.

"It takes dash and daring to dive down so deep into the hell put up by our flak," a German observed. "But the French know, as we do too, what it means if the bridge were to be destroyed. They failed …" The Allies lost 167 aircraft that day, long plumes of smoke trailing down through a cloudless sky until a flash of red and a column of oily smoke marked the end. The critical moment, the Germans thought, was when a pilot, his aircraft already hit, aimed it at the bridge and jumped at the last moment. "He floated five metres above the Panzer that happened to be crossing the bridge," a German said. "Not far away, he plunged into the Meuse, never to be seen again." His aircraft missed the bridge and exploded on the bank.

If the bridge survived, there was still another way of undoing Rubarth's handiwork: with a counterattack.

Even before Rubarth had crossed, General Grandsard of the French X Corps, had ordered reserves to be moved to Peak 322, which commanded the approaches to Bulson. French tanks should have been in position within a few hours. It was a practised move.

An exercise simulating a similar counterattack to throw the enemy back over the Meuse had been held three weeks before. It took 17 hours, however, and the Panzers beat the French to the heights by ten minutes.

The order to the 213th Infantry Regiment was sent by Grandsard by a motorcycle courier a little after 15:00. It arrived at 17:30. The commander of the regiment ordered the advance to start at 20:00. By then, the flood of Bulson *paniquards* was underway, delaying the move. The 7th Tank Battalion, ordered to move forward at 18:00, did not set out until 21:30, for fear of German aircraft, and also became mired in the panic. General Lafontaine of the 55th DI was ordered to take command of these reserves by telephone at 20:00. He refused to issue orders for the counterattack until this had been confirmed in writing. This took more time, and it was not until 05:00 on 14 May that Lafontaine finally issued the orders to counterattack.

When the counterattack finally got under way, at 07:30, the French tanks moved with their supporting infantry at a walking pace, taking 90 minutes to go 3 kilometres to the watershed on Peak 322.

German reconnaissance pilots saw the attack being mounted. Within ten minutes of the report being received, at 08:00, German tanks were making fast for the peak. They had 9 kilometres to travel, with some fighting on the way, but they took possession of the peak, and immediately began shelling the French tanks, which were still a few hundred metres from the top.

Even now, all was not lost. The powerful 21st Army Corps was assigned as reinforcements to Huntziger during the day. This gave him an armoured division, the 3rd DCR, a motorized infantry division, a light cavalry division and a cavalry brigade. The 3rd DCR was a formidable force, with B-1 bis and Hotchkiss 39 tanks, which outgunned the Germans and had thicker armour. The counterattack was entrusted to General de Flavigny.

It was due to get underway at noon on 14 May. It was delayed because of fuel shortages. The first tanks were not in their combat positions until 13:00 and the whole division was only in place at 17:30. It faced the Gross Deutschland infantry regiment, first-class troops, but no match for an armoured division. Had de Flavigny attacked hard, he could have closed the Sedan pocket and cut off Guderian and his army. He did not. He strung out his forces along at 20-kilometre line, and called off the assault.

By dusk on 14 May, Guderian had been able to get the main body of his corps across the river. It proved unstoppable. "The front is broken near Sedan," Paul Reynaud, the French premier, told Winston Churchill on 15 May. "They are pouring through in great numbers with tanks and armoured cars ..."

The great breakout from Sedan was under way. Instead of turning east to attack the heavily defended fortresses of the Maginot Line, Guderian wheeled west, driving a 35-kilometre wide rent between the French 2nd and 9th Armies. Sedan was the pivot, between the southern and northern armies, and Rubarth's breach had ripped it off its hinge. Each time the French tried to reform, the Panzers of Guderian and Rommel slammed into them, keeping them off balance.

The roads along which French reinforcements tried to move became blocked with millions of refugees. A *grande peur*, a flight of refugees so immense that it resembled a "geological cataclysm", seized the country. It seemed to the French poet-pilot Antoine de Saint-Exupéry, as he looked down from his aircraft, that a gigantic boot had scattered an anthill somewhere in northern France. Below him, the "ants were on the march. Without panic. Without hope. Without despair. On the march as if duty bound."

On 20 May, the Germans reached the Channel near Abbeville. A colossal pocket formed along the coast, 200 kilometres long and up to 140 kilometres wide in places. Inside it were trapped the Belgian army, the French 1st Army Group and the British Expeditionary Force, and the French 1st and 7th Armies together with parts of the 9th.

In all, 338,266 French and British troops were evacuated from the beaches at Dunkirk before the Germans overran the pocket. Paris fell on 14 June. The French asked for an armistice three days later.

WALTER RUBARTH WAS AWARDED THE Knight's Cross on 3 June. The citation left no doubt that his was the decisive role in the break-through. "Rubarth led the first and only *Stosstrupp* to reach the west bank of the Meuse, under heavy enemy fire," it said. It credited him with destroying six bunkers – the war diary spoke of seven – despite strong resistance. The crux followed: "Rubarth and his men opened a breach in the enemy defence line and held this bridgehead for three hours until the arrival of other forces. Through this single action, the attack of 10th Panzer Division, which had been halted, was transformed into a success. Feldwebel Rubarth decided the nature and tactics of the mission entirely, and seized the initiative." For this feat, he was awarded the *Ritterkreuz* and promoted to lieutenant.

A British liaison officer with the French, Major Philip Gribble, had walked through the fortifications along the Sedan front in early May. He estimated that a well-organized and resolute defence would cost the Germans half a million casualties, and even then it was far from certain that they would manage to achieve a break-through. "But what happened?" he wrote in his diary. "The Germans marched through the five-mile deep fortifications with a loss of perhaps 500 men."

He was more accurate than he knew. Guderian's Panzer Corps lost about 120 dead and 400 wounded on 13 and 14 May. In those two days, they achieved a decisive breakthrough, something that their forebears in the First World War had failed to do in four years, at a cost of millions of lives – just one of these doomed attempts, at Verdun, had resulted in 330,000 dead, wounded and missing.

There is no doubt that, in breaking a regiment and inducing a division to panic, in the critical area and at the most critical moment, when the German attack seemed to have stalled, Rubarth ensured the Fall of France.

He was not technically the first German across the Meuse. Men from Rommel's 7th Panzer succeeded in crossing the river over an old weir at Dinant during the early hours of 13 May. But the position far downstream made it of much less consequence. Sedan was pivotal, sowing panic and confusion right across the French rear.

Speed, and the astonishing absence of casualties, marked Rubarth's establishment of the bridgehead and the Panzer breakout as a new form of warfare. The two aspects were linked. Because the attack was so swift – straight off the march – and because it so stunned the enemy, there were almost no major combat actions, none of the hard-pounding battles in which the dead and wounded are piled high.

In another sense, though, Rubarth helped to engineer the ultimate defeat of the Third Reich. Fall Gelb was hugely risky. Hitler knew it. "This is a miracle, an absolute miracle!" he cried when told of the Sedan breakthrough. Guderian himself was only marginally less surprised: "The success of our attack," he wrote, "struck me as almost a miracle."

Not only had the French more tanks, Guderian said, but "theirs were superior both in armour and gun-calibre, if inferior in control facilities and speed". Control – notably through having many more radios and spotter aircraft – was indeed a factor. So was a great deal of good fortune. It was luck that the Allies pursued the wrong *Schwerpunkt* for so long, and that Huntziger positioned his best troops safely out of Guderian's way. It was luck that Major

Knoppf did not run out of pontoons. And Rubarth was luck, too, the final great slice of it.

But to achieve in four days in the Second World War what four years of the First had failed to do was so stunning – "the most sweeping victory in modern history," said Liddell Hart – that it seemed the rules had changed. It persuaded Hitler that Blitzkrieg – the "lightning war" that mesmerized the enemy, and which was soon credited as "the very own personal work of the Führer" – was an infallible way to wage war on the cheap. The success of the campaign in the West tempted Hitler to squeeze his limited resources in men and machines across ever-widening fronts, in Yugoslavia, Greece and North Africa, and on into the oceanic vastnesses of Soviet Russia.

Hitler became one of those whose "vague emotions and even vaguer minds", Clausewitz had noted with disdain, "impel them to expect everything from attack and movement, and whose idea of war is summed up by a galloping hussar waving his sword". After initial successes as stunning as Sedan, and on a vaster scale, the realities of industrial strength and manpower established themselves in Russia, and they did for the galloping Hitler and his Reich.

For the Sturmpionier, too. Walter Rubarth was killed in Russia on 26 October 1941.

2 · ACTION, ACTION, ACTION! PROMPTITUDE!

The lieutenant who defied orders to raise his own army of tribesmen – and won

The "plan of the war comprehends the whole
military act" (BOOK VIII, CHAPTER II). Seldom has a whole
military   campaign – planning, mustering forces,
recruiting allies, setting strategy and pursuing it,
commanding in battle – rested so much on
one man. And never, perhaps, on one so junior and
so far from home.

KINEYRI, INDIA ∗ 7 A.M. – 4 P.M. ∗ 18 JUNE 1848

IT BEGAN WITH MURDER.

In the late afternoon of 22 April 1848, a young British political officer called Herbert Edwardes was camped beside the mighty River Indus at Dera Futteh Khan, in India's Punjab. He was hearing a banal court case, and his tent was packed with curious Baluchi tribesmen, murmuring and straining to listen to witnesses. An exhausted dispatch rider galloped into the camp, his horse blown and streaked with froth and sweat.

He carried a letter. He said he had been ordered to deliver it to the senior British officer in Bannu, not far distant. Edwardes – pale, slightly bookish-seeming – was a mere lieutenant, but he was the only British officer for miles around. He was the son of a country rector, from Frodesley in Shropshire, a university graduate with a flair for writing who had dabbled in a little journalism on the *Delhi Gazette* after coming out to India as a cadet of the Honourable East India Company, through which British India was governed. He was 29, and he looked younger. Yet, as a political officer, he was expected to administer, legislate, raise revenues and levies, and uphold justice, acting as a sort of regional government-in-miniature for proud and restless natives.

Everyone knew the letter must contain dramatic news. "No one spoke, not a pen moved, and there was the kind of hush which comes over an assembly under some infinite feeling of alarm," he wrote.

Edwardes opened the letter. It was written in the elegant copperplate hand of an HEIC *munshi*, or clerk. It was from Patrick Vans Agnew, a fellow lieutenant of Edwardes, who was with William Anderson, another lieutenant, about 55 miles to the east in the city of Multan.

Vans Agnew wrote that they had been attacked "by a couple of soldiers who wounded us both pretty sharply. Anderson is worse off, poor fellow. He has a severe wound on the thigh, another on the shoulder, one on the back of the neck, and one in the face. I think it most necessary that a doctor should be sent down, though I hope not to need one myself." There was grave political news. "The whole [of the] Multan troops have mutinied," Vans Agnew wrote, "but we hope to get them round."

A few lines had been added in pencil in Vans Agnew's own hand. He asked for a regiment to be sent. "Pray let it march instantly, or, if gone, hasten it to top speed. If you can spare another, pray send it also. I am responsible for the measure. I am cut up a little, and on my back. Lieutenant Anderson is much

52

worse. He has five sword wounds. I have two in my left arm from warding sabre cuts and a poke in the ribs with a spear." It was signed "in haste", and dated at 2 p.m. on 19 April.

Edwardes was conscious that he had never been more moved in his life, and that never had it been so necessary not to betray the slightest emotion, or the tongues in the turbaned heads pressing in on him would begin to wag, and the mutiny spread. He looked up to the dispatch rider, and told him that he would attend to him shortly. Then he told the witness in front of him to continue with the evidence. As the "disappointed crowd" focused on the court case again, Edwardes fixed his eyes mechanically on the speakers, though "my thoughts were at Multan with my wounded countrymen".

BRITISH INDIA IN 1848 WAS A patchwork of semi-independent states, principalities, fiefdoms and territories. British power was exercised through the Honourable East India Company. The HEIC had started off by pioneering trade with India and China, but had begun to acquire territory after winning the Battle of Plassey and consolidating its hold on Calcutta and Bengal almost a century before. By 1848 it was regulated by Parliament in London, and was effectively a department of state acting as governor in India.

Morsel by morsel, the British writ was lapping towards the sub-continent's natural mountain boundaries. In the northwest, their eyes were on the Punjab and the plains and fertile valleys that ran up to the Afghan hills. British influence here was centred on the British resident (the representative of the governor general), in Lahore, and his young aides and political officers like Edwardes.

The wounded lieutenants were in the ancient city of Multan. It lay 200 miles southwest of Lahore, on the western edge of the Punjab. It had been seized from the Afghans in 1818 by Ranjit Singh, the great Sikh ruler who had consolidated the Sikh provinces into his kingdom, based on the Sikh durbar or court in Lahore. Multan was governed by Dewan Mulraj, a Hindu appointed by Ranjit Singh.

Mulraj paid a tribute to Lahore, but he had become rich, secure in his position of power, and self-satisfied. Ranjit Singh had died in 1839. Henry Lawrence, the resident in Lahore, set about exploiting the death of the "Lion of the Punjab" by undermining the new young maharajah, Dalip Singh, and extending British influence.

Political instability accelerated. It was clear to the Sikh *sirdars*, the leaders, that the British were aiming to take control of the Sikh lands. Dalip Singh's mother, Rani Jindan, realized this and had begun efforts to restore her son's power. Lawrence had put her under house arrest in the autumn of 1847. "Why do you take possession of the kingdom by underhand means?" she wrote bitterly to him. "Why do you not do it openly?" In Multan, Dewan Mulraj sensed a chance to be rid of both the British and his annual tribute to Lahore. He stopped paying it.

Lawrence sailed for leave in England in January 1848, the Punjab hot with rumour and intrigue. Lord Hardinge, the governor general of India, left on the same ship. His replacement, Lord Dalhousie, was an expert on railway regulation and a former president of the Board of Trade. He appointed an equally inexperienced bureaucrat, Sir Frederick Currie, to the most sensitive political post in India. An "office-wallah from Calcutta", a "regular Pecksniff" as his staff contemptuously dubbed him, Currie became resident at Lahore.

Currie at once announced that Mulraj would be replaced by a new Sikh governor of Multan, Sirdar Khan Singh, who was to take local levies and troops from Lahore with him. This guaranteed the fury not only of Mulraj, but also, avoidably, of the forces and mercenaries in Multan who were to be disbanded. Currie ordered two young HEIC lieutenants, Patrick Vans Agnew and

William Anderson, to accompany the new governor. It was a death sentence.

The Punjab is drained by the great Indus and by four main tributaries to its east that flow into it some miles south of Multan. The most westerly of these is the Jhelum, followed by the Chenab and the Ravi, on whose banks Lahore stands, and the Sutlej furthest to the east.

The two lieutenants sailed down the Ravi for part of their journey. Khan Singh and the escort, 500 Ghurkha infantry and a troop of cavalry, marched separately. It was a mistake. Neither did they realize that Dewan Mulraj and his Multani forces might see them as most unwelcome visitors. "We do not yet know precisely what our duties are to be," Anderson wrote to an old friend from his regiment as he went downriver, "but I fancy I shall be obliged to disband some 3,000 or 4,000 irregular troops of Mulraj, the late jaradar, tax collector ... To say that I am a lucky fellow is less than the truth ..."

They reached Multan on 18 April. Mulraj greeted them with flamboyant displays of friendship. The following day they were taken on a tour of the Multan fort, where Mulraj, apparently acquiescent, made a ceremony of handing over the keys to Sirdar Khan Singh. As the British officers rode back on the bridge over the moat, a sentry darted past their escort and stabbed at Vans Agnew with a spear. It was the sign for a general attack. Anderson was pulled from his horse and badly sabred. Khan Singh rallied the escort, and rescued the wounded men. He carried them to the Idgah, an open-air mosque a small way outside the city walls. Vans Agnew dictated a letter to Currie in Lahore, and gave the second with its pencilled postscript to a rider whom he told to cross the River Chenab and the Indus and make for Bannu.

Vans Agnew was dead before the rider found Edwardes on his way to Bannu. After a fitful night, the two lieutenants woke at dawn to find that almost all their escort of Ghurkhas had melted away. It was the first and only time that Ghurkhas have been known to desert British officers. It may be that Vans Agnew and Anderson paid for taking the river boat rather than marching with the men, so that the bond that normally tied the tough mountain men to their officers did not develop. It was not a mistake that Edwardes ever made. The open-sided Idgah, too, was a difficult place to defend.

In any event, as Edwardes found later, with the sun came violence. "An indistinct and distant murmur reached the ears of the few remaining inmates of the Idgah ... Louder and louder it grew, until it became a cry – the cry of the multitude for blood," he wrote. Khan Singh saw the howling mob approach. He begged Vans Agnew to be allowed to wave a sheet and beg for mercy. "Though weak in body from loss of blood, Vans Agnew's heart failed him not," Edwardes recorded. "He replied: 'The time for mercy is gone, let none be asked for. They can kill us two if they like, but we will not be the last of the English: thousands of Englishmen will come down here when we are gone, and annihilate Mulraj and his soldiers and his fort ...'"

It was to be a brave death, and in a sense a victorious one: it upheld the pride and prestige of the Englishman, and preserved his status, without which, so hopelessly outnumbered – at the height of empire, the sub-continent and its 300 million people were governed by a mere 5,000 of Vans Agnew's successors – the British would have been swept away in an instant.

Vans Agnew was sitting at Anderson's bedside, holding his hand and comforting him, when the mob burst in. He was struck repeatedly with a *tulwar*, a curved sabre, until his head was severed from his body. Anderson was hacked to death where he lay. At his durbar the next day, 21 April, Mulraj presented Vans Agnew's head to Khan Singh in a bag. He told him to go back to Lahore with "the head of the youth he had brought down to govern at Multan".

THIRTY-SIX HOURS AFTER READING Vans Agnew's letter, acting on his own initiative, Edwardes had raised a force of 3,000 irregulars from scratch, in order to mount a punitive exhibition. They were, he said, "bold villains ready to risk their own throats and cut those of anyone else".

He wrote of his men with deep affection, in a passage that is a distillation of the art of the infantry officer, and the reason why India could be held by so few British soldiers and administrators. "I learned to know them well," he wrote, "their characters, their circumstances and their wants; and, by living the same life as they did, wearing the same dress, talking the same language, and sharing with them all dangers and fatigues, they became attached to me, and I to them."

On 24 April he learned that it was too late to save Vans Agnew and Anderson. He expected the resident and governor general, Currie and Dalhousie, to avenge them by immediately despatching an army. If Mulraj was not at once brought to account, further Sikh mutinies and revolts would break out, and the whole British position would be threatened.

The other young political officers in the Punjab – James Abbott, John Nicholson, George Lawrence, Reynell Taylor, an extraordinary breed of men in their late twenties and early thirties – thought it a necessity. The murders and mutiny threatened their own lives.

Currie would have none of it. The "Hot Weather" was now upon them, he said. The commander-in-chief, the irascible and blimpish if splendidly titled Baron Gough of Ching-Keangfoo, had decided not to risk marching British troops over the Indian plains whilst it lasted. No troops would be sent into the Punjab, he said, "until the close of the Summer and Rainy Seasons". That meant not for six months.

The young men would have to fend for themselves. "As we learned from Lahore that no army would advance for the next six months," Abbott wrote, "it was manifest that upon the district officers lay the onus of preventing the threatened chaos." He wrote to Currie to let him know that "the opinion entertained by *all* his district officers, upon the feeble and un-English policy of deferring to punish an outrage so atrocious upon British honour ..."

Edwardes wrote letter after letter to Currie begging for action. He received no reply. He pressed on with raising his own small army. He was an excellent diplomat, fluent in the local languages, with a flair for understanding local custom and honour, and a fondness for the wild Baluchi and Afghans who joined him. He found a powerful ally in Bahawal Khan, the Nawab of Bahawalpur, who held lands east of the Indus.

Edwardes was a natural leader, who attracted the loyalty and affection of the rough Baluchis. He made sure that their leaders were sent letters of praise and thanks, and that they were awarded the "dearly-loved title of 'Ali Ja' or 'Of high degree'." As a result, he noted, they "followed me after to the wars, with four hundred Baluchi horsemen of their own tribe, and shared with me many months of exposure and hard fighting, without any recompense than their food!"

Edwardes secured the well-sited fort at Dera Ghazi Khan. He explained his strategy in a letter to his colleague William Hodson in Lahore, later famous as leader of "Hodson's Horse", a force of irregular light cavalry. His early success, Edwardes wrote, "should be followed up by Bahawal Khan crossing the Sutlej, my crossing the Indus, and driving all Mulraj's troops into the fort" at Multan. As for Hodson and the others in Lahore, he added sarcastically, once Mulraj was safely bottled up, "You might wait as many months as you choose with both safety and dignity until you are ready with a siege."

This he would do, orders or no orders – "Every post I urge this to the Resident, and I am quite sick of every post bringing no reply!" And indeed this is precisely what he did do.

THE SITUATION DETERIORATED AS Edwardes prepared his force. A further flood of Sikh troops deserted, and former sepoys and *sowers* of the Sikh regiments, infantrymen and cavalry, turned against the British.

Hodson himself was well aware of what was amiss. On 7 May he wrote to his father, the canon of Lichfield (like Edwardes, he was another son of the cloth who shone at war), that Lahore was surrounded with treachery. "No man can say who is implicated, or how far the treason has spread," he said. "The life of no British officer, away from Lahore, is worth a week's purchase." It was imperative that all the strategic forts still garrisoned by Sikh regulars should be taken over by HEIC troops before they went over to the rebels.

Edwardes warned that Mulraj was "daily adding to his means of resistance". He was digging up and mounting "long-buried guns", enlisting "an average of 100 men per diem", and collecting revenue. "Is this the sort of 'standstill' you all contemplate for five months?" he asked. And he added a colourful little postscript: "While I write this, the rebels are firing a salvo on the opposite side of the river, and have already fired nearly 100 rounds!"

He was furious to read in newspapers that reached him that brigades would eventually be mustered for the postponed assault on Multan. "Postpone a rebellion!" he wrote. "Was ever such a thing heard of in any government? Postpone avenging the blood of two British officers? *Should* ever such a thing be ever heard of in British Asia? ... Forsooth, to do nothing for five months! It is a burlesque upon politics, war and government. Give me two of all these prophesied brigades, and Bahawal Khan and I will fight and campaign for you while you are perspiring behind tatties, sun-screens, in Lahore and bottling up your British indignation on the slaughter of our countrymen. Action, action, action! Promptitude!"

Having heard that another regiment of Sikh cavalry had joined the rebels at Multan on 8 June, Edwardes had another go at the resident. "The event is most unfortunate and commences a new crisis," he warned, spelling out the perils to his colleagues. "It is painful to think what the consequences may be to Lieutenant Taylor in Bannu, Major Lawrence and Lieutenant Nicholson in Peshawar, and Captain Abbott in Huzara ... In the territory of which I have charge, I consider it to be my immediate duty to extricate my junior and assistant, Lieutenant Taylor, from the meshes of the army in Bannu."

Reynell Taylor had sent most of his troops south to bolster Edwardes's force. This left him desperately vulnerable to the Sikh infantry and artillery at Bannu. Edwardes ordered Taylor to ride to Peshawar for safety. He replaced him with Fatteh Khan. This was an old friend – "of all others the man for desperate times" – whom he had freed from the murderous clutches of the Maharajah of Kashmir the year before. When Edwardes asked him to go to Bannu, they both knew it probably meant death, but there was no time for sentiment. "I shall never forget the ghastly smile with which he replied, grasping me by the knees," Edwardes wrote.

"I would have wished to go with you to Multan, but as there is work to do in Bannu, I will go," Fatteh Khan told him. "I owe you both life, and honour, and as there is a God in heaven, I will pay my debt!" And pay he did, struck down by a chestful of musket balls shortly after getting to Bannu, having refused to make terms with the Sikhs because he had promised Taylor not to surrender.

Having added the Nawab of Bahawalpur's force to his own irregulars, Edwardes gained further reinforcement with the promise of two regiments of Sikh infantry and some field guns. These were commanded by Colonel Van Cortlandt, an officer of mixed race who had served the old Ranjit Singh as an independent commander. Edwardes still had no authority to march on Multan, and indeed was expressly forbidden to cross the River Chenab to get to it.

NONETHELESS, ON 11 JUNE EDWARDES began crossing the Indus, en route for the Chenab. He was lucky. A brisk and favourable southerly wind was blowing. "I effected the passage before nightfall," he reported, "with about two thousand five hundred of my newly raised Pathans and ten guns." Cortlandt and the remainder of the force were safely across the mighty river by the afternoon of 14 June. Edwardes estimated the river crossing as "nine koss wide", or about 13 miles. The sail-driven ferries would have taken more than twice that had the wind been foul.

He marched from the Indus to the right bank of the Chenab, arriving on the morning of 15 June. He had his Pathan irregulars with him, horse and foot, and 20 zumbooruks, native swivel guns mounted on camels. Van Cortlandt was still some distance behind him.

Currie had at last agreed, in a letter written to Edwardes from Lahore on 10 June, to allow him "to act as you think best, as circumstances arise". The letter did not reach him until he was making camp on the Chenab. Edwardes was amused to see that the resident had adopted his plan as if it were his own: "The best plan is undoubtedly to shut Mulraj up in his fort till the British force arrives there." Currie added, "If you have an opportunity of cooperating with Bahawal Khan (the Nawab of Bahawalpur), you should do so."

Edwardes already had, of course, as Currie knew full well, and his reply made clear how belated the permission was. "I have been obliged to incur the, at all times, dangerous responsibility to a political officer, of acting contrary to orders," he said, "and it is a relief to me, on the very bank of the forbidden river, to receive your kind and considerate carte blanche ..."

He now took stock. His force was now formidable, as long as he could combine its elements. The appointment of a young English officer, Lieutenant William Lake, to take "the political charge" of Bahawal Khan's force made this more likely. Between the three of them, Edwardes, Van Cortlandt and Lake should be able to fight a coordinated action. Edwardes estimated on the afternoon of 17 June that it would take three days to get all his men and guns across the Chenab.

Over that time, he still hoped that diplomacy and intrigue might allow him to avoid bloodshed. He wrote to Rung Ram, whom Mulraj had appointed commander of his force, urging him to desert. "Should he come over, I have assured him of every kindness," he said.

Far from that, though, he received warning on the evening of 17 June that he could not delay an instant. It came from Peer Ibraheem Khan, whose lengthy title – "Native Political Agent of the British Government at the Court of Bahawalpur" – made him Edwardes's close contact with Bahawal Khan's force.

Again, Edwardes's deep local understanding and friendships paid rich dividends. "The Peer was one of those men who are found only on frontiers, as the chamois is found only amid snows," he wrote. "On one side of his girdle was a pen, and on the other a sword; and he had a head, a hand and a heart, ready to wield either with vigour." The Peer warned that Rung Ram was moving down the left bank of the river towards the ferry, hoping to annihilate the Bahawalpur forces that had already crossed, whilst the rest watched impotently from the other bank.

Edwardes gave orders for the Bahawalpur commander "to strike his tents, and march down to this ferry at whatever hour of the night this letter reaches you ... *It must be done*, and there is no time for correspondence." He realized he could not get his own guns across the river during the night. He therefore filled the ferry boats "chock full of picked Irregular Infantry and dismounted cavalry, whose chief officers should take their horses, but no other horse were to go until morning". He got across a division of 3,000 Pathan irregulars, with 50 mounted chiefs, to the left bank during the night. They met up with the Bahawalpur force a little before sunrise.

EDWARDES SLEPT ON THE RIGHT BANK of the river, intending to take the second division across the following morning. At 6 a.m. on 18 June, though, no fleet of ferries was to be seen. Two little boats appeared. Edwardes got aboard, with a few horsemen and servants, leaving Cortlandt to bring across the remainder of the force as rapidly as he could.

With that, he pushed off for Kineyri on the left bank. About a hundred yards out, he said, "I was roused from a 'brown study', not unnatural amid plans so doubtful in their issue, so heavy in their responsibility, by a burst of artillery fire within a mile or two of the shore."

Columns of white smoke rose out of the jungle. The servants hoped anxiously that it was only a "salute", as the advance guard linked up with the Bahawalpur men, but the horsemen aboard the little ferry "knit their brows, and devoutly cried 'Al-lah! Al-lah!' at every shot, with an emphasis quite like pain on the last syllable. They quite *felt* there was a fight going on."

For his part, Edwardes felt it, too. "As I stepped on shore, and buckled the strap of my cap under my chin," he wrote, "I remember thinking that no Englishman could be beaten on the 18th of June." For it was Waterloo Day, the day that Wellington had beaten Napoleon. Edwardes added that he was not ashamed to say that he thought, too, of a "far more powerful aid – the goodness of our cause, and the God who defends the right." The dangers he faced were manifest. "A young lieutenant who had seen but one campaign ... alone ... to take command, in the midst of a battle, not only of one force whose courage I had never tried, but of another which I had never seen ..."

Yet, at that extreme moment, he said, "I doubted only for a moment – one of those long moments to which some angel seems to hold a microscope ... It came and went between the stirrup and the saddle ... I knew that I was fighting for the right. I asked God to help me do my duty, and I rode on, certain that He would do it."

The odds were so stacked against a man like Edwardes, a solitary 29-year-old English lieutenant commanding 18,000 men in a critical battle, that survival was impossible without such prodigious self-confidence and sense of purpose. It drifted very close to arrogance – how could Edwardes, a rector's boy from distant Shropshire, describe Mulraj's Sikhs as "rebels", as though they and not he were the interlopers? But his self-confidence was stopped short of vainglory by his empathy with his men, and by his faith.

Edwardes saw himself as a "pioneer of Christian civilization", and this sense of mission gave him the reckless courage that was the hallmark of his generation on the frontier. "A horse and a sword were all that were needful, and one never gave a thought as to danger," wrote Neville Chamberlain, another political officer, and namesake of the later prime minister. "Not that there was any levity in facing death. It was simply that one was possessed of a light heart to meet anything that came. There was nothing but God above and duty below."

Edwardes found the Bahawalpur force drawn up in a line on a "jungly plain", with his own Pathans on the left. He rode down the whole line, speaking to the Nawab's officers, making a point of praising them, begging them to be patient, and not to make any rash attack until the evening. By then, Cortlandt would have got his men and guns and horses across the river, and would arrive to support them. As they lay in the line, the men were restless under continuous fire from the Sikh guns.

After noon, the situation was becoming critical. The enemy had come close enough to reconnoitre their position. Edwardes had no cavalry to drive them back, and they identified the weak point in the line as Edwardes's Pathan irregulars. "The galling volleys poured into the new levies at this time were enough to shake older troops," Edwardes said, "and their impatience to be led on to strike a blow in their own defence was most difficult to restrain."

Edwardes dismounted. His *munshi* was behind him, "pulling out a Cachmere pen-box and paper from his girdle, just as quietly as if he had been in *cutcherry*", the law courts where he normally served. "A more striking instance of the quiet endurance of the Hindu character I never saw," Edwardes said, as he dictated a note to Cortlandt "informing him of our critical position", which he did not think he could hold after 3 p.m.

At 3.30 p.m. shot was tearing through Pathans and plough-ing up the ground they were lying on. "They were now perfectly mad," said Edwardes. Then he saw a force of enemy cavalry closing on his front in numbers his crude zumbooruk cannon could not deal with. He whispered to Foujdar Khan, a Pathan chief, to take his mounted officers and charge the enemy cavalry before they could reach his line, and force them back. "Put off the fight," he whispered, "or not a man of us will leave this field."

The "noble band" of Pathan horsemen – Edwardes was unstint-ing in his praise – spread their hands to heaven, "repeated the creed of their religion as if it were their last act on earth", passed their hands over their beards "with the haughtiness of martyrs", drew their swords and charged out of the jungle into the enemy horsemen. They caught them by surprise, and drove them back to their own line of infantry.

The rebels quickly rallied, though, and Edwardes in desperation decided on a charge of his whole line, unsupported by a single gun. It could have only one result, he said: "our total annihila-tion". The few minutes gained by Foujdar Khan – who had been severely wounded, and several of his men killed – proved decisive.

At "that moment of moments", when all seemed lost,

Edwardes heard the note of an artillery bugle from the rear. He made out "the rattling of wheels … the crack of whips and clank of chains …" Cortlandt had arrived. Six guns came with him, horses galloping them forward, and "panting after them, with clattering cartridge-boxes, might be seen two regiments of regular infantry …"

As they got nearer, the gunners shouted: "Grape! Grape! It's close enough for grape." The enemy thought so, too, Edwardes noted, for the next round rushed over his head, disturbing the air "like a flight of eagles". The enemy aimed high, and did little damage. Cortlandt's artillerymen were well trained and steady, and they quickly silenced two enemy guns. "A happy charge might carry all," Edwardes thought, and he ordered his infantry to rush the rebel artillery. Before they could reach the battery, half a dozen of his irregular cavalry galloped out of the trees behind him. Their leader took a ball straight in his mouth, but the enemy position was taken.

The guns continued to pour grape into the cover where the rebel infantry were lying, but the enemy rallied. A small body of cavalry approached Edwardes. He mistook them for the mounted chiefs of his Pathans. He rode towards them. "A single horseman advanced, and, taking a deliberate aim, discharged a matchlock at me … The ball passed through the sleeve of the brown holland blouse which I had on, then through my shirt …" The horsemen paid dearly for their daring, for two guns were instantly laid on them.

"And now," Edwardes wrote in his report, "I gave the word for the whole line of wild Pathans to be let loose upon the enemy. One volley from our battery, and they plunged into the smoke-enveloped space between the armies with a yell that had been gathering malice through hours of impatient suffering …" Once more, the artillery galloped to the front and laid into the rebels. "Our infantry was upon them, and another and another gun was abandoned in flight ..." The fight was hand-to-hand, and Edwardes was thrilled to see men "whom I had only enlisted a month ago" shaking their swords with "the most desperate and irresistible valour".

Rung Ram was not with his men. He had looked down safely on the fight below from his perch on an elephant in the surrounding hills. He fled, and the rebels began to give way. When they reached the cover of a hill, "they threw aside shame and arms, and fled, without once halting" to Multan.

"And so ended the Battle of Kineyri," Edwardes recorded, "which began a little after seven a.m. and was not decided until four p.m."

THE AFTERMATH OF BATTLE WAS TERRIBLE. "There was no European doctor to alleviate the horrors of war, by taking up lacerated vessels, amputating shivered limbs, extracting balls," Edwardes wrote. The air became pestilential, "from the action of intense heat on the dead bodies of men, horses, camels and gun-bullocks, in the thickets round about".

Dewan Mulraj's army abandoned 500 bodies on the battle-field, along with six guns and their ammunition, and many more bodies were found on the paths leading back towards Multan. Young Edwardes had won a mighty victory, and he followed it with another large skirmish, forcing Mulraj's men back into the fort at Multan, where they were bottled up. He had done what he had set himself to do.

His own reading of what would have happened if he had lost is an accurate view of his achievement: "Defeat would immeasurably extend the rebellion which I had undertaken to suppress, and embarrass the Government which I had volunteered to serve." To an extraordinary degree, too, his was a solely personal effort. He was inexperienced; prior to the Multan rebellion, he had taken a minor part in one battle, and had been wounded. He raised his own force, nourished it and led it, in a foreign land in foreign languages. He decided his own strategy. He acted in defiance or in the absence of orders. Most telling of his qualities was the way he won the respect and loyalty-to-death of Pathan tribesmen he had commanded for a month or less. And thus, single-mindedly, he avenged his countrymen's honour, and upheld their prestige.

IN THE EVENT, CURRIE CONTINUED to dither with a half-hearted siege of Multan. It was not until 22 January 1849 that the city, by now in ruins, finally fell. Dewan Mulraj surrendered, and Edwardes escorted him away for trial for the murders of Vans Agnew and Anderson. He was convicted and sentenced to death, but this was commuted to lifetime exile. During the Indian Mutiny, Edwardes raised another large force in the Punjab, which took part in the siege and capture of Delhi. He declined the governorship of the Punjab on health grounds, and in 1865 returned to England, where he was knighted. He died in 1868.

3 · PAVLOV'S HOUSE

A marathon of defiance

"For the conqueror the combat can never be finished too quickly, for the vanquished it can never last too long ..." (BOOK IV, CHAPTER VI). One man, over 58 days, personified this in an epic of house-to-house and room-to-room fighting across the ruins of a great city.

STALINGRAD ∗ 27 SEPTEMBER – 24 NOVEMBER 1942

THE GERMANS FELT THAT THEY HAD to be done with the Russians in 1942. The stunning victories of the early months of the invasion in the summer of 1941 had brought no end to the campaign. The Germans found something diabolical about the "stubborn, violent gestures" of an enemy who fought on to a terrible and inevitable death. The immensity of the Russian plains unnerved them, too, a "landscape always the same ... One can't bear it any more, the rain, the ankle-deep mud, the eternal sameness of the villages."

Before they returned to the front from leave in Germany, taking the long train ride back through country devastated by burnings and deportations, their families looked at them "with a certain look in their eyes, that animal curiosity when you gaze on something condemned ... and deep down so many of us believed it".

The German strategic situation had deteriorated greatly. Hitler had been able to concentrate his forces against Russia in the summer and autumn of 1941, with the British contained, and the Americans still neutral. In 1942, he faced war on far-flung fronts against a coalition with far greater industrial muscle than Germany, and with the certainty of an immense American build-up to come.

Both strategy and morale demanded that the knock-out blows be delivered before winter set in. This knowledge ran through the ranks, and gave a desperate edge to the year's campaigns. The Russians sensed it, too: hold on now, at any cost, and the future would see them saved. That idea, as we shall see, had a particular hold on the 13th Guards Infantry Division, on its commander, General Rodimtsev, and on Yakov Pavlov, a sergeant in a machine-gun squad.

Hitler moved to attack in the south, crippling Soviet industry by seizing the Donets industrial belt and the Caucasian oilfields. The penetration would be as deep as Baku on the Caspian. Stalingrad would be taken, so that the Germans could swing north up the Volga to cut off the Red armies around Moscow.

Operation Blau opened on 28 June, the German armour and divebombers smashing into four Russian armies. The flat steppe and cornfields offered no natural defences or protection, and the Soviet 40th Army disintegrated, isolated units wandering until their fuel or strength ran out. Tracked by German pilots through the clear dry air, they clustered by a stream or a farm building and awaited their fate.

The pit towns and steelworks of the Donets Basin were overwhelmed by the eighth day. With their whole southwestern front falling apart, the Russians set up a Stalingrad Front. It was allotted three reserve armies, the 62nd, 63rd and 64th, though they were badly mauled and split up in getting into position. On 20 July, Hitler told his chief of staff: "The Russian is finished." A vast encirclement battle was fought east of Rostov, which fell to the Germans on 23 July.

The German 6th Army, commanded by Field Marshal Friedrich Paulus, continued on for Stalingrad. The Don was crossed, Soviet aircraft – like the British and French on the Meuse in May 1940 – failing to destroy the pontoon bridge across which the Panzers flowed. General Vasily Chuikov, assigned to the front, came across two divisional staffs, travelling at speed in trucks packed with fuel cans. "When I asked them where the Germans were, and where they were going," he said, "they could not give me a sensible reply ..." The Red Army was showing signs of cracking. The first retreating units reached Stalingrad, in trucks with crumpled wings and staff cars with crazed windscreens, with "shreds of hay and tall weeds hanging from them", filled with the wounded and the belongings of fleeing headquarters staff. They drove down the broad avenues of the quietly expectant city, past the shop windows and the light-blue kiosks selling mineral water and syrups.

At 4:30 a.m. on 23 August the 16th Panzer Division broke out of the bridgehead on the great bend of the Don, and raced as a pack across 56 kilometres of parched steppe for the Volga. Stukas shrieked above, dealing with Russian strongpoints, whilst at 18:00 the bombers of Richthofen's 8th Air Corps dropped thousands of incendiaries, setting Stalingrad on fire, the wooden suburbs burning through to their brick chimneys, which stood erect above the ashes like ghostly regiments. Shortly before midnight, a Panzer unit radioed that it had penetrated the northern suburbs of Stalingrad and had reached the river that flowed on to the Caspian.

The Germans were on the Volga. They had arrived at the very heart of Russia.

STALINGRAD, LONG AND THIN, STRETCHED for 40 kilometres along the high western bank of the river. Three huge industrial complexes, the Tractor, Barricades and Red October factories, with surrounding garden suburbs of schools and apartment blocks, dominated the north of the city. The steeply banked River Tsaritsa ran at right angles into the Volga in the centre of the city, bisecting it near the hill of the Mamayev Kurgan, an old burial ground. This marked the rough division of the city between the industrial north and the business and administrative south, with its big department stores, grain silos and power stations. The city centre included Stalingrad-1, the main railway station, and the central landing stage for the ferries that crossed from Krasnaya Sloboda on the left or east bank. The river was 3 kilometres wide in places, with islands cutting up its flow into channels.

Far to the south, 640 kilometres from Stalingrad, in the central Caucasus, German mountain troops were unfurling the swastika flag on the 5,484-metre summit of Mount Elbrus, the highest mountain in Europe. Red Army Cossack divisions were mutinying, and minority peoples – Crimean Tartars, Karachais, Chechens, Kalmyks – were welcoming the Wehrmacht generals with gifts of white stallions.

The Soviet state seemed within a whisker of being swept away. That the Germans had reached the Volga, the third of its great rivers, beyond the Dnieper and the Don, gave fresh grounds for defeatism. Space, the traditional saviour of Russian armies, was running out.

There could be no further retreats. *"Ni shagu nazad!"* Stalin ordered the defenders of Stalingrad. "Not a step backward!" It was not rhetoric. His decree, Stalin Order No. 227, instructed army commands to form heavily armed "blocking detachments" of up to 200 men apiece. They were to form lines in the rear of the front, with standing orders to "combat cowardice" by shooting any Soviet soldier who tried to flee. They form a ghastly backdrop to the valour of those in the combat zone. Many troops – estimates range well into the thousands – were executed at Stalingrad, most in the early weeks. Ghoulishly, one man – a rifleman in the 45th Rifle Division – was executed twice. An execution squad stripped him of his uniform so that it could be re-used, then shot him, burying him in a shell-hole. They failed to kill him, it seems because they were drunk. The man dug himself out of his grave. "At night," the war correspondent Vasily Grossman wrote, "he came back to his unit in his bloodstained underwear. They shot him again."

The Red Army had young and able commanders now. Georgy Zhukov, a tank expert who had outfought the Japanese in the clashes in Mongolia in 1939, was appointed deputy supreme commander to Stalin in Moscow in August. Vasily Chuikov, in command in Stalingrad itself, was a peasant's son who had been a 19-year-old Red regimental commander in the Civil War. His optimism and tactical brilliance were untouched by the humiliations of 1941, when he was serving as a military attaché in China.

Paulus's 6th Army had problems as well as strength. The front extended for more than 3,200 kilometres, from Leningrad and the Baltic to the Caucasus, with the fresh and immense bulge at Stalingrad. The lines of communication were long and vulnerable. Paulus was dependent on two overworked railway lines for supplies and reinforcements, and one of them, from Rostov, was frequently cut by partisans.

The Germans failed to take the city by storm at the end of August. Their Panzers had swept over the bare steppe like ships at sea, navigating across the emptiness by compass, falling on Red units when the reconnaissance pilots found them, smashing them, and leaving the remnants to be swept up by the infantry. In the city, the tank commander was no longer a lofty sunburnt figure, master of all he surveyed from his turret. He was buttoned up inside the hull, and his horizon shrank from the immense blue skies of the steppe to the end of streets grey and black with dust and smoke and clogged with the debris of terror bombings. Blitzkrieg ran into the sands of house-to-house fighting. The Russians in the city had, just, a fighting chance.

Volga ferries transfusing men and supplies from the east bank were the key to Russian survival on the west bank. The crossings were bombed by day, and shelled both by day and night. Civilian casualties were terrible. The men were drafted into ill-armed and untrained emergency factory units, and many died during the early fighting. Women and children faced a fearsome journey across the city to get to the west bank. They were shelled whilst they waited, and again on the boats. More than a thousand died when the steamer *Iosif Stalin* was sunk. Many of the wounded died on the bank waiting to be evacuated. Hundreds who thought themselves saved by getting aboard another steamer, the *Borodino*, were drowned when she went down in midstream.

Chuikov was appointed commander of the 62nd Army on 11 September, crossing into the burning city by boat, whilst shrapnel splashed in the water "like trout". The temperature rose by several degrees as they approached the flames. Anyone without experience of war, Chuikov thought, must "think that in the blazing city there is not longer anywhere to live, that everything is burnt out". An awful scene awaited him on the west bank. A mass of women and children, covered with dust and soot, came out of their hiding places in shell holes and warrens in the debris to watch as the ferry drew in, with the "one desire of getting away to the other side of the river, away from their wrecked houses, away from a city that had become a hell …" The children were not crying, but "simply whining, and stretching out their arms to the water of the Volga".

Paulus was at Hitler's Werewolf headquarters at Vinnitsa on 12 September. Hitler was anxious to know when Stalingrad would fall. Paulus estimated that he needed another ten days of fighting, and then a fortnight to regroup. Early the next morning, he set 11 divisions, 3 of them panzer, at the Russians. The Germans had battered their way through to the Volga at the suburb of Kuporosnoye, at the junction of the 62nd and 64th Army fronts. The 62nd was isolated for the first time.

Three divisions of *Landsers*, German infantry, supported by tanks and aircraft, advanced block by block, smashing through the central part of the city towards the river. They took the crest of the Mamayev Kurgan and the engineers' house by Stalingrad-1 railway station. From here they laid down heavy machine-gun fire on the central landing stage. Some of the 62nd's 10,000-man divisions were reduced to a few hundred riflemen and machine-gunners. An entire tank corps had fewer than 50 tanks, and most of these were non-runners, dug in for static defence.

Chuikov's command bunker filled with dust from shellfire as he peered out through periscope binoculars. The field telephones were cut so often that he lost contact with his divisional commanders, except when a runner survived racing through the shrapnel-blasted open with a message. Both the cookhouse and the field kitchen took direct hits, so that Chuikov and his staff went hungry that day. During the night he moved from the Mamayev Kurgan to the "Tsaritsa bunker" sunk deep into the side of the ravine of the Tsaritsa River.

Next day, the Germans focused on Stalingrad-1. Stukas wheeled in groups of 50 and 60, subjecting the Russians to such an attack that an infantryman said no none could believe that "even a mouse was left alive". "This was an attack of exceptional strength," Chuikov recorded. "Despite enormous losses, the Germans were now crashing ahead. Whole columns of tanks and motorized infantry were breaking into the centre of the city ..." The *Landsers* of the 71st and 76th Infantry Division thought that they had won, rushing "to grab some souvenirs for themselves". Chuikov's men, lying in their hides in the ruins of houses and cellars, watched the "drunken Nazis jumping off the trucks, playing mouth organs, bellowing and dancing on the pavements ..." In Hitler's Werewolf HQ, staff cheered at the news.

The fighting was now within 800 metres of the 62nd Army's new command post. Chuikov threw in his last reserves to stop the Germans from overrunning him and getting to the river. A major with six tanks was ordered to hold the streets leading from the railway station to the landing stage, whilst a lieutenant colonel with three tanks attempted to deal with the machine-gunners in the engineers' house.

Stalingrad had almost fallen before Sergeant Pavlov reached it.

YAKOV FEDOROVICH PAVLOV WAS born on 17 October 1917 to a peasant family in the village of Krestovaya in the Valdai region of Novgorod. As he entered his teens, he would have witnessed the suffering and chaos caused by the confiscation of peasant land and livestock and the imposition of collective farms by Stalin. Those with initiative left the villages rather than toil as farm labourers for the state. Pavlov was among them. He joined the Red Army in 1938, as the worst of Stalin's purges of officers was passing.

He had been fighting since Hitler invaded in June 1941, in the southwest and on the Don Front. By now, shortly before his 25th birthday, he was a senior sergeant commanding a machine-gun squad of the 42nd Guards Rifle Regiment of the 13th Guards Division. This was attached to the 62nd Army. He was a versatile soldier, though he had no more than an elementary-school education, and had also served as a gun layer and the chief of a reconnaissance squad.

His division began to move to Stalingrad on 11 September, from Kamyshin, an important rail centre upstream on the Volga. It was a rough and sleepless ride. They crossed the bare steppe, the trucks and the pack camels kicking up dust clouds that attracted German aircraft. From far off they saw the towering plumes of black smoke that marked Stalingrad like a giant funeral pyre. In the afternoon of 14 September, as they got closer to Krasnaya Sloboda, the crossing point on the east bank, they passed through orchards and stands of willow.

Chuikov was already meeting in his command post with the 13th's commander. General Alexander Rodimtsev was only 37, though his grey hair made him seem older, and he was a veteran of the Spanish Civil War, where he had gained experience of street fighting in the Madrid University City in 1936. Many of the officers who had fought in Spain were purged the moment they returned, but Rodimtsev had been lucky, and his men worshipped him. His uniform was filthy from jumping into shell holes on the short but dangerous journey from the landing point. Chuikov told him to start getting his men across the river immediately. His orders were to "clear the centre of Stalingrad". He was to leave his heavy equipment and artillery on the east bank. His men would need rifles, sub-machine-guns, anti-tank rifles, knives and as many grenades as they could carry. This was to be close-quarters killing.

Pavlov's regiment was the first to cross. He and his comrades were issued with ammunition, grenades, sausage and bread. The battle was too critical to allow them to wait for dark. Men of the 1st Battalion under Lieutenant Chervyakov, reinforced with machine-gunners and anti-tank riflemen, went straight off the march onto the boats and barges at 19:00. On the water, they cursed the thin blueness of the smoke canisters, which gave no cover from the aircraft in the clear air above them. As they looked across at the blazing city, the ruined buildings were in sharp silhouette against the yellow flames and the smoke-streaked orange of the setting sun. Bombs and shells threw up gouts of water, and a boat was hit. There were screams as men were flung into the water, through the scum of oil and dead fish. When the surviving guardsmen got to the other side they jumped off the boats and fought their way forward. The air, Konstantin Simonov said, had "the sad smell of burnt iron".

The rest of the regiment came over during the night. Seven men were found guilty of trying to avoid the fighting with self-inflicted wounds, and were shot. A burning half-sunken barge lit the waters for several hundred metres, illuminating the motley armada of barges, fishing boats, small motor boats and rowing boats for the German gunners, who started shelling and machine-gunning when the fleet was about half-way across. A barge took a direct hit and sank, with 41 drowned and only 21 surviving. From the landing points, they were sent immediately into action by battalions. At dawn, the bombers came back looking for them.

The battle imposed its own natural selection on the newcomers. "They'd stand there on the shore, shivering with cold and fear," Viktor Nekrasov, the future novelist, recollected. "By the time they reached the line, five or ten out of twenty had already been killed by German shells, for with those German flares over the Volga and our front lines, there was never complete darkness. But the peculiar thing was that those who reached the front line very quickly became wonderfully hardened soldiers. Real *frontoviks*."

They fought the *Landsers* of the German 71st and 295th Infantry Divisions, from the landing stage, in the railway station, and on the slopes of the Mamayev Kurgan, whose crest, 90 metres above the Volga, commanded the crossing.

At a terrible price, the German onslaught on the city centre was held for the moment. Those who crossed suffered 30 percent casualties in their first 24 hours in the city. They were plugging the bloodiest gaps in Chiukov's line. By the end of the battle, Pavlov's division could count 329 out of the 10,000 who had crossed on and after 14 September. The rest were dead or wounded.

Many were killed in Stalingrad-1. The fighting on 15 October was exceptionally violent. At 07:50 the Russians logged the enemy approaching the station. At 08:00 the station was in enemy hands. At 08:40, the Russians retook it, only to lose it again by 09:40. By 10:40 the enemy were in the Pushkinskaya Ulitsa, 600 metres from Chuikov's command post.

On the evening of 16 September, the text of an intercepted radio message from Berlin was put on Stalin's desk in the Kremlin. "Stalingrad has been taken by brilliant German forces," it read. Russia "will soon collapse in her death throes". Stalin demanded to know if it was true. It took some time to establish that it was not quite so. Rodimtsev's men had staved off collapse.

Those of Rodimtsev's guardsmen still alive on 18 September were still fighting in Stalingrad-1, setting up their weapons in burnt-out carriages and along the low platforms. That night, the station was lost after five days of hand-to-hand fighting. By now, Chuikov recalled, "we had nothing left to counterattack with. Rodimtsev's division had been bled white." The guardsmen had abandoned several blocks of houses inside the city centre, but Chuikov said this could not be described as a withdrawal or a retreat: "There was nobody left to retreat." Only the heavily wounded crawled away, and it was from these that Chuikov learned how the men cut off from the rest of the division had made little groups of two or three, and entrenched themselves under railway carriages, in the ruined booking halls and waiting rooms, and had fought on until their end came.

They fought for days and nights at the giant grain elevator just to the south. "The grain was on fire, the water in the machine-guns evaporated, the wounded were thirsty, but there was no water," a survivor recollected. "Heat, smoke, thirst – our lips were cracked. During the day many of us climbed to the highest points in the elevator and fired out ..."

Two days later, the bombers concentrated from first light to pummel the remains of Stalingrad-1 into even finer rubble. "The station buildings were on fire, the walls burst apart, the iron buckled," the Russians reported, "but men went on fighting." German sub-machine-gunners and snipers got in behind the remnants of Chervyakov's battalion. He was wounded, and the man who took over from him, Fedoseyev, was killed in hand-to-hand fighting the next morning in the remains of the Univermag department store. The battalion was cut in half, and its remnants pulled back metre by metre to the Volga. Its last position was a three-storey building on the corner of Krasnopiterskaya and Komsomolskaya streets, defended by 40 men who held out for five days.

With 28 seriously wounded men in the basement, and the battalion's female nurse dying of a chest wound, German tanks brought the last walls crashing to the ground. At night, six wounded guardsmen broke out through the rubble, and crawled over a minefield and railway tracks to reach the river.

In the early hours of 23 September, a further 2,000 of Rodimt-sev's 13th Guardsmen crossed the river. German aircraft dropped parachute flares to illuminate them for the artillery, and for the sub-machine-gunners and Panzers who were within 150 metres of the bank as they scrambled ashore. During the day, Paulus extended the assault to include the industrial north of the city, with three giant factories and their suburbs. The Germans called this the *Tennisschläger*, the tennis racket, after the looping shape of its railway network, and its mesh of chemical plants, workers' housing and railway sidings. During the day, the Stukas set the oil storage tanks on the steepest part of the bank on fire, and burning oil tumbled into the river.

A fresh assault began on 27 September, a Sunday. The Panzers broke through to the Volga south of the Tsaritsa, and occupied an eight-kilometre sector of the river bank. By the evening, German troops had advanced 3,000 metres into Russian positions, leaving a "trail of two thousand dead men and some fifty blazing tanks".

That evening, sergeant pavlov was given a mission by Lieu-tenant I.I. Naumov, his company commander in the 42nd Infantry Regiment. The company command post was in a ruined mill a few hundred metres from 9 January Square. Pavlov was told to make a reconnaissance into German lines in the area around the square. This was at the heart of the city, close to the river, just north of the ruined grain elevator and Stalingrad-1, and a few hundred metres southeast of the Mamayev Kurgan, on the left flank of the 13th Guards front. The depth of divisional positions at this point were between 300 and 500 metres.

Individual buildings acted as strongpoints, little fortresses set into the line. The Germans had seized two, the "L-shaped House" and the "Railwaymen's House". The Russians had tried frantically to drive them out – the strongpoints provided the enemy with observation posts as well as firing points – but they had failed. There was a piercing danger that the Germans would make a further breakthrough to the Volga from the 9 January Square. As darkness fell on 27 September, 62nd Army had not a single reserve detachment. Even the training battalions had been flung into the pit. To launch a local counterattack, at Samarkandskaya Street, Chuikov drafted a dozen men from his own headquarters, and 30 riflemen who were recovering from wounds at aid posts. "One more attack like that and we'll be in the Volga," the general said.

Pavlov took three men with him, a lance corporal, V.S. Gluschenko, and two guardsmen, A.P. Alexandrandrov and N.Ya. Chernogolovy. They took with them sharpened spades, knives, sub-machine-guns, a light machine-gun and grenades. As he worked his way up from the river towards 9 January Square, Pavlov slipped into No. 61 Penzenskaya Street, a block that faces the square. It was very lightly held. There were two wounded Russians in the cellar, and a tenant, a sanitary specialist called Dmitry Kalinin. A few Germans were in the house as well, and Pavlov pursued them with grenades from one apartment to another, until they left. Pavlov worked his way to the top of the building. He realized its position, squarely across the line of advance from the square to the Volga, blocked the line the Germans were taking in their efforts to break through to the river. He sent a message to the command post the next morning: "Dislodged the Germans. Need reinforcements. Pavlov."

None came for three days. Pavlov was fortunate that the Germans shifted their attention further north for the moment. They cut into the northern industrial suburbs and factories on 29 September, bringing in a further Panzer and infantry division. Hitler gave a speech at the Sportpalast in Berlin the next day, boasting of having reached the Volga, and promising that "no man will shift us from this spot". Every day, though, the air had a little more of the chill of the coming winter to it, and fresh crosses bloomed atop the dead in the German cemeteries, from where, the survivors knew too well, they would indeed never be shifted.

The building Pavlov held, the "House of Specialists" to give it its pre-war name, had been one of the most prestigious blocks of flats in the city. It was in the airiest part of town, with officers' clubs and the promenade on the bank of the Volga within easy walking distance. Elite party *chinovniks* and senior industry bosses had apartments in it, with high ceilings and metal and stone balconies, some of them giving views to the river. The building fronted the 9 January Square, running back to Penzenskaya Street. It had four separate groups of apartments, each with its own entrances and entrance halls and staircases.

On 1 October, Pavlov was sent Lieutenant Afanasyev and men from the 3rd Machine-Gun Company, a group of anti-tank riflemen and some sub-machine-gunners. The little garrison now numbered 24 men. They crept forward and laid mines across the frontage on the square, but the activity seems to have alerted the Germans, who began to launch violent attacks. In one of the first of these, Afanasyev was killed. Pavlov retained command.

The front wall of the building that gave onto the square was pounded by artillery and tank fire. It slowly collapsed, revealing the apartments behind it, a bizarre sight, with pictures and mirrors still hanging on the back walls and furniture and carpets at crazy angles on the sagging floors, like a doll's house trashed by a delinquent child. Pavlov had his men smash through the walls between the adjacent blocks, so that they could move through the whole building from the inside. Sub-machine-gunners were placed at shell holes and windows in the first three blocks, closest to the Germans. A heavy machine-gun was sited in the semi-basement in the third block, in a good position to repel infantry attacking along the side of the building, but less vulnerable to German tank fire, since the Panzers could not depress their barrels enough to shell it. Two mortars were well forward towards the square. Anti-tank riflemen were posted in the semi-basement, and also at the top of the building, from where they could fire and throw grenades down onto the lightly armoured rear decks of the Panzers. A 45mm gun was sited in a ruined warehouse just behind the building, and three light machine-guns were carried from window to window. Four underground passages were driven out from the semi-basement, so that the defenders could get into positions in the rubble outside the building. A trench led back 200 metres towards the command post, where two men would go at a time to bring back rusks, ammunition, sugar and tobacco, carried back in a groundsheet.

Attacks were constant. The enemy infantry came first, to draw fire and identify positions. Then the Panzers came up and battered the building. Armour-piercing shot passed straight through, leaving no more than a jagged hole, but the tanks could not carry high-explosive rounds alone, for fear of meeting a T-34. The tanks could only hit the first three floors, because of the limited elevation of the turret, so that the anti-tank riflemen could operate both low and high in the building. The greatest threat to Pavlov's House, as it was called after it miraculously lasted out its first week, were the *Flammenwerfers*, the German flamethrowers. Their specific task was to set fire to the higher storeys of buildings that the tanks could not reach. All fire was concentrated on them as soon as they were spotted, with a single bullet enough to immolate them in their own flames. The mortarman, A.N. Chernyshenko, made a specialty of seeking out the flamethrowers.

Snipers roamed the attics and stairwells of the Pavlov House. The war correspondent Vasily Grossman watched the crack 13th Guards sniper, Anatoly Chekhov, in action. The 19-year-old was a frequent visitor to the Pavlov House. A German-occupied house was about a hundred metres away. Chekhov started his work as it got light. He sat on the landing of a staircase, with his rifle behind a grille to dissipate the smoke and muzzle flash. He looked at the Germans' uniforms, not their faces. His first kill was a soldier who had gone to get some water for the officers to wash. At first, the Germans walked. As his tally mounted, they began to run. After he had knocked down 17 in two days, they stopped coming out to lay mines or fetch water. On his third day, he spotted a German sniper. "I waited and fired. He fell down and cried out in German."

When it was sunny, he cast a shadow. So he didn't shoot when the sun was bright. "When I first killed, I was shaking all over: the man was only walking to get some water!" he said. "I felt scared. I'd killed a person! Then I remembered our people and started killing them without mercy ... I've become a beast of a man: I kill, I hate them as if it is a normal thing in my life. I've killed 40 men, three in the chest, the others in the head."

Other Russian-held houses were overrun one by one. The men scratched a message on the wall in one of them in their last moments: "Here died Rodimtsev's guardsmen faithful to the last."

A reckless bravado took hold of Pavlov's men. They expected to die. "They bombarded us from the air," Pavlov said. "Our house was assaulted by heavy tanks, we lived under heavy artillery fire. Machine-guns were firing without stop. Sometimes we ran out of ammunition. We didn't have enough water and food. We couldn't breathe, because of dust and ashes." Six of his men were killed in the first week. "We were not frightened at all, but we were tired," said Ilia Voronov, and it seems that the fighting was so intense that they had ceased to think in terms of personal survival. "You shoot day and night, then you try to build yourself a bunker to hide from fire. We slept on the ground. Rest? What rest could we have ...? Everything burns, everything rumbles, the house walls collapse ..."

Voronov was Pavlov's heavy-machine-gunner. He was a prime target, firing burst after burst of destructive fire, and the Germans got to within 12 metres of him, but he survived without a scratch. "They stop shooting, it gets boring," he told a newspaper. "They start shooting – that's fun." He was frantic that he could not get at the Nazi machine-gunners – "They were sitting in their holes, so we couldn't get at them." But there was no panic. In the moments of calm "We would sit together and say, almost praying: We won't let them through!"

The same determination, and the same phrase – "*Ils ne passeront pas!*" – had marked the French at Verdun. The *poilus*, though, were regularly rotated, and were rarely in the front for more than a fortnight. Pavlov saw almost two months crawl by, transfixed in a single ruined building. When he was asked why he fought, he replied with one word: *Rodina* – Motherland.

The Germans, so far from home, had no such consolation, and slowly the endurance of Pavlov and the guardsmen ground them down. "Are the Russians really going to fight on the very bank of the Volga? It's madness," a *Landser* wrote in his diary on 1 September. "Insane stubbornness ... Fanatics ... Wild beasts ... Barbarians," he wrote later in September. Then, as October wore on, he noted that: "The Russians are not men, but some kind of cast-iron creatures; they never get tired and are not afraid of fire." A day later, he added: "Every soldier sees himself as a condemned man."

Small assault squads of six or so men slipped out of Pavlov's House at night, killing with knives and sharpened spades as well as grenades. The night was Russian. In the darkness, they scuttled through the ruins and through the sewers and across ruined culverts, to knife and club – "like rats," the Germans said, "coming out to forage in the dark". Chuikov wrote of the "Stalingrad Academy" in house-to-house fighting. "Get close to the enemy's positions," he urged his men. "Move on all fours, making use of craters and ruins ... Go in grenade first, you after, go through the whole house ... A burst from your sub-machine-gun around what's left; a bit further – a grenade, then on again!"

By day, the Germans came back with their tanks and infantry. The grid plan of the city, with the streets running west–east to the Volga, helped them because a single tank at the western end controlled movement. The Pavlov House had become the key position for Pavlov's own regiment, and in turn the main effort of the division. It blocked the line through to the river, acting as a breakwater, dividing German assaults. Its very survival gave hope to Russian hearts, but chilled the Germans to the core. It began to figure on German maps, as a "fortress", at 48 degrees 42 minutes 57.88 seconds north and 44 degrees 31 minutes 58.59 seconds east, at an elevation above the river of 19.5 metres.

Luftwaffe pilots were flying four and sometimes five missions a day. They had so damaged the landscape that they were finding it more and more difficult to distinguish the targets given to them by the forward observers. "A saying from the Gospel often passes through my thoughts," a German wrote. "'No stone will be left standing one upon another.' Here it is the truth." The whole city was a mass of ruins and fires and smoke, with the only clues to one's position coming from the outlines of the main avenues and the few reinforced concrete buildings like the grain elevators that remained standing. Chuikov urged his troops to keep in as close an embrace with the enemy as possible, so that the fighters could not strafe and the bomber pilots could not release their loads for fear of hitting their own side.

The Stukas were never able to flatten the Pavlov House. It was at the most forward edge of no-man's-land, rubbing on the German line, within it during ground attacks, when German assault squads from the 295th Infantry Division broke in and occupied a floor or a room before being forced out. The two sides were so close that the Russians could sometimes hear the enemy arguing and eating, and make out the "tap dance of a German sentry in his torn boots".

THE GERMANS WERE BLEEDING. The 94th Infantry Division fighting on the south side of the Pavlov House was down to fewer than 550 active troops, its battalions reduced to 75 officers and men. Armour, no longer a spearhead, had become a sullen battering ram that was burning out in the street battles. General Kurt Zeitzler, chief of the general staff, called for the Stalingrad offensive to be aborted. Hitler would have none of it. Not "a single metre" was to be given up. Paulus called for three fresh divisions. All he got were a few engineer battalions flown in from Germany to dig saps to blow up Russian strongpoints. The Pavlov House was protected by the open spaces of 9 January Square. The sappers could not burrow their way to it.

Cloudbanks were building in the mornings. "The days were shortening again, you could definitely sense it. And in the mornings the air was quite cold," a German wrote. "Were we really going to have to fight through another of those dreadful winters? I think that was behind our efforts. Many of us felt it was worth anything, any price, if we could get it over before the winter."

They still thought that an all-out offensive would finish it. "*Rus, skoro bul-bul u Volga*," they shouted at the defenders of the Pavlov House and along the front. "Russian, you'll soon be blowing bubbles in the Volga."

It began on the morning of 14 October. It was a sunny autumnal day, but the smoke and soot from the massive air strikes reduced the visibility to 100 metres in places. The sky itself became "threatening and severe, with purple flames ..." The Germans crouched in their trenches as every available aircraft and artillery piece bounced gouts of masonry and rubble over the Russian positions. When the *Landsers* joined the battle in mid-morning, they could not distinguish individual shots and explosions in the general cascade of the bombardment. By noon, German sub-machine-gunners supported by 200 tanks had broken through to the Tractor factory. By midnight, they were fighting in the machine shops and assembly halls. In the night, General Zholudev's 37th Guards was torn to pierces. The general himself was dug out alive from the ruins of his command post.

Only a single regiment of fresh riflemen were fed into Stalingrad from across the river that night. With daylight, German aircraft and six-barrelled mortars interdicted the Tractor factory crossings. Nikita Khrushchev, the political commissar on the east bank, was in radio contact with Chuikov and agreed that the men trapped round the factory would have to fend for themselves. On the night of 15 October, 3,500 wounded were evacuated over the river. Hundreds of wounded soldiers and civilians lay untreated in the open on the river islands. The 37th Guards Division had only 200 or so men left alive, with one regiment down to 30 men.

A Panzer officer wrote of tanks that "crept screeching through chaotically destroyed workshops" in a battle fought "on and below the ground, in ruins, cellars and factory sewers ..."

Men driven beyond exhaustion slid into depression or, fuelled with amphetamine and schnapps, drove forward with wild exhilaration. "Supported by tanks, entire battalions would hurl themselves into the attacks," Chuikov recollected. "This enabled us to concentrate our fire on them."

Only a few pockets of the city still held out. None was much deeper than 300 metres from the Volga. In the north, the Red October plant had fallen. The Barricades metal works was half-gone, the Germans in the foundry facing Russians in the coke ovens. The Russians in the Tractor factory were split in three.

And in the centre, Pavlov's House still stood, defending a little scoop of land down to the river. It had worn the Germans down, into the profound exhaustion a Panzer officer blamed on fighting for a single house for 15 days. "The front is a corridor between burnt-out rooms; it is the thin ceiling between two floors," Lieutenant Weiner wrote. "From storey to storey, faces black with sweat, we bombard each other with grenades in the middle of explosions, clouds of dust and smoke, heaps of mortar, floods of blood, fragments of furniture and human beings ... The street is no longer measured by metres but by corpses ... Stalingrad is no longer a town. By day it is an enormous cloud of burning, blinding smoke; it is a vast furnace lit by the reflection of the flames. And when night arrives, one of those screeching howling bleeding nights, the dogs plunge into the Volga and swim desperately to gain the other bank. The nights of Stalingrad are a terror for them. Animals flee this hell; the hardest stones cannot bear it for long; only men endure."

By the evening of 29 October, having lasted 15 days, the momentum of the German onslaught was slowly dying away. Both sides stood "limp and exhausted from their murderous grappling in the misshapen, smoking ruins". The Germans were numbed by the thunder, the fire and smoke and blood, and the number of comrades they had sent back at night to be buried.

The names of ten of Pavlov's men who died in his House are known. Two Russians, Alexandrov and Afanasyev, the Ukrainians Sabgaida and Luschenko, the Georgians Mosiashvily and Stepanishvily, the Uzbek Turgunov, the Kazakh Murzeav, the Tajik Turdiev, Ramazanov from Tatarstan ... But Pavlov's House had held. Pavlov knew they had fended off the catastrophe with a few metres to spare.

ON 8 NOVEMBER, HITLER GAVE A LONG speech in the Bürgerbraukel-
lar in Munich. He spoke of Stalingrad. "I wanted to capture it and,
you ought to know, we are quite happy, we've as good as got it,"
he said. "There are only a couple of little bits left ..." It was broadcast, and its unspeakable and fatuous vanity was heard by 6th
Army soldiers as they huddled in their nests among the rubble,
or in the earth bunkers they had built in the sides of ravines. The
following day, 9 November, the temperature dropped to minus
18 degrees centigrade, and ice floes ground against each other in
the Volga.

In Pavlov's sector, Germans were seen to hold their hands out
of windows and over trench tops, in the hope of a wound that
would see them evacuated. Others came forward to surrender.
Men of the 13th Guards shot at least one, who had come forward
from his defended house whilst he and his comrades shouted
"*Rus*! Don't shoot!" Officers had to remind the men that this did
not encourage the Germans to desert.

Sometimes a silence "more disturbing than the roar of explosions" settled on the city. But there was an intensity to it, for,
from the attics of the Pavlov House and other vantage points,
snipers' eyes were scanning for the slightest movement, ready for
the single shot, to be followed by the scream "*Sani! Hilfe!*" as the
cry went out for a medical orderly. More and more, the men were
confined underground, in cellars and sewers and saps, with only
the tanks stalking the surface.

At 06:30 on 11 November, German aircraft and artillery
signalled the last desperate German assault. Only 1500 of Rodimtsev's guardsmen, with other burnt-out remnants, were left to
counter it in the southern sector. Shortly before noon, assault
troops with combat engineers and tanks reached the Volga on a
500-metre front, by-passing the Pavlov House, so that it and the
rest of Chuikov's left flank were cut off. The *Landsers* were filthy
and tattered, dragging assault guns with them, lashed by wind

and sleet. Chuikov admitted that "we were at our last gasp". Nowhere were the Germans more than 200 metres from the river: the Pavlov House was behind the front. But the bridgeheads held, and the attack dissipated in the downpours into bitter but formless skirmishes. By the evening of 18 November, an exhausted silence fell across the city, disturbed only by gusts of freezing rain and a sharply falling temperature.

The fighters in the city awoke next morning, 19 November, to the distant drumfire of 3,500 guns and mortars to the far northwest. At the most silent hour, when the Russian-dominated night gave way to the German day, the Russian defenders listened to the far-off ferocity of the guns with "frantic joy, hope and excitement". It went on for 80 minutes. Hitler had mocked the generals of the First World War, who had allowed themselves to become "besotted by an advance of a thousand metres". Now, in the limitless spaces of Russia, he had been lured into a contest for every metre, by an adversary who had drip-fed reinforcements into the city, relying on Pavlov and his ilk to bleed the Germans, whilst he had secretly built up his own forces to spring a giant trap.

For Operation Uranus, to cut off Paulus and the 6th Army, the Russians had assembled 1 million men, 13,541 guns, 894 tanks and 1,115 aircraft. Almost all this equipment was brand new, produced by plants in the Urals and Siberia over the summer and early autumn. In the breakthrough sectors, the Russians had over-whelming superiority. Zhukov had concentrated over 500,000 men with 250 regiments of field artillery and hundreds of Katyusha rocket launchers and new T-34s on an attack frontage of less than 65 kilometres.

As the opening barrage lifted, tanks with sub-machine-gunners riding atop them crashed through freezing fog onto the Romani-ans who were holding part of the long, thin flank created by the Stalingrad salient. By mid-morning, a wind was dispersing the mists and Russian aircraft bombed the still-fighting Romanians. The rout began at midday. General Konstantin Rokossovsky's men tore open a 13-kilometre-wide gap. Three Romanian divisions melted away in confusion and panic, hopelessly outgunned and out-tanked. The Russian T-34s raced on, steering by compass across the snowy wastes of the Don steppe, heading southeast for Kalach, infantry following in their tracks.

Paulus broke off the attack in Stalingrad. As he looked to his crumbling left flank, Russian forces under General Andrei Yeremenko prepared to bash in his right. At 10:00 on 20 November, two armoured corps and nine infantry divisions fell upon the 4th Romanian Army. By evening, the Russians were pouring through the bloody rents in both flanks, driving southeast and northwest towards each other over 30 kilometres in Paulus's rear.

Rokossovsky's tanks raced on across the steppe for the bridge over the Don at Kalach. The bridge was close to a German anti-tank training school, where captured Russian tanks were often seen. Driving through the pre-dawn darkness on 23 November, the T-34s were mistaken for captured machines. They burst over the bridge, machine-gunning the guards before they could blow it up. At 14:00, green rockets identifying each other, Rokossovsky and Yeremenko linked up. Paulus was surrounded, together with his army, 100 surviving tanks, 2,000 guns, 20 infantry and armoured divisions, elements of two Romanian divisions, a Croat infantry regiment, interpreters, surgeons, cartographers, dogs and dog handlers.

In the Berghof, his Alpine retreat, where snow meant winter sports rather than frozen flesh, Hitler mocked the generals who warned that the 6th Army was in mortal peril, and insisted it had to break out before the Russian ring around it set solid. "They always overestimate the strength of the Russians," he said. Hermann Goering, fat, drug-ridden, promised that the Luftwaffe could supply Stalingrad with 500 tonnes of supplies a day by air.

In truth, he had less than half the necessary aircraft, and the flying conditions were appalling, the pilots making approaches to rough airstrips through severe turbulence and snowstorms.

ON THE MORNING OF 24 NOVEMBER Hitler ordered Paulus to stand firm on the Volga. That day, Sergeant Pavlov was relieved. He had held his House for 58 days.

It was not over yet, since the Germans would neither break out nor surrender. They had to be shot and starved and frozen into defeat, a terrible process that took a further two months, but leading to a result that was by now inevitable. A relief force under General Hermann Hoth set out across the frozen steppe, strewn with dead horses and wrecked tanks, with buses for the wounded and carts of food and ammunition towed behind tractors. On 19 December, one of Hoth's Panzer divisions was close enough to see the flares hanging over the Stalingrad perimeter.

On Christmas Day, 1942, Hoth was forced to retreat by Russian attacks deep in his rear. The 6th Army knew it was doomed. In the ruins, a chaplain celebrated communion on an altar made from an ammunition box. "Yesterday the box still held anti-aircraft shells; today my hand spread over it the field-grey tunic of a comrade whose eyes I closed last Friday in this very room," he wrote. "I read my boys the Christmas story according to the gospel of Luke ... The men sat on footstools and looked up to me from large eyes in their starved faces."

Only instinct kept the 6th Army alive. A meteorologist continued to make notes on cloud ceilings for aircraft that never came. "Around me, everything is collapsing, a whole army is dying, day and night are on fire," he wrote. A Russian call for surrender was refused on 8 January 1943. At dawn on 26 January, tanks from the 21st Army met up with the survivors of the Guards 13th near Pavlov's House and the Mamayev Kurgan. The 62nd Army, fighting in isolation for almost five months, had company again, celebrated with tears of joy and vodka.

The end was very close now. It came at four in the afternoon of 2 February. Paulus, with 23 generals, 2,500 other officers and 90,000 other ranks surrendered.

IT COULD NOT, OF COURSE, BE SAID that Yakov Pavlov won the Battle of Stalingrad, nor even that he prevented it being lost, though after it was all over Chuikov wrote of Pavlov's House as the symbol of Soviet courage, and credited the sergeant and his men with personally killing more of the enemy than the Germans had lost in taking Paris.

Pavlov's House, which for almost two months served to block a German sweep through the central sector, was of unquestioned military significance. It broke up major German assaults, and, on quieter days, its snipers preyed on German nerves and lives. In purely military terms, though, the Russian guns and rocket launchers on the east bank of the Volga were fundamental to the victory on the right bank. The novelist Konstantin Simonov said: "We certainly could not have held Stalingrad had we not been supported by artillery and the Katyushas on the other bank all the time. I can hardly describe the soldiers' love for them."

But morale and nerve were the critical elements in this drawn-out and ghastly contest. Here Pavlov was key. Rodimtsev's guardsmen disappeared by the battalion into the belly of the beast. Each night, as both sides buried their dead, after the frenzies of the German-dominated day, Pavlov was still among the living, though in the most exposed spot of all. He was a touchstone, a symbol, an amulet. The Russians believed that his House was marked as a fortress on Paulus's personal maps. And, in a battle of this length, which had no single decisive moment, continuity was more important than momentum. Pavlov, to an extraordinary degree, provided continuity of resistance. Fifty-eight days, one position, and one sergeant, always, reliably, still fighting. And he was continuity, of the most abrasive, soul-destroying kind, for the other side, too, since the Germans were aware that his House was a rock on which their daily efforts were dashed.

Pavlov and his House were the distillation of Clausewitz's great martial virtue of perseverance:

> There is hardly any celebrated enterprise in war which was not achieved by endless exertion, pains and privation; and as here the weakness of the physical and moral man is ever disposed to yield, only an immense force of will, which manifests itself in perseverance … can conduct us to our goal.
>
> BOOK III, CHAPTER VII

Yakov Pavlov went on to serve with the 3rd Ukrainian and 2nd Byelorussian Fronts. He survived the war. He was awarded the Hero of the Soviet Union with the Order of Lenin and the Golden Star medal, by an edict of the Presidium of the Supreme Soviet, on 27 June 1945. He was demobilized in 1946, and, after graduating from the Central Committee's Higher Party school, was an official in national economic affairs. He is sometimes confused with Ivan Dmitriyevich Pavlov, also a much-decorated sergeant in Stalingrad, who later became famous as Archimandrite Kyrill of the Orthodox Church at Zagorsk. After Stalingrad had been rechristened Volgograd, Yakov Pavlov was made an honorary citizen of the city. A boarding school for orphans and a fishing factory ship were named after him. He died in 1981.

4 · THE FIELD MARSHAL, THE PRIME MINISTER AND THE SERGEANT

Saviour of France in one war, traitor in the next

Information is vital in war. It is "the knowledge which we have of the enemy … therefore, in fact, the foundation of all our ideas and actions." It can be dangerous – "a great part is contradictory, a still greater part is false" (BOOK I, CHAPTER VI) – but when it is right it can see a sergeant help win a war.

THE CHAMPAGNE FRONT, FRANCE ★ 14 JULY 1918

A WIRY MAN IN A GREY CIVILIAN SUIT, shiny and threadbare but smartly pressed, was decorated in the great Court of Honour of Les Invalides in Paris on a blustery spring morning in 1927. In his left hand he held, not a sword as the others on parade did, but his felt hat.

The Great War was long over, and he was now working for a furniture maker in the provinces. Experts analysing the war, however, had examined his actions as a 21-year-old sergeant at the front on Bastille Day 1918. As a result, he had been summoned to this place, the spiritual heart of the French army, where *gloire* and the body of Napoleon are enshrined.

His name was Joseph Darnand. His wartime commander, General Gouraud, invested him with the Légion d'honneur, dubbing him on the shoulder with his sword. It was a commonplace enough award, but a letter from Raymond Poincaré, the French president, regretting his absence from the ceremony, made it quite clear that Darnand was very far from ordinary.

"I would like to have joined my homage to that rendered to Sergeant Darnand," President Poincaré wrote, "as an *artisan de la victoire.*"

That title, "craftsman of victory", was the greatest honour that France bestowed after a war that had cost her one and a half million dead. It was given to three men. Georges Clemenceau, the fearless wartime prime minister was one. So was Marshal Foch, the supreme commander of Allied forces. Darnand was the third.

Gouraud met another great figure of the war, Marshal Pétain, a few days later. The two men shared their recollections of the sergeant "with eulogy". Pétain said that Darnand's deed "was the turning point of the war". Gouraud agreed, praising the young man's "courage and audacity" as a "prime cause of victory".

Later, much later, Joseph Darnand would be shot for treason.

AT 00:10 ON 15 JULY 1918, ON THE Champagne Front in eastern France, the German Crown Prince Wilhelm heard a "thunderous roar, as if the end of the world was come". More than two thousand German batteries of all calibres created, he said, "an overwhelming scene, the pitch-black sky stabbed by quivering flashes of lightning, bursts of flame, an apocalyptic symphony of destruction". Sleeping Parisians were woken by the rumble of the guns. Housewives hurried to turn off gas meters, and bridge players shaded their lamps. They thought the city was being bombed by Zeppelins, so loud were the explosions and vivid the flashes in the sky.

This was the start of Operation Friedensturm ("Peace Assault").

The Germans had tried three times earlier in the year to break the Allied armies. It was their last throw of the dice. General Ludendorff, the driving force of the German High Command, knew that American troops would soon be arriving in France at the rate of 300,000 a month. His own troops were weakened by the fierce battles they had fought in the spring, but he thought that the French and British had suffered worse. German strength was "still high enough to allow us to strike one more blow," he said, that would "make the enemy ready for peace. There was no other way."

Troops who had fought on the now defunct Eastern Front were still being transferred to the west. They helped give Ludendorff a distinct superiority in numbers over the British and French for the first time. They included men from Alsace and Lorraine, the two French regions that had been forcibly incorporated into the German Empire after the Franco-Prussian War of 1870. Their loyalty to their new masters was suspect. A unit had deserted en masse to the French at the start of the war. The Germans were careful thereafter to station them on the Eastern Front against the Russians. When the Bolsheviks sued for peace in 1917, there was no need for them there, and they were brought back to the west.

Planning for Ludendorff's desperate do-or-die offensive was completed by the end of June 1918. Crown Prince Wilhelm's army group was to attack the French armies on both sides of Reims, crossing the Marne on a broad front from Château-Thierry to Châlons-sur-Marne. The salient that dug into the German line at Reims would be sliced off, surrounding the city and trapping large numbers of Allied troops, whilst the crossing of the Marne would so threaten Paris that the British would be forced to transfer divisions from Flanders. Having broken the French and the two American divisions on the Marne, Ludendorff planned to finish the war by breaking the now under-manned British in Flanders in Operation Hagen, a linked offensive.

He was right in believing that the troops commanded by General Gouraud on the Reims Front were vulnerable. The French had been bled white. The pre-war regulars had been massacred in the First Battle of the Marne in September 1914, and draft after draft had gone to their deaths since then. Because units were rotated regularly, many of the troops around Reims had fought in 1916 in the ten-month meat-grinder of a battle at Verdun. One fresh unit after another had marched along the hallowed *Voie Sacrée* into the zone of eternal dust and flares and the constant din of shelling – "*Trommelfeuer*", they said, using the German word for "drumfire". As they marched they passed the survivors of the slaughter returning from the front. The sight of one such revenant, beyond speech, mouth pursed, eyes glittering in their sockets, his face the colour of his grey-blue greatcoat, warned the men moving up what was to come. "He waved an emaciated arm to take in the horizon," a lieutenant wrote. "We knew this mute gesture exposed a horror beyond words."

Awful sights abounded. "Helmets full of blood," one *poilu* wrote, "rifles splashed with blood, a white shirt spotted with red. Near a tree, a head." Another saw a great pile of earth after a shell exploded, and sticking out of it, to a distance of 40 centimetres, were "legs, arms, hands and heads like the bloody cogs of some monstrous capstan". The novelist Henri Barbusse spoke of "super-human exhaustion, water up to your belly, unspeakable filth, rotting faces and flesh in tatters".

When Verdun was over, the French had lost 61,238 dead and 101,151 missing, vaporized by direct hits, entombed in mud, rotted beyond recognition. Four months later, the French went onto the offensive on the Chemin des Dames, between Reims and Soissons. When the *poilus* went over the top, they found the German wire largely intact, and German machine-gunners and mortar crews dug in on the heights. The creeping French artillery barrage hit the advancing infantry it was designed to protect. By the second day, 120,000 French troops were dead on the battlefield.

Units now began to mutiny, not while they were at the front, but in "collective indiscipline" in the rear. A battalion near Reims refused to march when ordered back into the line after only five days rest. Other battalions moved up, but bleated like sheep as they did so. The movement spread quickly. A division that had fought repeatedly at Verdun refused to move to the front at Reims. Within a month, eight divisions had disobeyed orders. The mutiny was defused by Marshal Pétain, the victor of Verdun. He used the stick sparingly: of the 554 men sentenced to death by court martials, only 49 were shot, *pour encourager les autres*. Mainly, though, he used the carrot. He improved the quality of army food and wine, and mattresses, and increased leave. Above all, he reassured the troops that there would be no more great blood-drenched attempts to break through the German lines. The French would wait "for the Americans and the tanks".

The troops of the French 4th Army facing the Germans in the Reims sector were fatigued. They were waiting, for the "Sammies", the Americans, to take the brunt of any fresh fighting, and for the new Renault 17 light assault tanks that were intended to take the lead in any attacks. Where the Americans brought "a fresh, surging vigour to the body of France, bled almost to death," a French officer wrote, the *poilus* "in torn uniforms, hungry and hollow-eyed, were scarcely able to hold themselves upright". Ludendorff had every prospect of breaking them.

The German commander moved up his own troops and guns in the greatest secrecy. The wheels of all vehicles were wrapped in sacking. Reconnaissance, ammunition delivery and all movements were to be made "without any noise whatever". An order to the German 7th Army on 7 July stated that movement by day, "even by headquarters, small units or single vehicles", was now prohibited.

German regiments were given their attack orders on 12 July. They were to go over the top at 04:30 on 15 July, after one of the most violent artillery barrages of the war, orchestrated by the barrage specialist Colonel Georg Bruchmüller, known as Durchbruchmüller, "Breakthrough Müller". The Germans were confident that their build-up, with 48 divisions poised to assault, had passed unnoticed by the French armies facing them. "Our offensive intentions have been kept hidden from the enemy," the 7th Army war diary noted on 14 July. "We may expect to take him by surprise."

Paris enjoyed Bastille Day on 14 July. There was sadness at the death of Quentin Roosevelt, son of the former president, whose plane went down in flames during a dogfight over the German lines near Château-Thierry, but the parade was more magnificent than ever. Troops from a dozen nations marched or rode from the Arc de Triomphe to the Place de la Concorde – Italian Bersagliere in cockerel-tail hats, resplendent British Life Guards, Greeks in stiff white skirts, and Americans, the cause of Ludendorff's gamble on the Marne, in battle-stained uniforms and tin hats.

Allied officers crowded the Paris restaurants on a still and luminous summer night. To their east, Crown Prince Wilhelm was being driven to an artillery observation post, to oversee his armies' advance. His father, Wilhelm II, was celebrating the 30th anniversary of his accession to the throne of Imperial Germany at his own observation post a few miles north of Reims. He issued a message describing the war as "a conflict between the two approaches to the world. Either the Prussian-German approach – Right, Freedom, Honour, Morality – is to remain respected, or the Anglo-Saxon, which means enthroning the worship of gold."

As Bruchmüller's mighty barrage began, it seemed that the Kaiser's approach must triumph. Colonel Billy Mitchell, commander of the American Air Service, heard the rumbling as he dined late in Paris. He looked at his watch. It was exactly 00:10

on 15 July. He saw tremendous flashes in the sky as he tumbled out of the restaurant and into his staff car to race off to his headquarters. The noise at first reminded Pearl Adams, an Englishwoman living in Paris, of an immense symphony, and then a funeral march, until it settled into a roar like a heavy truck. "The front," her neighbours whispered fearfully, as Crown Prince Wilhelm praised his batteries in ecstasy as they "hurled their iron hail at the foe". Who could survive it?

It was falling, in fact, on empty trenches.

THIS WAS DARNAND'S WORK. HE WAS just 21, a lean figure, straight-backed with a countryman's big hands, and an intense simplicity and directness to the dark eyes. He came from Coligny, a small railway stop on the line from Paris to Bourg-en-Bresse, where the fields run westward to the Saône and the woods roll eastward to the foothills of the Jura. His grandfather had been the village cartwright, and his father was the stationmaster's assistant. His family were good Catholics. He was sent to a Church college, and his mother used his father's railwayman's concession to take the children to Paris and High Mass at Sacré-Coeur for days out. At 14, his parents too poor to keep him at school, he was apprenticed to a cabinetmaker, at 20 sous a week.

He volunteered at the outbreak of war in 1914. But he was too young, and too small, weighing only 50 kilos. It was only in 1916 that he was reckoned *bon pour le service*. He joined the 35th Infantry Regiment. He was a natural soldier, corporal from April 1917, and sergeant from June the same year, transferring to the *grenadiers d'élite* of the 366th Infantry. These were the cream of the regiment, known as *nettoyeurs de tranchées*, "trench cleaners", but also used for night patrols, reconnaissance, ambushes and other *coups de main* or blows against the enemy front lines.

He had already earned the Croix de Guerre – in November 1917 for "distinguishing himself daily" in patrols – and five citations. In March 1918 he had "cleaned" 300 metres of enemy trenches and dugouts. A month later, his "valour, energy and remarkable tenacity" had seen him penetrate to the third German trench line, running a huge risk of being killed by French artillery, which was laying a barrage on the rear trenches to keep the Germans' heads down. In May, a stronger German force fell upon his own patrol, but he fought it off with pistol and grenades, and took four prisoners.

In July 1918, Darnand's regiment was in the line on the Reims salient on the Champagne Front. The city was all but destroyed. Only 20 of its 40,000 houses were left undamaged. It was protected from the Germans by a little group of small hills with grand, Alpine-sounding names – Mont Cornillet, le Casque, Mont Téton – that remained in French hands four miles beyond it.

The 366th held one of these ridges, le Mont-sans-Nom, the "nameless mountain", only 175 metres high. The ground between them and the Germans was deeply pitted where heavy shells had scooped out the earth, and criss-crossed with barbed wire. Clumps of wire smashed by shellfire lay rusting in the hollows. It was a forlorn place, and today it still has traces of shell holes and sunken casemates. Much of the area is now a *zone interdite*, forbidden to the public by the French atomic energy commission, which has installations among the old German positions.

The regiment was part of the French 4th Army, commanded by General Henri Gouraud. He feared an enemy offensive, for much the same reason that Ludendorff was promoting it: he felt that the Germans could smash straight through his weakened forces, and cross the Marne to have Paris at their mercy.

By 14 July, the general was convinced that an attack was imminent. There was one very perilous way to find out. Gouraud ordered the 366th's grenadiers to make patrols in depth to "capture live prisoners at all costs". Each battalion had an elite group of grenadiers, later called corps-franc and then commando. They provided the men for the three 12-man squads detailed to carry out the mission. One was commanded by Sergeant Darnand.

The men were briefed by Lieutenant Balestié, the officer responsible. He told them that they would leave their own trenches at 19:55. A section of infantry and some engineers were held in reserve, he said, but there would be no artillery support. "The mission is to take prisoners and to bring back maximum information," the lieutenant said.

DARNAND SLIPPED OVER THE TOP of the French trenches as the setting sun dazzled the Germans. He was lightly armed, with a pistol, grenades and a long-bladed hunting knife, and a whistle for communication. His face was blackened with mud. Speed and agility, the ability to slip rapidly in and out of trenches and bunkers, were paramount. He was slender and lithe, and a country boyhood catching rabbits had given him an eye for the lie of the land.

A small ravine offered some concealment for the first 200 metres. He and his men got beyond the first two German trench-lines without being spotted. Raiders usually grabbed their prisoners from the first trench they came upon. Darnand knew that the prizes – men of real intelligence value with knowledge of German plans and intentions – were not to be found in the front trenches, but in the bunkers and command posts in the rear. He kept going.

The Frenchmen were among the officers' dugouts and command posts in the fourth trench line when the first sentry spotted them. Hand-to-hand fighting broke out. Five Germans were killed. Darnand lost two grenadiers dead and four wounded, but he took 24 prisoners, including an adjutant. Some were Alsatians, happy to turn their coats and go with him. He ransacked a command post, taking telephone logs, message pouches, officers' satchels, maps and orders.

He hastened back as general firing broke out, the captured Germans, bayonets in their backs, acting as shields as they crossed the German trenches. He regained his own trenches 40 minutes after setting out. His battalion commander, Commandant Besnier, embraced him. The two other squads had returned five minutes earlier, with four prisoners between them, taken from the front line, and useless for intelligence.

Darnand's prisoners were interrogated immediately at the regimental command post. The Alsatians among them talked freely of the offensive that was about to break on the French line. The captured documents were sent with all speed to the Deuxième Bureau, the intelligence staff, at 4th Army. By 21:30 Gouraud realized that Darnand had struck gold.

The general knew that Bruchmüller's barrage was set to start in less than three hours, at ten minutes past midnight. He knew that Crown Prince Wilhelm's infantry would attack at 04:30. He knew, too, the direction of the attack, towards the Marne. That, at least, was the intelligence Darnand had brought back. Ought Gouraud believe it? Was it too good to be true?

Fake intelligence is often acted upon, whilst genuine evidence is set aside as planted. A few months before, the Germans had "accidentally" released a captive balloon from its moorings near Reims. The French shot it down, as the Germans hoped, and found orders for a major attack on the Champagne Front, supposedly to start a few days later, on 26 March 1918. This was sent to Marshal Pétain, commander of French reserves, who turned down a request to send reinforcements to the hard-pressed British in Flanders on the strength of it. Those orders turned out to be fake.

Gouraud was brave – he was fierce and red-bearded, and nicknamed *le lion d'Afrique*, after colonial campaigns that had cost him an arm and half a leg – and he decided that Darnand's haul was genuine. He ordered the immediate evacuation of the front lines, pulling back his troops 4 kilometres into the rear. Only a scattering of listening posts were left to observe the German advance.

At 23:30, he ran another huge risk, unmasking his own batteries by firing on the German mustering points. The German 5th Grenadier Regiment was caught in its jump-off positions so severely that two companies disintegrated and others were savaged. "Men, panic-stricken, run this way and that, seeking only one thing, to get under cover," recalled Lieutenant Hesse. "Again, the shells, the dull explosions of gas-grenades ..."

The staff at the French command post at Châlons-sur-Marne fretted as midnight passed. They feared Darnand's prisoners and papers had lied. Gouraud told them to wait. At 00:10 on 15 July, the thunder of heavy shells roared overhead, and the lights went out. The sergeant had brought back the truth. "All's well, old man," Gouraud told his deputy, General Prételas. "Let's go to bed."

AT 04:30 THE GERMAN INFANTRY moved forward. They found the trenches on the Mont-sans-Nom turned into a chalky moonscape by their own guns, but empty. French shells had started catching them as they had massed before midnight, and had been following them ever since. As they moved on, they were cut down by well-sited, hidden machine-gunners. They were exhausted before they reached the new positions where Darnand and his regiment, "fresh as paint", were waiting for them.

On the Marne, the American 38th Infantry Regiment knew from Darnand's treasure trove that the Germans would emerge from the reeds and bushes on the north bank at 04:30. Gas and smoke mingled with morning mist to cause a dense fog, but the Americans were expecting them and caught them with rifles, automatic weapons and shells when they were halfway across. "Scores of German boats were shattered or sunk," a doughboy wrote. "Hundreds of Huns jumped into the water and were drowned.

Those who swam to our side were either killed or wounded."

The chief of staff of the American Rainbow Division, Colonel Douglas MacArthur, watched the Germans storming the abandoned front-line trenches. They looked exhausted, done for, by the time they reached the real line. "Their legs are broken!" MacArthur told his sweating artillerymen as they shelled them. Colonel Mitchell, who had taken to the air at first light, saw "a great mass of artillery fire" hitting the banks of the Marne, and a "terrible combat taking place …"

German infantry had taken bridgeheads across the Marne on both sides of Dormans. Pétain was anxious, and wanted reserve divisions thrown in, and a planned counteroffensive shelved. Marshal Foch forbade it. Gouraud's men were holding, thanks to Darnand, and that was the crucial factor.

Crown Prince Wilhelm was deeply unhappy that the enemy had escaped his barrage by simply evacuating the front line. He drove to see his father. He found the Kaiser in the middle of a victory breakfast. "I regard the situation as unpromising," he felt obliged to report. Staff officers were "horrified", but the Crown Prince's chief of staff was telephoned, and confirmed that "our troops are being held up before the enemy's second line".

The Crown Prince ordered a fresh bombardment to prepare the second line for assault. "In my heart of hearts," he said, "I had to admit the bitter truth that the offensive had failed." Anxious and depressed, he returned to his own command post. "Here I found grave men," he wrote, who "confirmed on the map what I already knew", that the colossal barrage "had destroyed a trench system which had been almost entirely evacuated".

Ludendorff still hoped for a breakthrough. "If my blow at Reims succeeds now, we have won the war," he told a staff officer. He telephoned the chief of staff of the 3rd Army, held up by Gouraud east of Reims. "Why isn't the attack getting any further?" he demanded. "It must be pressed home at once." The officer replied that the army commander had ordered it to be halted. "The French have pulled their artillery back a long way," he added, and the enemy were "laughing at the withering fire" from the safety of their new positions.

The game was up. Ludendorff realized it. He agreed that it was right to discontinue the attack. "I am the last man to order an attack that merely costs blood," he said.

By late afternoon on 15 July, the men who had hoped to be in Châlons that evening, and on their way to Paris the following morning, were broken. "We lay exhausted and dispirited," wrote Georg Bucher, a four-year veteran of the war, who had crossed the Marne only to cower in a cornfield. "They had asked us for more than we could give – we had given all we could, our strength, our eagerness, our courage. For us, the end had come ..." They had been told that the future of Germany depended on them, but all their blood had bought was a tiny and unsustainable bridge-head. "Were we, I asked myself, really a nation's hope?" Bucher said. "I dared not believe it for we were at our very last gasp."

Another veteran, Lieutenant Hesse, had "never seen so many dead, never contemplated so frightful a spectacle" as the remains of the German reserve units, caught and blasted by artillery on the northern slopes of the Marne. On the southern side, the Americans, hiding in the wheat, had "let our men advance and then annihilated them from 30 or 40 metres". "I have lived through the most disheartening day of the whole war," Rudolf Binding, a lieutenant, noted in his diary. "How could one expect to put one's heart into such a business?"

At 5 p.m. Gouraud announced that he remained "in possession of the entire front of attack". A little later, it was confirmed that the Germans who had crossed the Marne near Château-Thierry had been repulsed. The Kaiser returned to his headquarters at 7 p.m., his mood, an aide said, "slightly less ebullient than usual".

Crown Prince Wilhelm called off the assault across the Marne on the evening of 16 July. Limited and futile attacks dragged on through 17 July, but all hope of breakthrough had gone. The Kaiser was distraught. Visiting him at his headquarters in Avesnes, Field Marshal Hindenburg had told him the "bitter truth, which conflicts with the optimistic communiqués". The failure was total, Hindenburg said, and the reason was the "betrayal of the offensive plans". The Kaiser slept badly and had disturbing dreams. He told his aides that he was "a defeated War Lord", and that he had "seen visions of English and Russian relatives and all the ministers and generals of his reign marching past and mocking him ... Only the little Queen of Norway had been friendly to him."

In three days, all Ludendorff's hopes in Champagne had been blown away. "Even the most optimistic among us knew that all was lost," wrote Georg von Hertling, the German chancellor. "The history of the world was played out in three days."

Ludendorff admitted as much in a telegraph stating that Operation Hagen, the planned twin assault in Flanders, "will probably never come to execution". Abandoning his cherished offensive meant that he had given up hope of winning the war.

He knew why he had failed. The French had somehow known that he was coming. Operation Friedensturm had been betrayed. He blamed his own men. "While the commanders were doing their utmost to keep these secrets," he railed, "the love of talking and boasting inborn in Germans betrayed to the world and to our enemies matters of the greatest weight and significance."

The Germans pulled out of their bridgeheads on the Marne on 26 July. They went "back, back", one of them bitterly observed, "riders in the blowing rain bent over in their saddles, cannoneers hanging on the limber of their guns", with fragments of infantry, the remnants of companies, knapsacks bulging beneath their ponchos like comic hunchbacks, so that "our dead alone remain ..."

BUT IT WAS NOT LOOSE-TONGUED Germans, of course, who had so dispirited the mighty – the Kaiser, the Crown Prince, Field Marshal Hindenburg, the Imperial General Staff – and helped change, as the chancellor had put it, the "history of the world". It was the obscure French sergeant, who had at Mont-sans-Nom so perfectly fulfilled Clausewitz's dictum of being in the right place at the right time.

In his report to Pétain on the "glorious day" of 15 July, Gouraud said of Darnand's work: "A historic *coup de main* with exceptional strategic results." The marshal himself came to present Darnand with the Médaille Militaire in front of the troops. "What a magnificent day, when Pétain gave me the accolade!" Darnand wrote to his father. "I could not stop myself weeping."

On 26 September, 4th Army began to clear the Germans out of the Champagne Front. The war was all but won. Gouraud proudly reminded his men that "on 15 July they won the battle that permitted all the successes that have followed for France and her allies on all fronts ... The hardiness and sang-froid of a single sergeant were an element that tilted the scales to the Allies ..."

It was not until military analysts examined Darnand's exploit nine years after the war that a grateful nation became aware of this. They concluded that, had Gouraud not pulled his front line back in response to the intelligence the sergeant had provided, and had he not begun shelling the enemy as it massed, the Germans would have broken through, or presented so great a threat to Paris that British divisions would have been called on, thus making the Flanders Front vulnerable to Ludendorff's Operation Hagen. As it was, the Germans were so decimated and demoralized on 15 July that they ceased all offensives, just at the moment when the Americans were tipping the whole balance of manpower.

A STRANGE AND TROUBLED FUTURE awaited Darnand.

He was wounded whilst attacking a heavily fortified position in Flanders in October 1918. After the Armistice, he went with his regiment on occupation duty to Germany. He then joined the French garrison at Marash in Turkey. He returned to France in 1921 and was demobilized, having achieved the rank of warrant officer. The peacetime army did not appeal to him.

He worked as a cabinetmaker and forester, before joining a furniture manufacturer. He moved to Nice, starting a transport business, and dabbling in far-right politics. He joined Action française, a monarchist, anti-democratic group, and the Cagoulards, right-wing extremists who carried out several terrorist attacks in the 1930s. Exactly 20 years after his *coup de main*, on 14 July 1938, he was arrested on the Italian frontier. He had been smuggling large quantities of arms and ammunition destined for the Cagoulards into France through San Remo. After six months in prison, he was released for lack of evidence.

At 42, with France again at war with Germany, Darnand rejoined the army, now as a lieutenant. He served with the corps-franc, the commando unit, of the 29th Infantry Division. During the winter of the "phoney war", the period of inactivity before the German Blitzkrieg began, he was stationed in the abandoned village of Morsbach in Lorraine, three kilometres from the German line.

He was on an intelligence-gathering patrol commanded by his close friend Félix Agnely when it was spotted by a superior German force on 8 February 1940. A fierce firefight ensued. Darnand was credited with killing four Germans, but Agnely and six other French soldiers were killed. Nine others were missing, believed to have been taken prisoner. Darnand took command of the survivors, and beat a fighting retreat. At huge risk, Darnand returned to the scene, amidst the now thoroughly alerted enemy, to recover his friend's body and carry it back. For this, he was made an officer of the Légion d'honneur. His picture was splashed across the cover of *Match*, forerunner of the magazine *Paris Match*, to bolster French morale.

He fought on hard after the Germans broke through the front in May, and began to overrun France. On 7 June he rescued a wounded French pilot who had crash-landed behind enemy lines. Three days later, he received another citation, leading a counter-attack that prevented his unit from being cut off, causing the enemy severe losses. On 19 June the remnants of his company were finally surrounded in Sologne. Four days later, Marshal Pétain signed the armistice and set up a collaborationist regime in the spa town of Vichy. Darnand considered joining the Resistance.

Fatally, though, he felt a personal loyalty to Marshal Pétain, who had presented him with his Military Medal in the field in 1918. The Resistance was often Communist-led, and Darnand was leery of it, as a Catholic and right-wing ultra. He had no ties to de Gaulle and the Free French. Troubled, face pale, lips tight, he remained faithful to the marshal. Darnand, as the arch-collaborator Pierre Laval remarked, was "a fine soldier with as much political sense as a kerbstone".

Laval and Pétain used him to do the dirty work of repression for them. Darnand organized and led the black-uniformed *milice*, the pro-German Vichy militia that engaged in a murderous struggle with the *résistants* from 1943 on. It numbered about 30,000, with fanatical anti-communists bolstered by large numbers of thugs and petty criminals. Darnand himself swore a personal oath of loyalty to Hitler. He was rewarded with the rank of Sturmbannführer in the Waffen-SS, and with arms and money for his men.

The day of reckoning for the collaborators grew ever closer as the British and Americans began the liberation. Pétain began trying to shift the blame, writing to Darnand on 6 August 1944, expressing his "horror" at hearing "for several months" of rape, murder and theft by the *milice*, and of their cooperation with the Gestapo. For four years, Darnand replied, "I received your compliments and congratulations … And today, because the Americans are at the gates of Paris, you start to say that I am going to be a blot on the history of France." He might, Darnand said, have "made up his mind a little earlier".

Both of them fled to Germany a few days before Paris was liberated. They spent the rest of the war with other senior collaborators in the castle of Siegmaringen on the Danube. As the Allies closed in, Darnand fled with a few men to the Alto Adige in Italy. The Swiss refused him asylum. He went on the run after the German surrender in northern Italy. The French expeditionary force in Italy was on the look-out for him, but it was a British intelligence officer who spotted him in Milan. He was arrested, and sent back to France in chains.

At his trial, he stressed that he had never practised "*la politique du double jeu*", of pretending to serve the Germans the better to foil them, thus denying himself the standard defence used by Vichy officials. He accepted responsibility for all his actions; he had never, he said, given an order that was against his conscience, or that he secretly disavowed; he had always believed in what he said and did; patriotism was his only guide.

In short, he condemned himself. He was shot for treason at the fort of Châtillon on 10 October 1945. His best friend was a witness, and it was typical of this complex, driven man that this should be Father Bruckberger, "Bruck", a Dominican and a famous hero of the Resistance, who had fought in Darnand's unit against the Germans in 1940, and had then fought against Darnand's *milice*, but who bore his old comrade no malice.

5 · THE BIPLANE AND THE BATTLESHIP

A man takes on a steel mountain

The stunning impact of the individual seen here reflects to the full the observation that: "War is the province of chance. In no sphere of human activity is such a margin to be left for this intruder, because none is so much in contact with him ..." (BOOK I, CHAPTER III).

THE NORTH ATLANTIC FROM 63° 21′ N 31° 47′ W
TO 48° 09′ N 16° 07′ W ⋆ 23–27 MAY 1941

THE MISTS OVER THE ICEFIELDS TO the west of the Denmark Strait dispersed in the evening of Friday 23 May 1941. The tops of the Greenland mountains were clearly visible to the crew of the battleship *Bismarck* as they thundered south towards the open Atlantic. To the east, though, towards Iceland, walls of moisture lingered on, yellow and dense.

At 19:22 the battleship's alarm sounded. A shape was seen disappearing into the fogbanks. The Germans did not have time enough to identify it or to bring their guns to bear. It was a British cruiser, the *Suffolk*, and it knew who they were, and was glad to have escaped them.

Two thousand miles to the south, as the early summer sun slid down the rocky slopes and aromatic shrubs of Gibraltar, Royal Navy shore patrols began to round up the seamen and aircrew from the aircraft carrier *Ark Royal*. The carrier had just returned from a mission, flying off fighters for the defence of Malta, and most of the crew were ashore. The Admiralty in London wanted them back at sea, urgently.

Orders for the crew were flashed onto cinema screens, shouted out in pubs and bars, and whispered more discreetly to the officers dining in the Rock Hotel. Liberty boats waited to ferry them out to their darkened ship.

John Moffat, a 22-year-old pilot, boyish and eager, was among them. A Scot, born in Kelso, his heroes as a schoolboy had been the record-breaking long-distance fliers of the day. "All my school prizes were books on flying," he said, "and I always wanted to be a pilot." His father had been in the navy, and he set his heart on becoming a naval pilot, "the best of two worlds", he said, "because you have a ship and the sea as well as the air". At the outbreak of war, newly commissioned a sublieutenant, he was learning fighter techniques near Southampton. Later, he joined 818 Squadron aboard *Ark Royal*.

The squadron flew Fairey Swordfish torpedo-bombers, antiquated biplanes with open cockpits and canvas wings kept in place by struts and rigging wires. Flat out, the Swordfish only managed 138mph, but it was the love of Moffat's life. "We called it the Stringbag, like the bags old ladies carried to go shopping," he said. "It didn't matter what you put in them, they just kept getting bigger and bigger. The Swordfish was like that. It was a torpedo bomber, a divebomber, a high bomber, the lot. All it had was a single nine-cylinder radial engine, but it carried a big load, and three of us."

Ark Royal slipped out to sea in the early hours of Saturday. She did not turn east, into the clear Mediterranean skies where she had spent the past months. She turned west, passing midway between Tangier and Cadiz, and then northwest, into the sullen, slopping North Atlantic. At dawn, she was off Cape St Vincent.

She, and the battlecruiser *Renown* and the destroyers with her, were under orders to meet and escort a high-value convoy outbound from the Clyde for Suez, via the Cape. But Moffat was to find a very different rendezvous awaited him and his Stringbag.

THE ADMIRALTY HAD REASON TO be fretful. The *Bismarck*, the most powerful German ship afloat, was about to break out into the open North Atlantic on her maiden operation. She had been launched, in the presence of Adolf Hitler, on St Valentine's Day six months before the war, and handed over to the navy, her fitting out completed, in late August 1940. This was the first time, though, that she had gone to sea to make war.

She was a ship of great grace and beauty, and immense destructive power. Let her loose in a convoy protected by lesser ships, and she could sink almost at will, naval escorts included. Her eight 15-inch guns threw three-quarter ton shells to a maximum range of 36,000 metres or 22 miles. Her secondary battery of twelve 5.9-inch guns had a range of 23,000 metres. She was fast, working her way up to 30 knots in trials, despite her 50,900-ton displacement.

The high quality of her rangefinders and fire-control systems was established during her trials. She was unusually beamy, 36 metres for a length of 251 metres, and she proved a stable gun platform. Her gunnery was brilliant. "We usually succeeded in straddling the target on the first fall of shot," said Burkard von Müllenheim-Rechberg, one of her gunnery officers.

Only one minor weakness had cropped up. When her electric-drive steering gear had been immobilized to simulate an emergency, her two huge parallel rudders, each with an area of 24 square metres, were locked amidships. It was found to be extremely difficult to hold a course using the engines alone, even in a calm sea. Running the starboard propeller at full ahead, and port full astern, with the central screw idle, produced only a weak turning movement. Locked rudders, though, were only the remotest possibility. What mattered were guns and armour, and here *Bismarck* was more than a match for any ship afloat.

Her primary role was to sink enemy merchantmen. The British were islanders. All their oil, and much of their food and machinery, came by sea. They moved their troops by sea. By May 1941, they had been fighting Germany on their own for almost a year, aided only by their empire, and that was all overseas. The Atlantic supply lines were their lifeline. All the routes from the empire and the United States came together here. Cut them – scatter and sink the convoys, by U-boat or surface raider – and the British would be beaten.

They had already been given a taste of this "commerce raiding". Earlier in the year, Admiral Günther Lütjens had taken the battlecruisers *Gneisenau* and *Scharnhorst* from Germany into the Arctic Ocean, and then swung south through the Denmark Strait. Lütjens, tall, pencil-lean, precise, allowed a little light to shine through his habitual fatalism. "For the first time in military history," he signalled his ships, "German warships have succeeded in breaking out into the Atlantic. Now go to it!" In a single day, 15 March, his crews sank or took as prizes 16 ships. After 60 days at sea, having accounted for 116,000 tons of merchant ships, Lütjens reached port at Brest in German-occupied France.

He was soon ordered to return to the Atlantic, taking with him the *Bismarck* on her first operational cruise, and the battlecruiser *Prinz Eugen*. This pair could play havoc with any convoy, unless protected by British capital ships, and those the raiders would try to avoid. The operational area given in their orders was defined as "the entire North Atlantic north of the equator". The target for the operation, codenamed Rheinübung, was enemy merchant shipping. They were only to engage enemy warships if they were forced to, for the "decisive objective in our struggle with England is to destroy her trade".

On 18 May, a Sunday, *Bismarck* was at anchor at Gotenhafen, on the Baltic, Hitler having paid her a personal visit a fortnight before. In the afternoon, a band on the quarterdeck struck up *"Muss i' Denn?"* ("Must I go?"), the traditional lament at the start of a long cruise. She sailed at 02:00 on Monday 19 May. She had a crew of 103 officers and 1,962 petty officers and men, under Captain Ernst Lindemann. The number of souls aboard was brought up to over 2,200 by war correspondents, the Luftwaffe pilots and mechanics for her two float planes, prize crews for captured merchantmen, and Lütjens's staff.

BY LATE ON TUESDAY THE BRITISH knew *Bismarck* and *Prinz Eugen* were on the move. The two ships were spotted by a Swedish cruiser as they steamed through the Kattegat. Word was passed to the British naval attaché in Stockholm. In the early hours of Wednesday 21 May, the news reached Scapa Flow. This was the base of the British Home Fleet, strategically positioned where the Atlantic meets the North Sea to the north of Scotland, a lonely sweep of water protected from violent gales by the wind-scoured heather and stunted grasses of the Orkney Islands.

The commander of the Home Fleet, Admiral John Tovey, brought his ships to short notice to steam. The cruiser *Suffolk*, already off Iceland with the *Norfolk*, was ordered to keep especial watch along the ice edge of the Denmark Strait. Reconnaissance aircraft were sent to Norway. At 13:15, the pilot of a Spitfire flying high above the Norwegian coast spotted and photographed the German ships in a fjord. That same evening, Tovey sent the brand-new battleship *Prince of Wales* and the "mighty *Hood*", the best-known, best-loved and biggest of all British warships, to reinforce his patrol lines off Iceland against a German breakout.

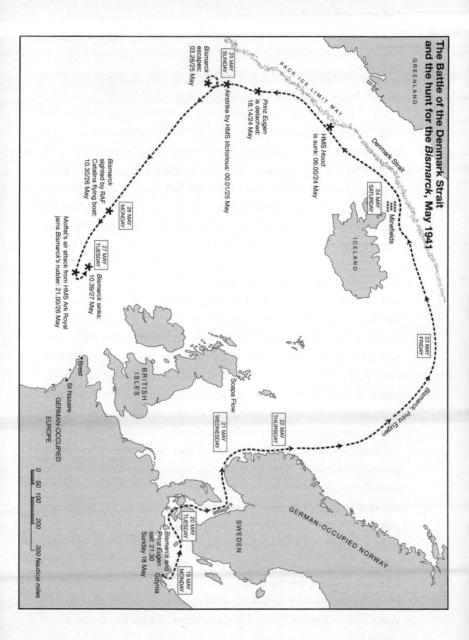

The Battle of the Denmark Strait and the hunt for the *Bismarck*, May 1941

GREENLAND

PACK ICE LIMIT MAY

Denmark Strait

Minefields

24 MAY
SATURDAY

ICELAND

Bismarck
escapes:
03.26/25 May

25 MAY
SUNDAY

Airstrike by HMS Victorious: 00.01/25 May

Prinz Eugen
is detached:
18.14/24 May

HMS Hood
is sunk: 06.00/24 May

23 MAY
FRIDAY

Bismarck, Prinz Eugen

Bismarck
sighted by RAF
Catalina flying boat:
10.30/26 May

26 MAY
MONDAY

27 MAY
TUESDAY

Bismarck sinks:
10.39/27 May

Moffat's air attack from HMS Ark Royal
jams *Bismarck*'s rudder: 21.00/26 May

BRITISH
ISLES

Scapa Flow

21 MAY
WEDNESDAY

22 MAY
THURSDAY

Brest

St Nazaire

GERMAN-OCCUPIED
EUROPE

GERMAN-OCCUPIED NORWAY

SWEDEN

20 MAY
TUESDAY

Bismarck and
Prinz Eugen
sail: 21.30
Sunday 18 May

Gdynia

19 MAY
MONDAY

0 50 100 200 300 Nautical miles

An air search of the Norwegian coast on Thursday afternoon showed that Lütjens had gone. Tovey guessed that he was steaming almost due north, high into the Arctic, before turning southwest to squeeze past the Greenland pack ice. He was right – as they progressed north beyond the range of German aircraft, *Bismarck*'s crew spent the afternoon painting out the air recognition markings and the giant Nazi swastika on the quarterdeck – but he could not be sure. The German admiral could equally be making for the open Atlantic between Iceland and the Faeroes, or, even closer to home, the Faeroes–Shetlands gap.

Shortly before midnight on Thursday, the gigantic anti-submarine netting that protected the Scapa Flow anchorage was parted. Tovey sailed out aboard his flagship *King George V*, with the aircraft carrier *Victorious* and four cruisers. As he did so, Lütjens was turning southwest from Arctic waters to position himself for his dash through the Denmark Strait.

On Friday morning, 23 May, *Bismarck* and *Prinz Eugen* entered mushy ice and reduced speed. The narrow passage between the westernmost tip of Iceland, and the Greenland pack ice was the place of greatest danger. A British minefield reduced the Strait to a width of 40 miles or less. The fog had lifted a little, but the lookouts could see no more than 400 or 500 yards. Dim shapes loomed from the mists, sometimes ship-like, until they resolved themselves into ice floes, and the helms were put over violently to avoid propeller damage.

After her brief appearance in the early evening, *Suffolk* ducked back into the fog banks. She was radar-equipped, and took up position to shadow the Germans from astern. *Norfolk* put on speed to join her, breaking clear of the fog at 20:30 to find *Bismarck* coming straight for her. *Bismarck* opened fire, the 15-inch shells throwing up waterspouts about the cruiser, close enough for splinters to hit, as she made back at speed into the murk. All through the long gloaming of a summer evening in high latitudes, the Germans and their shadowers thundered south, as the *Prince of Wales* and the *Hood* made course to intercept them, and, far off in Gibraltar, Moffat and the crew of *Ark Royal* were summoned to return to their ship.

THE BATTLE, AT DAWN ON SATURDAY, lasted just 21 minutes.

Through snow showers and the brief darkness of the northern night, *Suffolk's* radar and lookouts guided the two British heavy ships onto the Germans. At 05:30, the four ships sighted one another, and hurtled on, 7,000 men trembling with anticipation within their armoured entrails, white battle ensigns snapping stiffly beneath the black funnel gases of the British ships, white water seething from the propellers at the stern, bows smashing into a head sea in explosions of spray that sluiced and stung those whose battle stations exposed them to it.

The *Hood* fired first at a range of 13 miles, at 05:52, the flashes visible to *Bismarck's* crew as "great, fiery rings like suns". Their own guns straddled *Hood* with their second salvo. Three minutes into the engagement, a hit was seen amidships on *Hood's* boat deck, a "blood-red rectangle" that gave off thick fumes. *Bismarck* fired a fifth salvo at 06:01. A huge pillar of flame soared from the base of *Hood's* mainmast, so high that the crew of the *Suffolk* saw it from 30 miles away, a catastrophic strike by a shell that had burst deep in her innards, exploding 112 tons of cordite in the aft magazines. A seabed investigation of the wreck suggests that the explosion – so violent that the ship's 650-ton conning tower was found over a mile away from the ship's middle section – vented forward as well as upward, and set off the forward magazines as well.

On the *Prince of Wales*, only 1,600 yards away, it was seen as a "vast blow lamp", hurling parts of gun turrets and the mainmast into the air, with *Hood's* own shells flying upwards and bursting like fireworks in the smoke. Then, suddenly, the *Hood* was gone,

121

had evaporated, noiselessly, like a ghost, leaving a shroud of yellow vapours drifting on the sea.

A minute later, a shell smashed straight through the bridge of the *Prince of Wales*, exploding as it exited, leaving it a slaughter-house, so that blood, sprayed into a bridge voice pipe, ran down to stain the chart of the plotting officer on the deck below. Command was re-established on the lower bridge, but the fire controllers were blinded by smoke and spray, and the salvos were ragged. At 06:13, her captain, one of only three to have survived on the bridge, turned away under the cover of smoke.

Destroyers came later to pick up *Hood*'s survivors. They expected to find hundreds. They found three.

One of them was Bob Tilburn, who had manned the *Hood*'s anti-aircraft guns. He recalled *Bismarck*'s shells getting closer and closer until they began to hit. "The ship shook like mad. Bits of bodies were falling over the deck, and one hit me on the legs," he said. "I thought 'I'm going to be sick', so I got up and went to the ship's side to throw up." He heard no explosion, no noise to mark the enormity of what was happening to the ship.

"I looked up and saw the bows coming out of the water. The *Hood* was turning over," he said. "I looked round and saw the ship rolling over on top of me ... The radio aerial wrapped round the back of my legs and started pulling me down. I had my knife in my hand so I cut my sea boots off and shot to the surface. I looked up to see the *Hood* with her bows in the air. Then she slid under."

He saw a seaman and a midshipman on rafts. "There was nobody else, no bodies, nobody else alive or dead," Tilburn said. "No people drowning or anything which you would expect."

They were found by the destroyer *Electra*. "1,418 people were killed," said Tilburn, "so why should I boast when each of those 1,418 had seven or eight relations who were saying, 'Why you? Why not my son, my brother, my husband?' I kept quiet about it for a long, long time."

A NEW URGENCY, BEYOND THE protection of the Atlantic convoys, was added to the imperative of sinking the *Bismarck*. If left unavenged, the loss of the *Hood* would corrode British morale and reputation.

Hood was more than the great symbol of British sea power. She was loved – for her elegance, for the happy peacetime cruises she had made to show the flag – on every ocean, in every corner of the empire, and beyond. When she arrived in San Francisco, the mayor was captivated by her beauty: "We surrender our city unto you. We capitulate," he said. Millions had visited her, for dances, dinners, receptions, or simply for sightseeing, to be photographed with her immense and burnished guns, or to let the children scamper round her holystoned decks.

She was named after a family that had given the Royal Navy four famous admirals since the 18th century. The last of the line was Horace Hood, killed at Jutland in 1916, when his flagship *Invincible* exploded after a German shell penetrated her magazine, a fate eerily similar to *Hood*'s own end. *Hood* herself had been launched by Lady Hood, Horace's widow, in 1918. Though the great ship was elderly by the time the Second World War broke out, her flowing lines had still given her 32 knots, a knot or two faster than *Bismarck*, and, at 860 feet, 32 feet more in length.

Her vulnerability lay in her armour. It was spread over three decks, the top deck designed to explode the shells and draw their venom before they met the next two. Since then, shells with time delays had been perfected, which enabled them to penetrate the layers of weak armour and explode deep in the bowels of the ship.

Now, she was gone, snuffed out. Admiral Wake-Walker on the *Norfolk* signalled baldly "*Hood* has blown up." The shock was traumatic.

Ten convoys were crossing the Atlantic at the moment *Hood* had disappeared. It was a huge risk to tamper with their escorting battleships, cruisers and destroyers, but the British were determined to send all they could against *Bismarck*. The cruiser *Edinburgh*, which had just captured a German blockade runner off the Azores, was also deployed, though she was short of fuel. Hundreds of miles to the northwest, the battleship *Ramillies* was instructed to leave the convoy she was escorting. West of Ireland, the battleship *Rodney*, on her way to the United States for repairs, and escorting the troop transport *Britannia*, was ordered against the *Bismarck*.

For the moment, the Admiralty did not call on *Ark Royal*. She, with Moffat and her pilots, was off Cape St Vincent when the *Hood* went down. But she could be summoned to join the chase if need be.

As THE *PRINCE OF WALES* RACED AWAY, licking her wounds, the "All clear" was sounded on *Bismarck*. The men celebrated with a triple "Hurrah!" The officers met in the wardroom, and drank a champagne toast to Adalbert Schneider, the chief gunnery officer. They were in high spirits, expecting *Bismarck* to hold her breakout course into the open Atlantic, and anticipating the merchantmen they would find. But *Prince of Wales* had landed shells, too, and although only three had hit *Bismarck*, and no one was killed or injured, they had ruined her prospects as a commerce raider.

The first shell had struck well forward, passing directly through the ship from port to starboard, above the waterline but below the bow wave. It left an exit hole one and a half metres wide. Two thousand tons of seawater from the bow wave cascaded into the forecastle. The second shell flooded a generator room and ripped several fuel tanks.

The ship had a list to port, and was down three degrees by the bow from the flooding. The tips of the starboard propeller blades were coming out of the water as they turned. A thousand tons of fuel in the forward tanks were isolated from the service tanks near the boilers, and unusable. The ship's trim was improved by flooding her trim tanks, and collision matting reduced the inflow of water, but her top speed was reduced from 30 to 28 knots because of the water pressure on the forward bulkheads, and her range was compromised by the fuel shortfall.

Lütjens knew the game was up. His ship was in no condition to continue with the operation, even had he been able to take on more fuel from one of the fleet oilers. To rectify the damage forward, *Bismarck* would have to be stopped in the water, and heeled first one side and then the other to patch the holes. That was not an option with an angry enemy about her ears. She needed to be dry-docked for repairs.

At 08:01 on Saturday morning, two hours after sinking the *Hood*, Lütjens signalled: "Intention to proceed to St Nazaire. *Prinz Eugen* cruiser warfare." Rheinübung was over. *Bismarck* was to retire to France for repairs, leaving her consort on her own to see what pickings she could find as a commerce raider. Lütjens planned to lead the British shadowers westward, towards a line of six U-boats lying in wait south of Greenland, before swinging in a southeasterly curve for St Nazaire. He would separate his battleship from *Prinz Eugen*, hopefully unseen by her pursuers.

The two ships steamed on together through the morning, *Suffolk* shadowing them at 30,000 metres range. The weather worsened before noon and the sea rose. Visibility dropped from 18 nautical miles to 2 miles or less in the frequent rain squalls and banks of fog. *Bismarck* tried to break away from *Prinz Eugen* during a heavy rain squall in mid-afternoon, but the rain lifted when she was still in sight of *Suffolk*. At 18:14, she tried again, in a fog bank, firing at *Suffolk* when the mist parted for a moment, her shells close enough to loosen rivets in the cruiser's plating. The blast from her own guns shattered the windows on *Suffolk*'s bridge, opening her exhausted watch-keepers to the icy spray.

A gunnery officer on *Prinz Eugen* watched her "big brother" disappear with melancholy. "The flashes of his guns suddenly paint the sea, clouds and rain squalls dark red," he said. "In the fire of his after turrets, we clearly see the outline of the mighty ship, the long hull, the tower mast and stack, like a solid, sturdy building ... On the gaff below, waves the battle ensign, still recognizable as a dot. Then the curtain of rain squalls closes for the last time ..." *Prinz Eugen* was meant to be the decoy, to allow *Bismarck* to escape the shadowers, but *Suffolk*'s radar stayed glued to the battleship, and it was the smaller ship that escaped, eventually to reach safe haven in Brest a week later.

And so *Bismarck* thundered southwestward, drawing *Suffolk* and *Norfolk* and *Prince of Wales* behind her port quarter, hoping to deliver them to the U-boats waiting to the south of Greenland. At 19:30, as though conscious of the trap, the British ships began to zigzag, an anti-submarine drill in which they altered 30 degrees to each side of their mean course every ten minutes.

In the evening, *Bismarck*'s wireless room tuned in to a special broadcast from the Deutschlandsender in Berlin, and relayed it through her loudspeakers, so that the crew could share the news of their triumph with the millions of listeners in Germany. The distant radio band played the naval anthem, and the announcer read out the communiqué of the sinking of the mighty *Hood*. The first song of the evening's radio requests was dedicated to *Bismarck*'s men: "*Komme zurück!*" – "Come home!"

That, though, so his engineers told Lütjens, was becoming problematic. The lost thousand tons of fuel was a critical factor. If he continued southwestward, it was imperative that he refuelled from one of the four oilers waiting for him. If he did not – if he failed to shake off his pursuers, or the U-boat line failed to sink them – he would find himself in the the mid-Atlantic without enough oil to reach France. But if he turned now for St Nazaire, or for Brest, even closer, then he had fuel enough already.

In truth, the British were short of fuel, too, and had gunnery problems, but Lütjens knew only that they had stayed with him through every manoeuvre. "Shaking off contact impossible due to enemy radar," he signalled by radio at 20:56 on Saturday evening. "Due to fuel steering direct for St Nazaire."

THE PILOTS ON *VICTORIOUS* HAD SEEN *Hood* going off at high speed into the sunset as they had arrived at Scapa Flow. "A magnificent sight," said Sublieutenant Pat Jackson, "going so fast we were sure something was up." As Lütjens turned for France, Jackson and the other aircrew were being briefed to avenge her. *Bismarck* was 120 miles away, across a darkening and rising sea. "We were sent off," said Jackson, "to try to slow her down and do as much damage as possible."

The carrier turned into the wind to fly off nine Swordfish at 22:00. Jackson remembered the date, 24 May, because the next day was his birthday. Some of the pilots had made their first deck landings a few days before. Lieutenant Commander Eugene Esmonde led the aircraft to 1,500 feet, and after an hour his ASV (aircraft surface vessel) radar detected a target. He found *Bismarck* through a break in the cloud, but lost her again. Then his ASV picked up *Norfolk*, and she signalled him "enemy 14 miles on starboard bow". He left the cruiser at 23:50, picked up an ASV target, and began his descent for the attack. As he broke cloud, he saw the US Coast Guard cutter *Modoc*, flying an outsize and illuminated ensign to make plain her neutral status.

Bismarck was 6 miles away. She spotted the Swordfish and opened fire with everything she had. "Daringly, they flew through our fire, nearer to the fire-spitting mountain of the *Bismarck*, always nearer and nearer," said Müllenheim-Rechberg. "They were moving so slowly they seemed to be standing still in the air, and they looked so antiquated." Esmonde's starboard lower aileron was shot away, and he attacked at once, before he could suffer further damage. Heavy flak burst around Jackson's aircraft, and the air filled with the stench of burning explosive. He felt a tapping on his shoulder, and thought someone must have been hurt, but then he heard David Berrill, his observer, wishing him a happy birthday. "I looked at my watch," Jackson said. "It was 00:03 on Sunday May 25."

The noise from *Bismarck*'s guns was so deafening that the seaman at the ship's wheel could not hear Captain Lindemann's orders. So he "combed" the nine torpedo tracks himself, steering to minimize the size of the target.

There was only one confirmed hit, by Lieutenant Percy Gick. As he did his run in, he told his telegraphist air gunner, Les Sayer, over the speaking tube that he was not lined up properly, and he was going round again. The Swordfish returned out of the glare of the midnight sun. "We came back on our own," said Sayer. "I thought to myself, they've only got us to aim at, they're bound to hit us, this is your lot. But we went in and dropped the fish and turned away, and it was only then that they saw us and they let us have everything."

The battleship's big shells made huge waterspouts as they made to get away. They were only ten feet above the wave tops, and they flew right through one. "It came up underneath us and ripped out all the underside of the aircraft," said Sayer. "It was a bit draughty."

The torpedo hit the armoured belt amidships. The concussion killed a petty officer, *Bismarck*'s first fatality, but it did little other damage. Müllenheim-Rechberg was sure that the armour would not be "bothered by a little aerial torpedo", and a glance at the speed and rudder-position indicators showed nothing untoward. The violent changes of course, though, dislodged the collision matting forward and let in more water until speed was reduced and the matting made watertight again.

Morale in the ship after the attack, Müllenheim-Rechberg said, was outstanding. "The crew felt even better when they were told that five enemy aircraft had been shot down." In fact, none were lost. The Swordfish headed back to *Victorious*, and found her, after four hours in the air, just as they reached the limit of their endurance. "We all landed safely, even though it was dark, with rain and a pitching deck," said Jackson, "which was good because half the chaps hadn't landed at night before."

BISMARCK ESCAPED IN THE EARLY hours of Sunday 25 May. Her hydrophone operators reported that she had no enemy ships to starboard, and that the cruiser shadowing her to port was zigzagging, at times closing to within 12 miles of *Bismarck*, and then sheering away. Though he misidentified her as the *King George V*, Lütjens knew that the *Prince of Wales* was further out on his port quarter – he had exchanged salvoes with her at long range after the air attack – and he planned to avoid close contact with her when setting his course for St Nazaire, by first turning sharply to starboard and making west at increased speed before circling round to head for France.

He was in luck. Had *Suffolk* maintained continuous radar contact during her zigzags, she would have come dangerously close to the battleship. To keep her distance, she was losing contact for a few minutes on her outward leg, regaining it when she turned inward again.

At 03:06, *Suffolk* turned on her outward leg and Lütjens ordered the wheel to be put over. *Bismarck* faded from *Suffolk*'s radar screen, as expected. After ten minutes, *Suffolk* turned back, but her operators found no trace of the battleship. By 03:26 it was clear that her quarry had made away, it seemed to the west. Lütjens had unwittingly timed his turn to perfection, and he followed it with a great loop, heading through west to north and east before crossing his own wake, circling round behind his pursuers, and slipping away without trace. At 05:00 *Sheffield* signalled: "Have lost contact with enemy."

Bismarck was now heading southeast, on a course that would take her past the French Atlantic ports towards the southwest extremity of the Bay of Biscay.

As a sullen dawn broke on 25 May, *Bismarck* had slipped safely to the east of her pursuers and their trio of admirals – northeast of Sir John Tovey on *King George V*, due east of Frederic Wake-Walker's first cruiser squadron with *Norfolk* and *Suffolk*, southeast of Alban Curteis's second cruiser squadron with *Victorious*. As *Bismarck* continued to the southeast, the British steamed west. She had, however, acquired a new set of pursuers. During the night, Force H, ploughing northwards from Gibraltar, received a signal cancelling the instructions to escort Convoy WS8B. Instead, Moffat and the pilots aboard *Ark Royal* were to have a new target. The new orders read: "Steer to intercept *Bismarck*."

Lütjens, however, believed quite wrongly that he was still being shadowed. He thus committed two indiscretions that should have delivered him back to the enemy. At 07:27 on Sunday morning he radioed a short report to Group West in Paris. "One battleship and two heavy cruisers still in contact," he misreported. He followed this, in four bursts between 09:12 and 09:48, with a detailed account of his actions, including the destruction of the *Hood*. He stressed that his shadowers held him in a vice: "Enemy's possession of detection equipment with minimum range of 35,000 metres affects Atlantic operations in gravest way. Ship detected in thick fog in Denmark Strait and not let loose since. Escape attempts impossible ..."

Radio D/F (direction finding) teams in Britain were onto it in a flash. They computed *Bismarck*'s rough position, and rightly concluded that she was making for France. But, in another of the strange aberrations of war, the British let this diamond-hard intelligence shatter in their hand. The Admiralty sent the raw figures, and not the computed position, to Tovey in the *King George V*.

Tovey had asked for raw data, it is true, and the Admiralty thought that he had two destroyers newly equipped with D/F with him. These would enable him to pinpoint *Bismarck*'s position more accurately than could be done from 1500 miles away in London. But Tovey had no destroyers. They had left for Iceland at midnight owing to shortage of fuel, and of the two with D/F, one had a defective set and the other had withdrawn long since to Scapa Flow with boiler trouble.

The figures were wrongly computed by the tired men aboard *King George V*. They placed *Bismarck*, not where she was, to their southeast, but to the north. They calculated that *Bismarck* was steering, not for France, but in almost exactly the opposite direction, for the Iceland–Faeroes gap. Tovey's mighty ships steamed northwest into empty waters.

That, too, was where the pilots from *Victorious* went searching that Sunday morning. Seven Swordfish combed separate sectors of the ocean, and found nothing. Six returned after four hours. Jackson, the birthday boy, did not. Captain H.C. Bovell, *Victorious*'s much-loved captain, mourned one of his best crews. He wrote of the luck that David Berrill, Jackson's observer, had enjoyed – returning from an operation at Dunkirk where half the aircraft were lost, crash-landing in a Swordfish that turned upside-down, twice going over the side of his carrier. The captain also recalled that he had "never seen Berrill dismayed under any circumstances ..."

No one was to know it for nine days, but Berrill's luck had not run out. After a fruitless search, fuel low, the crew of Berrill's Swordfish had headed back for *Victorious*. They found no sign of her. It was the carrier pilot's ever-present nightmare. "We were lost halfway across the Atlantic," Jackson said. He was a Catholic, and when the fuel gauge read "E" for empty, he said three Hail Marys. He heard Berrill shout, and saw below them the outline of a ship's lifeboat with waves breaking over it.

"When someone gives you a lifeboat in the middle of the Atlantic," he said, "you don't muck about. I decided to ditch immediately. I came down as if I was doing a deck landing and landed in the water about 20 yards upwind. I stuffed my flying boots full of Very light pistols and cartridges ..." They bailed the lifeboat out with their flying boots and got aboard. It came from a Dutch ship. It had a bag with sails and a mast lashed to the thwarts, a rusty knife, a trilby hat, a tin of cigarettes, a bottle of 1890 Napoleon brandy, and a water beaker.

It was bitterly cold, and they had to bail continuously, but Berrill assured them that in nine days they would be saved. As the hunt for the *Bismarck* moved ever further away, they sailed on. They spotted another lifeboat, with Norwegians aboard, the only survivors of a convoy torpedoed a fortnight before. Everything about the Norwegian boat was black, the men with black rings around their eyes, and dead men on the bottom boards. Jackson gave them some biscuits and the cigarettes, and the Norwegians sailed off, never to be seen again.

On the ninth day, a violent breaking sea threatened to finish them off, but from atop one crest they saw a ship, the smoke from its funnel horizontal in the gale. Jackson fired off all his Very lights. The ship spotted the last of them, and gave a long blast on its siren. She was an Icelander, and took them to Reykjavik.

JACKSON SHARED HIS BIRTHDAY, 25 May, with Günther Lütjens. As the sublieutenant was watching his fuel gauge slide towards "E" on Sunday morning, the German admiral had a most welcome present. "Last enemy shadowing report was at 03:13," Group West informed him. "Type of enemy signals now being sent indicates shadowing vessels have been shaken off."

At last, Lütjens now knew, he had given his pursuers the slip. He received radioed greetings – mostly fulsome, but one, from the Führer, cold and aloof, "Best wishes on your birthday. Adolf Hitler" – and he held a little ceremony to award the helmsman with the Iron Cross for his seamanship during the Swordfish attack. Officers and men, at action stations for 36 hours, were able to wash and shave and eat hot food.

At noon, though, Lütjens was sombre as he addressed the crew. He confirmed that they were making for a French port. "On our way there, the enemy will gather and give us battle," he said. "The German people are with you, and we will fight until our gun barrels glow red-hot and the last shell has left the barrels. For us seamen, it is now a matter of victory or death!"

Most of the crew were in their early twenties, and, though Captain Lindemann tried to cheer them up with news that aircraft and U-boats were on their way, the speech deadened their natural optimism. "He spoke beautifully," said a seaman, Otto Maus, "but we discerned from his words that we'd already lost our last battle." Müllenheim-Rechberg, who was on duty and missed it, felt it created a "contagious depression" and he noticed that even officers on the admiral's staff began wearing life-jackets under their uniforms. He was given a précis by a petty officer: "The admiral says we haven't a hope, sir, the whole British fleet is after us and they're bound to find us."

But they didn't. The old battleship *Rodney*, with her nine 16-inch guns and destroyer screen, crossed 50 nautical miles ahead of her in mid-afternoon. The cruiser *Edinburgh*, coming up from the Azores to search the approaches to the Bay of Biscay, passed 30 miles under her stern at around 18:00. The troop convoy WS.8B sailed across her path less than 100 miles away. In the late evening, a Catalina flying boat of Coastal Command came within 50 miles of her. Nothing by air or sea disturbed her private world, its limits marked by the heaving horizons, as a stiff northwesterly drove her corkscrewing towards France and safety.

Spare hands were kept busy making a dummy funnel, from canvas and sheet metal, in the hope it would confuse British pilots into identifying her as one of their own King George-class battle-ships. The gale was too strong to hoist it, but it lifted spirits when the chief engineer said it must give off smoke like the real thing, and went on the loudspeakers: "Off-duty watch report to draw cigars to smoke in our second funnel!" The feedwater in the turbo-generators was successfully changed to prevent the danger of salt-water getting into the boilers. Divers in the flooded forward compartments managed to open valves to provide a few hundred tons more oil.

At about 19:30, Group West told *Bismarck* that the Luftwaffe was ready to cover her approach in force. Bombers could get as far out as 14 degrees west, and long-range reconnaissance aircraft to 25 degrees. In the middle of the night, the five destroyers of the flotilla escorting WS.8B were ordered to leave the convoy and join Tovey's force, and the battleship *Nelson* left Freetown in Sierra Leone to steam north.

Aboard *Bismarck*, spirits rose further as Sunday slid into Monday. At 04:30 on the new day, the bridge announced: "We have now passed three-quarters of Ireland on our way to St Nazaire. Around noon we will be in the U-boats' operational area and within range of German aircraft."

"This brought great joy," said seaman Georg Herzog. "No one thought of a bad outcome any more."

HOPE WAS PREMATURE.

At 02:00 on Monday 26 May, the crew of Catalina Z/209 had been woken to prepare to search for the *Bismarck*. By the time *Bismarck*'s crew heard the "joyous" news from the bridge, the flying boat had taken off from Lough Erne in Northern Ireland, and was heading southwest into the Atlantic. The crew – the co-pilot was an American, Ensign Leonard Smith – anticipated a long and probably futile day. They cooked bacon and eggs over a stove for breakfast, for flying boats had a leisurely pace, and reached their search area at 09:45.

It was further south than the navy had requested. The head

of Coastal Command, Air Marshal Sir Frederick Bowhill, was an ex-seaman, who had rounded Cape Horn under sail, and he felt that *Bismarck* would not close on the rocky Brittany coast at night, but would stand off southwards before turning east when on the latitude of St Nazaire or Brest.

His hunch was right. The Catalina was flying between the low cloud base and the rough seas, at 10:30, when the crew saw a dark shape on the limits of visibility 8 miles off. It was a warship. The Catalina climbed into the cloud and circled to come astern of the ship. *Bismarck* was no more than 500 yards off when a gap in the cloud revealed her below. Her gunners were as alert as ever and shrapnel rattled on the flying boat's hull. "I thought they had us," said Flying Officer Dennis Briggs, the pilot. "She put up the worst barrage I've ever seen. She seemed to be one big flash of fire from bow to stern. We were lucky to get back into the cloud." He dumped his four depth charges to gain height faster, and then had the crew stop the holes from the flak with rubber bungs, "so that we wouldn't sink when we landed ..."

Some of the bridge officers wanted to launch one of *Bismarck*'s Arado float planes to shoot him down. They knew the Catalina had great endurance, 28 hours with long-range tanks. They had picked up the message he had already sent, giving *Bismarck*'s course, speed and position, and they feared he would go on guiding the British towards them for hours to come. The two-man Arado was faster than the big Catalina with its bunks and galley and nine-man crew, and it was armed with two cannon and two machine-guns. It was launched by a powerful catapult that extended over the ship's side. Retrieval, though, was a dangerous manoeuvre at the best of times. The ship had to lie dead in the water as the seaplane landed close to her side, and then hoist it with a 12-ton crane. With a heavy sea running, it was all but impossible. Lindemann refused to allow it.

The Catalina in fact lost contact with *Bismarck* after its

desperate scramble into the cloud. Other aircraft and pilots were up now, though, John Moffat and *Ark Royal*'s Swordfish. They had had a miserable night. The northwesterly gale that was blowing *Bismarck* on her way threw up a harsh head sea for the carrier. Her captain, Loben Maund, was worried at the battering her plates were taking. Her shipwright was constantly fixing the cracks and loose rivets caused by near misses from bombs on her Mediterranean convoy work. At 23:15, speed had been reduced to 23 knots, and by 01:12 on 26 May the carrier was down to 17 knots.

At dawn, though her flight deck was 62 feet above the waterline, seas were coming clean over the bow. Maund had the rise and fall of her stern measured by sextant. She was pitching 56 feet, and she was rolling, too, by up to 30 degrees. The wind was blowing over the deck at 50 knots. The flight-deck crews struggled to prevent the Swordfish from being blown off the side as they manhandled them into their take-off positions. Whether conditions were at or beyond the limit, none could tell, but the imperative of finding *Bismarck* brooked no caution.

At 08:43, Maund had turned into the wind and begun the launch, the operations officer straining to sense the sea and wind as he flagged each aircraft to go. The pilots looked directly down into the breaking seas as the carrier plunged her bow, and then into the racing clouds as she rose to the next wave. The first aircraft away put its wheels through a wave top as it slowly gained the airspeed to climb. Others merely kissed the sea. Maund got them all off, and then worried how he would get them back.

They had been gone for more than an hour and a half, over a vile and still empty sea, when the Catalina's report came through. It showed the Swordfish to be searching in the right area. At 11:14, Müllenheim-Rechberg's heart sank. For 31 hours *Bismarck* had been free of surface shadowers. Now he saw a wheeled aircraft, a Swordfish. It could only mean that there was an aircraft carrier nearby, and so, he feared, happiness "had now, perhaps for good, come to an end".

The weather continued to deteriorate in the early afternoon, and one of the search planes was smashed by the carrier's rising stern as it came in to land, the crew unhurt, the flapping canvas and metal remnants pushed hurriedly over the side. *Ark Royal* was steaming parallel to *Bismarck*, about 50 miles off. She had the ageing *Renown* with her, but the battlecruiser was too under-armoured to take on *Bismarck*.

The pilots, briefed that *Bismarck* was the only ship in the target area, took off again at 14:50. An hour out, they picked up a ship on ASV, broke out of the cloud cover, and attacked it. Surprise seemed total. The ship did not fire back. Only after 11 torpedoes had been launched did the last three pilots realize why. They were attacking HMS *Sheffield*. Her captain, Charles Larcom, ordered his guns to "on no account fire". One pilot, penitent, signalled back by lamp: "Sorry for the kipper." Brilliant ship-handling saved the cruiser from the 6 torpedoes that ran at her. The others, fitted with magnetic pistols, exploded on hitting the water.

All the Swordfish got back safely. Maund did not blame them. "We were told to get some food in the wardroom, and that we'd be off again in an hour," said Moffat.

Aboard *King George V*, Tovey was waiting for the result of the strike with mounting anxiety. *Rodney* had joined him in the mid-afternoon, but, though the men in her engine room were fainting with heatstroke, the old battleship could barely make 20 knots, and *King George V* was short of fuel. At 18:21, Tovey signalled the Admiralty that he would have to return to harbour for fuel unless *Bismarck*'s speed was reduced by midnight, and that *Rodney* could remain only until 08:00 on Tuesday morning.

The only chance of slowing *Bismarck* was a torpedo hit. Ten minutes later, Tovey received a brief message on the strike force. It made no mention of the *Sheffield* debacle, but it was still the worst of news: "Flag Officer Force H to C-in-C Home Fleet. Estimate no hits." Not a word was said. It was pointless. *Bismarck* would escape.

They thought so on *Bismarck*, too, as afternoon gave way to evening and the promise of darkness. They had waited for the Swordfish, but none came, and hopes rose that the carrier was too far distant to launch an attack. In any event, the ship's armour had already shrugged off one torpedo strike. A bee sting, no more, Lütjens had said. The Luftwaffe reported that *Rodney* and three destroyers had been seen 200 miles astern. Word spread that no British battleship was within a hundred miles, and so had no chance of catching them before dawn next morning. They would be within 200 nautical miles of the French coast by then, and under the protection of the Luftwaffe. *Sheffield*'s presence, dimly visible through the squalls, was no more than an irritant. Cruisers do not frighten battleships.

Then, a little after 20:30, the alarm bells shrilled: "Aircraft alarm! Aircraft alarm!"

THIS WAS TOVEY'S LAST THROW OF the dice.

He had plotted for four days and nights, steamed more than 2,000 miles, and hunted *Bismarck* from the Denmark Strait almost to the Bay of Biscay, with the greatest pack of warships ever loosed on a single quarry at any time on any ocean. He had deployed them from the Orkneys, from Plymouth, from the Western Approaches, the South Atlantic and Gibraltar, summoning three battleships, three battlecruisers, two aircraft carriers, a dozen cruisers, and 32 destroyers. He had even deployed two ancient battleships from the American and West Indies Station.

He had lost a battleship and 1,418 men on *Hood*. *Bismarck* had lost one man.

Now, of the more than 30,000 seamen engaged, it had come down to John Moffat and 14 fellow pilots, together with their observers and telegraphist air gunners. Tovey had no great expectations. Other attacks had failed, and he gave himself until midnight before giving up the hunt.

Problems aboard *Ark Royal* delayed the launch. The carrier was steaming downwind at 25 knots, to make up the ground she had lost to *Bismarck* in turning to launch earlier in the day. Lubricating oil caught fire. Olive oil was poured over red-hot bits of machinery, and hoses played on the engine-casing. The big following seas were rolling and pitching her so badly from stem to stern that she had moments when she seemed uncontrollable. Refuelling and rearming the 15 aircraft, and bringing them up on deck, needed care and time.

The abortive strike on *Sheffield* brought one blessing, though. It had shown up the faulty magnetic firing pistols. The torpedoes were now fitted with older and more reliable contact pistols. And *Ark Royal*'s aircrews – the most experienced in the navy, who, a year before, had sunk the German light cruiser *Königsberg*, the first major warship ever lost to air attack – were mustard-keen to make amends for the afternoon's humiliation.

At 19:00 the carrier turned into the wind and reduced speed to 12 knots. *Bismarck* was 38 miles to the south-southeast. It was blowing a strong gale, Force 9, with storm-force gusts, low cloud and heavy rain. The Swordfish crews were exposed as they climbed into their open cockpits, water splashing from their leather helmets and sheepskin jackets, each fitted with a little red light and a whistle, as if that would bring rescue from a sea howling with wind and obscured by driving spray.

It was suggested that the carrier's Fulmar fighters be launched to create a diversion during the attack. The conditions were beyond them. Here, the apparent vices of the Swordfish, its antiquated design, its low speed, its flimsy canvas, became a supreme virtue.

"Only a Stringbag could get off," said Moffat. "No other aircraft had a chance. It really was an extraordinary aircraft. It flew so well. It had such stability and lifting power." Pilots could pull a Stringbag off the deck and put it in a climbing turn at 55 knots. It manoeuvred in a vertical plane as easily as straight and level. Even when diving from 10,000 feet, the indicated air speed never rose above 200 knots. The controls were not frozen stiff by the force of the slipstream. Moffat could dive within 200 feet of the sea before beginning to pull out. The approach to the carrier deck on landing could be made at astonishingly low speed – less than 30 knots when the headwind and the carrier's own forward speed were taken into account – and yet with a firm response from the controls.

The bow was pitching by the height of a house and spray was streaming over the bow as Moffat waited with the others on the flight deck, the Bristol Pegasus engine roaring in front of his shallow windscreen, the wind tugging at the canvas skin, the propeller wash whipping rain between the struts. At 19:10, the green flag on the bridge dropped for take-off.

"It all came down to timing," said Moffat. "The deck officer was the key man. He felt every roll of the ship and he knew when you could go and when not. We called him 'Bats', because he motioned with paddles like ping-pong bats. He was Pat Stringer, as tall as a giant, and he had a safety line on so he wasn't blown or tossed off the deck. We trusted him absolutely. When he said go, you went. A laden Swordfish could fly at 60 knots, so you could dip a bit going off the bow and still get airborne."

The strike leader, Lieutenant Commander Tim Coode, was first off. The aircraft flew in formations of three, and Moffat was Coode's wingman. They steered for *Sheffield*, to make sure there was no repeat of the afternoon's fiasco, and to get *Bismarck*'s exact position. They glimpsed the cruiser after about 45 minutes, lost her again in cloud, and refound her at 20:35. "The enemy is 12 miles dead ahead," she signalled them.

Coode led the aircraft up, expecting to break out of the cloud where they could manoeuvre so that each formation attacked from a different quarter, giving *Bismarck* less chance of combing the torpedo tracks. The battleship, though, was enveloped in a storm front, and the cloud above her towered almost from the surface of the sea to above ten thousand feet. Coode climbed, through six and seven to eight thousand feet, and still the grey dimness persisted. The 12 miles to *Bismarck* was a six-minute run, and the time was up. He gave a hand signal that each sub-flight should attack on its own. One aircraft lost its bearings and flew back to *Sheffield* to begin again.

Moffat followed Coode down as he dived, the altimeter unwinding, lower and lower, without a glimpse of sea or ship. "We got down to about 600 feet, and we were in a 45-degree dive," he said. "I wondered how the hell I'd be able to pull out in time. Then we came out of the cloud and levelled off at about a hundred feet. And then I saw the *Bismarck*, a massive dark thing."

They had hoped to break cloud astern of *Bismarck* for a downwind approach to her, but they found themselves 4 miles ahead and to leeward of her, the great bow smashing through the seas towards them. To attack upwind in such a wind force would leave them hopelessly slow and vulnerable. They were already under fire. They climbed round to attack from *Bismarck*'s port beam. On *Sheffield*'s bridge, they saw muzzle flashes and the stains of shellbursts through the gloom.

Surprise and coordination were lost to the little biplanes. They came in individually and in pairs, breaking cloud a mile out or less, and struggling to obtain the perfect approach, height 90 feet, speed 90 knots, range 1000 yards. "They looked like seagulls, wheeling in the air, they were so slow," the flak gunner Bruno Rzonca thought. *Bismarck* fired guns of every calibre at them. She had thirty-two 10.5cm and 3.7cm heavy and medium flak guns, and twenty 2cm light flak guns. And she fired the huge 15-inch guns that had sunk *Hood*, too, on a flat trajectory, throwing up hundred-foot-high waterspouts that could engulf a Swordfish and suck it down into the sea. The aircraft were so low that the spray from the heaving sea sometimes hid their wheels.

"Nearer and still nearer they came, into the midst of our fire," Müllenheim-Rechberg said. "It was as if their orders were, 'Get hits or don't come back!'" They were more reckless in the attack than those from *Victorious* had been two days earlier. "Every pilot seemed to know what this attack meant to Tovey," he thought. "It was the last chance to cripple the *Bismarck* so that the battle-ships could have at her. And they took it."

The ship heeled sharply as Lindemann sought to evade the torpedoes, "tin fish" to Moffat, malevolent "eels" to the Germans. The rudder indicator never came to rest, and the engine telegraphs danced: "All ahead full!" – "All stop!" – "All back full!" Müllen-heim-Rechberg heard two torpedoes explode in quick succession, well forward of his position in the aft fire-control station. He thought it "good fortune in misfortune", for he had absolute confidence in the armoured belt.

The attack had gone on for about 15 minutes, and he had a flood of confidence. The ship had shrugged off the two hits and was handling well. He thought all the Swordfish had completed their attacks. "Let's hope that's an end to it," he said.

But there was still Moffat to contend with. The guns picked him up as he began his approach, the heavy shells sending up sheets of water in front of him. "All one side of the ship was firing at me," he said. "It was like flying into hail with the tracer coming at us. I thought the lower we were, the better the chance of survival, so we dropped to 50 feet. You usually calculate the ship's speed and course to launch the torpedo. This time, I didn't. I just thought, I'll aim for the bow and it's bound to hit her, somewhere around amidships."

As Moffat prepared to drop, his observer, John "Dusty" Miller, shouted "Not yet! Not yet!" In a rough sea – and now a huge Atlantic swell was running – it was vital to drop the torpedo into the trough of a wave. If it hit the crest, it would "porpoise" and plunge deep.

"Dusty was hanging over the side of the aircraft, with his backside sticking up in the air, looking at the waves," Moffat said. "I realized what he was up to. He was waiting for the right one." The *Bismarck* was getting closer and closer – her crew reported Swordfish passing within 20 metres of the stern – and Moffat wondered if the right wave would ever come. "At last he said 'Let it go!' And did I!"

He did a flat turn to get away from the battleship, careful not to bank and increase his size as a target. He glanced back, and saw that *Bismarck* was not turning into the torpedo, but away from it, exposing her stern, but the glimpses the aircrew had of the ship were brief and obscured by gun smoke and rain squalls.

Moffat thought he had missed. Müllenheim-Rechberg knew better.

"The attack was almost over when it came, an explosion aft," he said. "My heart sank. I glanced at the rudder indicator. It showed 'left 12 degrees' … It did not change. Our increasing list to starboard soon told us we were in a continuous turn." It was not as dramatic as the two earlier hits. "It didn't make a big explosion," said Rzonca. "It was more of a 'thud'." The result, though, was immediate and chilling. The ship was still making 28 knots, but the angle of heel became so extreme some feared she would capsize, until the speed reduced.

The sky abruptly emptied of aircraft as the attack ended. As he flew back, Coode, the strike leader, sent a message: "Estimate no hits." When it reached Tovey's flagship, the admiral smiled sadly. He'd had two bites at the cherry, and it was too late now for a third. The cruiser *Edinburgh* turned for home, having reached her fuel safety margin. *King George V* herself was almost on the limit, too. On *Rodney*, the captain told the crew that he was "very sorry" to say that the second Swordfish attack had failed. "As a result," he added, "we have lost our last chance of slowing down the enemy and bringing him to action." He reduced his ship's state of readiness.

Indeed, the pilots were lucky to have a carrier to return to. The U-boat U-556 had spotted *Rodney* and *Ark Royal* while they were still airborne. Its captain, the ace Helmuth Wohlfahrt, was ideally positioned. "I could have manoeuvred between them," he wrote in his log, "and got both of them." He had a particular motive. U-556 was twinned with *Bismarck*, and Wohlfarht had signed a pledge for his submarine to "stand beside our big brother whatever may befall her". But he could offer no help now. He had used up all his torpedoes attacking a convoy. He watched as the great ships passed a few hundred metres away, and the deafening roar of their propellers in the hydrophones slowly grew faint.

Four of the Swordfish were badly damaged. One had a wounded crew and 175 holes in its fabric. All got safely back, though; they had flown so slowly that they were outside the parameters of the German fire predictors, and most of the *Bismarck*'s gunners had fired ahead of them. "It was ten o'clock at night, and we'd no idea what we'd done," said Moffat.

BISMARCK, THOUGH, WAS ALL TOO aware of Moffat's handiwork. She radioed at 20:54 that she was under attack by carrier aircraft. No mention was made of the torpedoes that struck the armoured belt, but at 21:05 she radioed: "Have torpedo hit aft." Ten minutes later, she radioed: "Ship no longer steerable." To his horror, his gaze drawn to the rudder indicator "like a magnet", Müllenheim-Rechberg saw that it still showed left 12 degrees. "At one stroke," he realized, "the world seemed to be irrevocably altered."

Moffat's 18-inch, 1,600-pound torpedo had hit right aft at least six metres below the waterline, so violently that the floor of

"Quivering flashes of lightning, bursts of flame, an apocalyptic symphony of destruction," wrote Crown Prince Wilhelm of the barrage that opened the final German offensive in France in July 1918. The shell bursts were heard 80 miles away in Paris, but they fell on empty trenches. This was the handiwork of **Joseph Darnand**, a 21-year-old who had led a trench raid deep into German lines a few hours before. The prisoners and documents he brought back revealed German plans in such detail that the French cut the attackers to ribbons. Marshal Pétain described Darnand's deed as "the turning point of the war". A grateful nation honoured him (left, above, in civilian suit) as one of just three "artisans of victory". After 1940, Darnand was faithful to Pétain's Vichy regime (below, behind the Marshal's right shoulder) as it collaborated with the Nazis. The hero of the First War was tried for treason (left) and shot at the end of the Second. (*See page 96.*)

For over three hours on 13 May 1940, **Walter Rubarth** (above, with the Knight's Cross he was awarded) was the flesh-and-blood speartip of the German invasion of the West. The tanks and guns of three German Panzer divisions were stalled on the right bank of the Meuse at Sedan behind him. The French had blown the bridges and shot up or sunk scores of German rubber assault boats (opposite, above). Rubarth got a solitary boat across under heavy fire. With a handful of men, he created his own bridgehead, destroying bunkers until at length the enemy "fled like ferrets, throwing away their arms and equipment ...". In an afternoon, an eager, 27-year-old platoon sergeant had tipped the balance of a struggle in which three million men were engaged. Within hours, the Germans had flung a bridge (opposite, below) over the river. The fall of France had begun. (*See page 12.*)

Herbert Edwardes (above) was painted in his Indian finery in 1850. It was no mere dressing up for the son of an English country vicar to appear like this. He owed his brilliant success as a young soldier in India to his empathy with the force of Muslim irregulars he raised. "By living the same life as they did, wearing the same dress, talking the same language, and sharing with them all dangers and fatigues," he wrote, "they became attached to me, and I to them." That is the very distillation of the art of the infantry officer, and it brought him victory against all odds. (*See page 51.*)

In the "screeching howling bleeding nights", a soldier wrote of Stalingrad, "the dogs plunge into the Volga ... animals flee this hell. Only men endure." Most notable among them was a young Red Army sergeant, **Yakov Pavlov**, seen here (top) in front of the ruins of No. 61 Penzenskaya Street. He held it for 58 days and nights, German assaults breaking around him like waves on a half-tide rock. To Russian infantry, here (above) launching a grenade attack with the white building seen behind them, it was simply "Pavlov's House". To the Germans, the defenders were at first "insane ... fanatics", but slowly they saw them as "not men, but cast-iron creatures ...". (*See page 69.*)

Bismarck, the greatest German warship afloat, fired this salvo (opposite, top) at HMS *Hood* early on 24 May 1941. *Hood* exploded, with the loss of 1,418 men. National prestige demanded vengeance. Swordfish biplanes (opposite) spotted her late that evening (opposite, below) but she escaped. Late on 26 May, *Bismarck* was close to reaching safety under German air cover. **John Moffat** (below, at war) flew a Swordfish from HMS *Ark Royal* in a final attack in a severe gale. "All one side of the ship was firing at me," he said, and he thought he had missed. But his was a 100,000:1 shot. He crippled *Bismarck*'s steering gear, and the Royal Navy closed in for the kill. Moffat flew over the survivors in the water – some were picked up by HMS *Dorsetshire* (above) – but he felt no exhilaration. "It was more, there but for the grace of God ..." Against the odds, too, he survived the war (below, right, in retirement). (*See page 114.*)

The scale of the Vietnam War was changed for ever at the hamlet of Ap Bac on 2 January 1963. Viet Cong guerrillas achieved two firsts. They shot down five helicopters (including those above), and, through the actions of an individual squad leader, **Nguyen Van Dung**, they resisted an assault by a company of M-113 armoured personnel carriers. They then escaped after paratroops were dropped in the wrong position (below). The shock waves reached Washington after the senior American adviser, John Paul Vann, summoned the Saigon press corps to the battlefield, and told them that the war would be lost without regime change and a massive American input of men and material. Vann, who stayed on in Vietnam (left) until his death in 1972, convinced President Kennedy to escalate. Dung's courage had an equal effect in Hanoi, persuading Ho Chi Minh to increase North Vietnamese involvement. (*See page 154.*)

the centre engine room buckled upwards by half a metre. Flood-water poured through split welds and cable ducts. The engines and the propellers were unharmed, though water gushed up the propeller shaft into the port engine room, and the starboard engine shut down for a few moments after the shock triggered a safety valve. But the rudders were jammed solid, and all the steering-gear compartments were flooded. The master carpenter and his mate thought they might be able to reach and disengage the jammed rudder motor coupling, wearing underwater escape and breathing apparatus. They opened the armoured hatch over the steering mechanism, and had terrifying confirmation that the stern was open to the sea. Seawater shot up as the stern fell in the seaway, and was then sucked down as the stern rose. No one could live, let alone work down there.

Heavy seas swept away the collision mats the crew tried to get over the hole. The ship kept turning until her bow faced into the northwesterly gale, on an almost perfect reciprocal for the south-easterly course she should have maintained for St Nazaire. The hull shuddered as Lindemann tried every combination of speeds and engines to get back on course: port engine half ahead, centre and starboard engines stop, port and centre half ahead, starboard engine back slow. She kept rounding up into the wind, as a ship without steering always will. The problems noticed on her trials – the difficulty of manoeuvre without the steering gear, the weak turning power of the propellers – became a crisis.

Lookouts on the *Sheffield* were the first to realize that something very strange was afoot. *Bismarck* suddenly loomed out of the swells broadside on and in range. Captain Charles Larcom pulled away at high speed and put down smoke. The second salvo from the battleship's 15-inch guns straddled the cruiser, with a lethal hail of splinters that killed three and wounded more. Larcom reported that *Bismarck* had reversed her course and was steering northwest. Tovey did not believe it. He said scornfully that Larcom had joined the "reciprocal club" of navigators who make 180-degree errors.

An hour after Moffat's strike, there was desperate talk on *Bismarck* of sending divers down to cut off the rudders, or to set explosives to blast them off. The ship might then be steered by her engines, it was hoped. But the sea was too high, and the suction under the stern too strong for either a free-swimming diver or one working down a line fixed from the stern. It was realized, too, that blowing the rudders off would probably damage the propellers, and might sink the ship.

Another idea was to take the door of the ship's aircraft hangar, and weld it to the starboard side of the stern at an angle to counter the left rudder. The gale made that impossible, too.

At 21:40, Lütjens signalled Group West: "Ship unable to manoeuvre. We will fight to the last round. Long live the Führer."

It was only at 23:25, when a Swordfish that had been shadowing *Bismarck* returned to *Ark Royal*, that the British had confirmation that the battleship had lost speed and was indeed steering erratically. Tovey, exhilaration replacing his despondency, prepared for the kill. He wrote a note for the commanding officer of his flagship to read out to his crew: "The sinking of the *Bismarck* may have an effect on the war as a whole out of proportion to the loss to the enemy of one battleship. May God be with you and grant you victory."

A moonless and gloomy night fell on his quarry. "Incapable of manoeuvring, we crept towards the superior forces coming to destroy us, a virtual journey to Golgotha," Müllenheim-Rechberg said. Shortly before midnight, destroyers were sighted. Word spread that work on the rudder had stopped, and the certainty that there was no escape became absolute. Lütjens sent a message to Hitler: "We will fight to the last in belief in you, my Führer, and in unshakeable confidence in Germany's victory."

Bismarck kept the destroyers at bay, but they always returned to attack with torpedoes, though the seas were breaking over their mess decks and spray deluged their bridges. They started firing star shells to illuminate their prey. U-556 surfaced. "I can see star shells being fired and flashes from *Bismarck*'s guns," Wohlfarht wrote in his war diary at midnight. "It is a terrible feeling to be near and not to be able to do anything."

The conditions in the heavy seas were poor for torpedoes, though, and the 16 fired at her that night all missed, ever-accurate gunnery keeping the tormentors at extreme range. *Bismarck* survived, as the temperature in the engine rooms rose to 50 °C, while the men, sweatbands on their heads and slices of lemon in their mouths, worked the throttles of the turbines to evade the torpedoes. A turbine that locked under extreme changes of power during one attack was freed with steam pressure at 58 times atmospheric pressure and 400 °C, without shedding a blade.

Hitler was far from the sea, amid the mountains at the Berghof, his Alpine eyrie. At 01:53 he sent a message to the crew: "All Germany is with you. What can be done, will be done ..." The star shells died away at 03:00. At 03:51, the Führer awarded Adalbert Schneider, the chief gunnery officer, the Knight's Cross for sinking the *Hood*. This was announced, with other messages of goodwill, and morale among the young seamen rallied. "We were told that 81 Junkers bombers would arrive by dawn, and four U-boats, a tanker and a tug," said Otto Maus, a seaman. "Our turret leader promised us he'd personally insist that we'd be given leave as soon as we got in. There was great joy." The men sang sailors' ballads and the *Bismarck* hymn, a homage to the old Iron Chancellor:

> *Bismarck Heil! Dem einzig Einer*
> *Uns'res Volkes treu'sten Mann ...*
>
> [Hail, Bismarck! One and only,
> Our people's most loyal man ...]

The older men knew what was coming. Between destroyer attacks, *Bismarck* lay athwart the seas, rolling so badly that waves were breaking over the port side, threatening to wash men overboard. It didn't matter whether she made headway or not, Müllenheim-Rechberg thought, "because when daylight came on 27 May, Tovey's battleships would find us one way or another." At 04:00, Wohlfarth wrote in U-556's war diary, "The seas are rising ever higher. *Bismarck* still fighting."

A few officers sat in the wardroom, whilst a soup tureen sloshed to the roll of the ship. "Today my wife will become a widow," one of them said, "but she doesn't know it." Men were lying stretched out, even on the bridge, where they should have been at their most alert. Lindemann was wearing a life jacket. In the chartroom, the ship's course was marked, running arrow-straight for St Nazaire up to the point where Moffat's torpedo had hit. Then it became a serpentine line swerving back to the northwest.

Dawn came, Müllenheim-Rechberg found, like "a succession of curtains being opened, each of which instantaneously disclosed a more distant view". A little before 06:00 it was light enough to see the destroyers around them, which made off to the west to remain hidden against the dark horizon and the rain squalls. An Arado was readied to fly *Bismarck*'s war diary and film of the sinking of the *Hood* to safety. Men gave scribbled notes to the pilot to give to wives and girlfriends. The compressed air pipe to the catapult was fractured, however, and the aircraft, useless without it, was dumped over the side.

The pack was gathering. The two battleships, *King George V* and *Rodney*, were close. Tovey did not want to fight until it was fully light, and he kept below the horizon, working to approach from the northwest. *Norfolk*, which had been on the hunt since the Denmark Strait, reached the scene at 07:53. Sighting a battleship to her southeast, she assumed that it was the *Rodney*. *Norfolk* was making visual recognition signals when her captain realized that he was steaming straight for the *Bismarck*, and had the helm put over sharply to get out of danger. The cruiser *Dorsetshire*, which had been escorting a convoy, arrived at high speed from the west, unannounced and unexpected by Tovey's forces. She was taken to be the *Prinz Eugen* for some moments, and narrowly avoided being fired on by her own side.

At 08:44 Müllenheim-Rechberg saw the two battleships through the eyepieces of his gun director at a range of 24,000 metres, coming straight for him, in line abreast, "as imperturbable as though they were on their way to an execution". He calculated that a single British broadside weighed 18,448 kilos against *Bismarck*'s 6,904 kilos. That was from the battleships only, without the two British heavy cruisers. But it no longer mattered how many ships were closing in: "We could be shot to pieces only once."

Rodney fired the first salvo, at 08:47. *King George V* followed a minute later. *Bismarck* returned fire at 08:50, concentrating on the *Rodney*. At 08:54 *Norfolk*'s 8-inch guns began firing from 20,000 metres, joined at 09:04 by the *Dorsetshire*.

Bismarck's third salvo was a straddle, a shell 20 yards from *Rodney*'s bridge sluicing it with foul-smelling water, and forcing her to make an elaborate series of manoeuvres to spoil German computations. By 08:59, though, both British battleships were on target, and four heavy salvoes were landing around *Bismarck* every minute, raising columns of water as high as her foretop. At 09:02, the whole of *Bismarck*'s forepart was swept by a sheet of flame from a 16-inch shell from *Rodney*. Her forward turrets were knocked out.

The shellfire was so intense that the eye saw *Bismarck* only as a maelstrom of waterspouts and smoke illuminated by a dull red glow when she returned fire. Salvo after salvo crashed into her port side. By 09:19, only one main turret was returning fire. At 09:31, this too fired its last salvo. A thick oily smoke poured from her funnel, obscuring her after end, flames flickering amidst it, and *King George V* and *Rodney* poured one-ton shells into her in a murderous crossfire.

They wanted it over quickly. A German reconnaissance aircraft had appeared overhead, and air-raid and U-boat warnings were in force. But it took a fraction under two hours – 115 minutes – to sink the *Bismarck*. The British did not much enjoy it. They were smashing to pulp a ship of great beauty, and what they were doing to her brave crew, they could not bear to imagine: "the ship full of fire, her people hurt", a watching destroyer officer said, "and surely all men are much the same when hurt".

The range closed to 3,000 metres. At 10:15 two heavy shells from the *King George V* penetrated the superstructure and the firestorm they caused swept up to ignite the signal rockets stowed on the bridge in bursts of colour. A third shell went through the face of a turret and blew the armour plate at the back over the side. The smoky red-orange of fires deep within her glowed through holes in her upper deck. She was listing to port, and men were washed off by the seas that boarded her. Others had begun jumping from the quarterdeck. When Bruno Rzonca came up to join them, he found "the whole deck was full of blood and body parts".

Admiral Tovey signalled: "Cannot sink her with guns." He wanted torpedoes used. Moffat had taken off from *Ark Royal* with another strike force to finish her off. The Swordfish arrived in driving rain to find four ships firing simultaneously at *Bismarck* from very short range. The trajectories were so flat that the shells might hit the low-flying biplanes if they attacked. The Swordfish held off until the *Dorsetshire* launched a final torpedo into her just after 10:30.

"When we got about a thousand yards from the ship, it suddenly turned on its side," said Moffat. "I flew over it, maybe fifty feet up, and all those poor people in the water, in the waves and wind, hundreds of them, terrible. We didn't feel exhilarated. It was more, there but for the grace of God ..."

At 10:38 *Bismarck*'s bow was momentarily visible, looming out of the water in a cloud of smoke. Her first and only voyage was almost over. At 10:39, colours still flying, she was gone.

MOFFAT'S TORPEDO HAD DELIVERED *Bismarck* to her executioners. Both sides agreed on that. Had he missed, she would have escaped.

It is also beyond dispute that Moffat fulfilled Clausewitz's dictum on the role of chance in warfare.

During trials, practices had been held for a "hit in the steering gear". The steering compartments were "flooded" during the simulation. The men in them asked the training officer if a hit would be catastrophic in actual combat. "Yes," he replied. "Put your caps on backwards and you'll be counted as dead." He thought for a moment, and added: "The odds against such a hit are a hundred thousand, practically nil."

When Moffat let go his torpedo, a moment itself defined only by the vagaries of the wave patterns and his observer's reading of them, *Bismarck* was making 28 knots. The torpedo had a window of about half a second to strike her Achilles heel. A fraction later, and it would have missed the stern altogether. A smidgen earlier, and it would have hit the ship's armoured belt.

The punishment *Bismarck* absorbed showed how well she was protected everywhere but where Moffat hit. The hull had 17,500 tons of armour plate, accounting for a quarter more of her total displacement than the newest British battleships. Torpedo bulkheads ran inside her outer armoured shell. Her main armoured belts covered 70 percent of her length, 13.75 cm thick at deck-edge level increasing to 32.5 cm at the waterline. Horizontal protection came from an armoured weather deck, and a main armoured deck that ran across the ship at waterline level, 8.75 cm thick at the centreline, and 10 cm where it sloped down to meet the belt armour below the waterline.

In her final fight, 2,876 shells were fired at her, and of these 719 were one-ton 14-inch and 16-inch monsters. She was the target of 59 other torpedoes. Moffat's Swordfish alone had left her helpless, able only, as Tovey wrote in his report, "to put up a most gallant fight against impossible odds".

Bismarck sank 4,700 metres to the deep ocean floor, making a vast impact crater where she hit, and then sliding a further 1,400 metres on the sloping bottom before coming to rest. All Lütjens's staff were among the 2,131 who lost their lives. Only 115 of the crew were saved.

Her sinking, both sides agreed, had a profound influence. Had *Bismarck* survived, Winston Churchill telegraphed Franklin Roosevelt, the Royal Navy would have had to keep its capital ships "practically tied to Scapa Flow against a sortie ... Now it is a different story." The sinking had an electrifying effect on public opinion in the United States, confirming that the British, though still fighting the Germans alone, were not beaten.

Hitler was acutely aware of the loss of German prestige. He forbade Grand Admiral Raeder, the Kriegsmarine commander, to risk other warships in like manner. Raeder admitted that the loss had a "decisive effect on the war at sea". German surface vessels would no longer undertake any major operations in the Atlantic.

ARK ROYAL'S OWN LUCK RAN OUT FIVE and a half months later. She capsized and sank off Gibraltar 13 hours after being torpedoed and taken in tow. The miracle of Swordfish invulnerability was soon over. In February 1942, the *Prinz Eugen*, together with the *Scharnhorst* and *Gneisenau*, left Brest to dash through the Channel to Germany. All six Swordfish of 825 Squadron were shot down when they intercepted the warships, and 13 of the 18 aircrew were lost. Eugene Esmonde, who had led the first strike against the *Bismarck*, was awarded a posthumous Victoria Cross.

John Moffat, who was belatedly credited with the *Bismarck* strike, survived the war with only one ditching. "I was told to drop two depth charges behind the convoy we were escorting," he said. "They should have gone off at a good depth and well behind us. They exploded immediately they hit the surface. They blew the arse straight out of the aeroplane. I was picked up by a destroyer."

He went into the hotel business after the war. He ran a hotel and restaurant at Kendal in the Lake District, and then had his own hotel at Grantully in Perthshire in his native Scotland.

At the age of 86, he was still flying a Piper light aircraft.

6 · CAST NET – THROW SPEAR

The squad leader who started the Vietnam War as we know it

The political consequences of an individual's action
may have an impact out of all proportion to
the military event. Seldom more so than here, a
near-perfect example of Clausewitz's dictum: "Wars
may all be regarded as political acts"
(BOOK I, CHAPTER XXVI).

MY THO PROVINCE, SOUTH VIETNAM ∗ 06:00 – 17:00 HOURS
2 JANUARY 1963

THE GUERRILLAS KNEW THE ENEMY was coming. Their spies in My
Tho, the provincial capital, counted 71 truckloads of ammunition and supplies arriving from Saigon in the last few days of the
year. They were destined for the South Vietnamese 7th Division,
whose operational zone covered the northern delta of the Mekong
River. This rice-rich region was the key to the war between the
Viet Cong and the forces of the Saigon regime, "puppet forces"
to the guerrillas, "the ARVN" (Army of the Republic of Vietnam)
in correct military jargon to the Americans who were advising
them.

An American radio detection team had picked up a Viet Cong

transmitter and located it 14 miles from My Tho, in the vicinity of the village of Tan Thoi and the nearby hamlet of Ap Bac. The intercepts suggested that it was serving as a headquarters of some sort. Viet Cong strength was estimated at a company of 120 or so men.

The villages lay close to Highway Four, the only major land route between Saigon and the fertile rice paddies and fish ponds and fruit groves of the Delta. They were close, too, to a wild and safe guerrilla sanctuary, at the eastern extremity of the Plain of Reeds, whose swamps and brackish reed beds stretched towards the Cambodian border.

Wooden huts with earth floors were scattered under shade trees, with roofs of thatched water palm that overhung the sides for protection in the monsoon. Storehouses held the rice crop. Black hogs and chickens and ducks rooted about. The villages were linked by canals, and dykes were raised above the paddy fields, to contain the water when the fields were flooded during the wet season. Thick stands of bamboo and coconut and water palms grew along the dyke tops, with groves of mangoes and grapefruit and limes. Sugar cane grew high and dense.

This was Viet Cong country. The main road could be travelled at some risk by a single car or jeep during daylight, but not after dark. The roads leading off it were mainly impassable. Ditches were dug across them and bridges destroyed. Deeper in towards Tan Thoi and Bac, the roads had disappeared completely, having been dug up and the soil scattered in the fields.

Water, thick and brown, or grey and soupy like gruel, was everywhere, in the rivers and streams, and in the many canals and dykes dug for irrigation. For centuries these waterways had been used by sampans taking people and produce to market. By the end of 1962, they were also carrying arms and ammunition to the battlefield. It was the dry season now, and the water level was below the tops of the dykes. Sampans could move under the thick vegetation without being seen from the paddies, or from the air.

In fact, the Viet Cong were in greater strength here than was suspected. They had about 340 men, the equivalent of a scratch but well-trained and motivated battalion. The VC commander, Hai Hoang, was not aware that his radio had been located. He knew, though, that the villages were prime targets for an enemy sweep. Their proximity to the Plain of Reeds offered him a safe place to withdraw after battle was done.

His men had grown up in this flat, moist landscape. Hoang had a company of the 514th Regional Battalion, the locally recruited home battalion of the province. The 1st Company of the 261st Main Force Battalion gave him a backbone of experienced regulars. They, too, were men from the Delta, largely from around My Tho and Ben Tre, just to the south. Reinforcing these two companies, he had two squads and a support unit of main-force troops, and guerrillas from local forces.

Hoang put the 514th men into positions just to the north of, and flanking, Tan Thoi. Further south, the regulars of the 261st were deployed in a semicircle round Bac. One group held a heavily wooded dyke that ran north to south just to the west of the hamlet, overlooking the open paddy fields in front of it. Within the dyke was an irrigation canal broad enough to take sampans. This tough, experienced company was commanded by Nguyen Bay. To the south of his foxhole line, and cutting east–west into the paddies at right angles to it, local guerrillas held the coconut groves of another tree line that commanded the approach from the south.

Hoang had them dig in throughout the day on 1 January. They burrowed into the sides of the dykes, making near-perfect fighting foxholes, protected by banks and camouflaged with thick foliage. They had captured American weapons, M-1 rifles, a 60mm mortar, about a dozen BAR light machine-guns, four .30 calibre machine-guns and – a prize beyond value – a heavy .50 calibre machine-gun. They set out aiming parameters for the automatic weapons, small wooden stakes topped with white tape, which designated the fields of fire.

Nguyen Van Dung, a young squad leader, was among those digging in among the trees of the dyke that overlooked the paddies west of Bac. He was typical of the Delta guerrilla, deceptively slight but wiry, toughened by farm work, familiar from boyhood with the mud and water and dykes, and with the hiding places in stands of trees and reeds. He had started as a village volunteer, acting as a scout or porter as need arose, and progressed to a main force unit. He had trained at a safe base in the Plain of Reeds, in weapons handling, first aid and the basics of infantry tactics. Recently, stress had been put on "leading" helicopters and fighter-bombers – aiming in front of them to compensate for their forward speed. Dung had impressed enough to be given his own eight-man squad of riflemen and a BAR gunner, with, it appears, a .30 calibre machine-gunner attached to it.

"The spiked traps and booby traps were checked anew," the Viet Cong chronicler of the coming battle wrote. "In the night, the gun nests and all the defence works were finished." Scouts were sent out. Women and children were taken to safe hiding places among the reeds. Dung and his comrades were ready for the "puppets" and the Americans.

THERE WERE TO BE MORE OF THEM than Hoang had reckoned on. He was himself a soldier of rare quality, as he was to show that day. The senior American adviser to the 7th Division, a brilliant and driven young lieutenant colonel called John Paul Vann, was a fitting adversary.

Vann had been in the country for less than a year. He was already hurting the Viet Cong badly with aggressive infantry sweeps given mobility and firepower by helicopters and M-113 armoured personnel carriers. Hoang knew what to expect of Vann: tactics that the guerrillas called "Cast net – throw spear". The net was cast by helicopter-borne infantry, trapping the guerrillas, who were then speared by helicopter gunships, fighter-bombers and M-113s.

The American was very good at it. Three months before, the 7th Division's M-113s had routed the Viet Cong 502nd Battalion in difficult, watery terrain in the Plain of Reeds. The guerrillas had tried to hide in the reed beds and the flooded paddies, breathing through reeds, but the carriers had charged straight into them, flushing them out by creating waves with their tracks. When the infantry dismounted from the machines, they found themselves bogged down knee-deep in mud and water. The initiative passed briefly to the enemy, who knew the terrain and moved to higher ground where there were underwater knolls. Once the ARVNs remounted, though, the slaughter continued, the infantry firing from the open hatches whilst the machine-gunners cut down the Viet Cong as they ran wildly for cover, only for the pursuing machines to catch up and crush them. When the ARVNs cleared the battlefield, they found more than 150 Viet Cong dead.

The memory of that battle was still fresh. It was, indeed, almost certainly one of the reasons that Hoang intended to stand and fight at Ap Bac. Viet Cong strategists, including Pham Xuan An, the most subtle of their agents in Saigon (where he masqueraded as a journalist), had a "dual-prong" approach to the war, part *chin tri*, "political", and part *vy trang*, "military".

From a purely *vy trang* stance, withdrawal made more sense than taking on Vann's awesome weaponry – rockets, napalm, bombs, quad machine-guns, a flamethrower. But *chin tri* demanded that the Viet Cong cope with Vann's sweeps, or lose their political credibility. Their forces were being burnt up at an unsustainable rate. The regional 514th Battalion had taken more than 30 percent casualties since the summer. It seemed incapable of protecting the local peasantry, and its impotence was slowly undermining support in the villages. Defeating "armoured vehicle and helicopter mobility", captured Viet Cong documents showed, was the most "urgent requirement" of the leadership. Melting away, as discretion demanded at Ap Bac, was no longer an option. Only in battle could they learn how to cope.

What Vann had in mind for them was terrifying indeed. A triple assault was planned. An infantry battalion from the 7th Division was to be landed in paddy fields north of Tan Thoi to squeeze southwards onto the guerrillas. This was a well-armed force of about 330 regulars. Two battalions of Civil Guards, a less well-trained and armed but nonetheless large body of men, was to march up across the fields from the south in two columns.

A company of 13 M-113s was also to move up from the south, along the western side of the battle zone, to block the Viet Cong when they started to retreat under pressure from the others. The big amphibians carried an infantry company in their armoured hulls, and could serve as mobile reserves as well as a strike force. Once the Viet Cong broke, the final instruments of their annihilation were to be the helicopter gunships and fighter-bombers that would be at hand throughout the day. The divisional commander, Colonel Bui Dinh Dam, had a further two infantry companies in reserve at the 7th Division's airstrip nearby at Tien Hiep which could be helicoptered in if reinforcements were needed. A paratroop battalion was also disposable as a reserve of last resort.

Had he suspected the scale of what Vann was to throw at him, Hoang might have slipped away. He did not know, until it was too late, but he did have long experience on his side.

This was an old war, dating back to the 1940s, and Hoang had fought the French in its first round. That had ended when the French withdrew from their Indochinese colonies after their defeat by Ho Chi Minh's communist Viet Minh at Dien Bien Phu in

1954. Vietnam was cut in two. Ho ruled the North from Hanoi. The pro-Western regime of Ngo Dinh Diem held shaky sway over the South from Saigon.

Round Two of the war began with attacks on Diem's forces by men like Hoang, communists who had stayed in the South and fought to unite Vietnam under Hanoi. The South Vietnam National Front for Liberation established its own army, the People's Liberation Armed Forces (PLAF) or Viet Cong, in 1961. American involvement on the other side deepened in May that year when the Kennedy administration promised Diem aid that would more than double the size of his armed forces. In November 1961 the US National Security Council voted to supply the ARVN with new weapons, and to send large numbers of military advisers and aircrew to Saigon. Among these was John Paul Vann.

At 04:00 on 2 January 1963, the first scouts reported to Hoang that they had heard truck and jeep engines at 7th Division bases. Dung's squad checked their weapons and their camouflage. A climactic battle, that would lead to the war's Round Three, was about to start.

TEN CH-21 HELICOPTERS WERE TO carry the 7th Division infantry in. They were ponderous old machines, whose aft fuselage bent upwards to prevent the two big rotors from hitting each other in flight, giving them a strange angular shape and the nickname of the "flying banana". They could carry 22 fully armed troops, plus a four-man American crew, but they were slow, and their control cables and fuel lines were vulnerable to small-arms fire. Five American-crewed UH-1B gunships flew escort for them, suppressing ground fire with their quad machine-guns and 2.75in rocket pods. These were "Hueys", the first turbine-engined helicopters to be mass produced, tough and brilliantly adaptable, as eager as gundogs, and a lasting symbol of the Vietnam War.

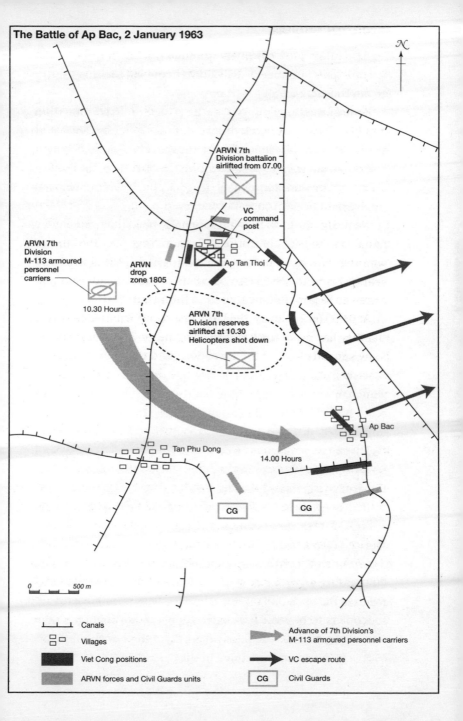

The Battle of Ap Bac, 2 January 1963

ARVN 7th Division battalion airlifted from 07.00

VC command post

ARVN 7th Division M-113 armoured personnel carriers

10.30 Hours

ARVN drop zone 1805

Ap Tan Thoi

ARVN 7th Division reserves airlifted at 10.30 Helicopters shot down

Ap Bac

Tan Phu Dong

14.00 Hours

CG

CG

0   500 m

	Canals
	Villages
	Viet Cong positions
	ARVN forces and Civil Guards units

Advance of 7th Division's M-113 armoured personnel carriers

VC escape route

CG   Civil Guards

𝒩

The pilots took off in the pre-dawn from Tan Son Nhut, Saigon's sprawling airfield, to fly down to the 7th Division's airstrip at Tan Hiep to load up the troops.

One of the Huey pilots, Charlie Ostick, noticed something odd on the way. He was flying at and below treetop level at 90 knots. This gave very little time for anyone on the ground to react, and he did not want to make it known that Tan Hiep was the pick-up zone, as would have been clear had he flown safely above small-arms fire at 1,500 feet or higher.

As he dropped low over a paddy field, he found himself a few feet above the heads of a platoon of Viet Cong. "Now, in the past when we flew over Viet Cong they scattered and left us alone," he said. "This time, they rolled onto their backs as we went over them and immediately started firing into the air." It was an effective infantry tactic, because the Hueys flew in pairs, and the second one would fly into the bullets if it was in trail formation astern.

Ostick had learnt not to do this in earlier operations, and his wingman was not behind him, but flying in echelon a 100 yards off to his left. "So I told my door gunner, 'Drop smoke,' and he immediately dropped a red smoke canister out of the chopper," Ostick said. He radioed his wingman: "From my smoke, 6 o'clock, 50 metres, enemy troops in the open. Circle right, follow my lead, fire machine-guns and rockets at will."

The Hueys went into steep right turns and circled back on the red smoke. "I saw the troops in the open still firing at us," Ostick said. "So we opened up with our quad M-60 machine-guns, hosed down the area, fired a pair of rockets, and then broke off maybe 200 yards short of the target." His wingman followed, and they repeated the operation on several passes, with machine-guns and rockets on each pass. "It wasn't long before we could tell there was no return fire," the pilot noted, "and there were numerous Viet Cong killed and wounded in the open field."

He flew on to Tan Hiep and refuelled and rearmed. He was still surprised that the Viet Cong had not scattered. Was it a signal? A sea change?

A LITTLE BEFORE 07:00, THE CH-21S began airlifting the infantry battalion into the rice paddies north of Tan Thoi. Vann had taken off in an L-19 spotter plane to watch them. It was going to take four lifts to carry all of the men, and ground fog blanketed the area after the first lift passed without incident. Flying ten of the big two-rotor machines in the white-out would invite a mid-air collision. So the machines and the rest of the battalion waited at Tan Hiep for it to burn off as the sun rose.

The Civil Guards, however, had begun their operation and were still advancing towards Tan Thoi from the south. The Viet Cong followed their progress through runners and by listening in to their radio traffic. The ARVN transmitted in clear. Hoang had Dung and his regulars in the Bac tree line, and a platoon of district guerrillas in coconut groves, between the Civil Guards and Tan Thoi. They let the guardsmen get within 30 metres of them before opening fire. The company commander and his executive officer were killed in the first few moments. The rest of the battalion went to ground, cowering behind a low dyke. Occasionally one would raise an arm and fire wildly over the top, so that their wounded comrades out front and those as yet un-hit and trying to get back were being fired on by both friend and foe.

By 07:45 the Civil Guard battalion had reached an unhappy stalemate, stalled in front of the enemy-held tree line to the south and west of Bac. Artillery was called in, but the shells fell behind the guerrillas. The feeble efforts to dislodge or outflank the guerrillas ceased altogether when the captain in command was wounded at 10:00. He had 8 dead and 14 wounded. He radioed Colonel Dam asking him to fly in the two companies being held as a division reserve at Tan Hiep. He wanted them landed behind the guerrillas he was facing in the tree line.

The fog had burnt off and the CH-21s had completed lifting the 7th Division battalion north of Tan Thoi without incident. Vann, though, was worried at lifting the reserve companies to the paddies just to the west and south of Bac. He had his little spotter plane make pass after pass over the deserted hamlet, down to treetop level. In particular, he flew down the tree line to the west of the hamlet. He could see nothing; but then he could see nothing of the Viet Cong dug into the southern tree line, though he knew they were there, because he could see the Civil Guards sheltering from their fire.

At length, Vann advised the CH-21 pilots to come in tight from the south, and to land at least 300 yards away from the western tree line. He was still suspicious. Three hundred yards is a fair safety margin for small arms and .30 calibre fire. Two hundred is not. And the Viet Cong were waiting for the "Angle Worms", their name for the "flying bananas", and "Dippers", as they called the Hueys. Dung and his men in the western tree line knew the significance of the little spotter plane that had tried so hard to tempt them into betraying their position. Hoang's radio operators, too, had picked up ARVN transmissions on the lift.

The lead pilot ignored Vann. The CH-21s came in from the north, reckless, directly over Tan Thoi and down the creek that linked it to Bac, where they swung to land 200 yards west of the hamlet. They took enemy fire all along this flight path. As the ARVN infantry jumped into the paddy, up to their knees in water, a drum roll of fire pounded above the roar of the engines from all along the western tree line. "The puppet troops," the chronicler exulted, "found themselves in a pell-mell like frogs in a basket." The regulars of the 261st had never had a target like it, ten large, ungainly machines, 52 feet long, almost 16 feet high, flopping in front and below them at a range where even their small arms could do real damage, disgorging frightened enemy troops into the killing zone.

The Hueys did what they could. "We'd had no return fire until this lift," said Ostick. "Then the Viet Cong decided to ambush the CH-21s as they were coming into the landing zone. Now this is a very difficult situation, as the ARVN were already on the ground and were moving towards the tree lines and some were in the open field." The gunships strafed the tree lines and fired their rockets, but the guerrillas were dug in deep, and invisible beneath the foliage, and they fired back with their machine guns and BARs, so that tracer came streaking back out of the trees, a novel experience.

All the CH-21s took multiple hits. Nine shuddered back into the air. The controls on the tenth were shot away. The pilot radioed that he and his co-pilot and the two crewmen were taking to the paddy with the ARVN. Honour dictated that they be rescued at once. A CH-21 circled back and landed to pick them up. Its pilot put it, like a plump duck, between the crippled machine and the tree line. It was swiftly too damaged to fly. Ostick and his fellow gunship pilots strafed both tree lines as the Huey leader now attempted a rescue. He landed behind the two CH-21s, away from Dung and the men in the western tree line, but they hit the Huey time after time until they got the main rotor, and the helicopter crashed onto its side. In the meantime, a CH-21 that had limped into the air had crash-landed in a paddy a mile away.

"So now we also had an aircrew on the ground under enemy fire and our pucker factor went way up," said Ostick. "We had never lost an aircrew and we never had a downed Huey up to that time." It was now 10:30. In five minutes, the Viet Cong had shot down four helicopters. Ostick's premonition was right. Nothing like this had ever happened before.

An adviser, Arnold Bowers, who had jumped from a CH-21 with an ARVN squad, made his way over to the crashed machines.

The engine on the Huey, freed from the drag of the rotor, was burning itself out in wild whinings. Bowers helped the dazed pilots get behind a mound that protected them from the shots that were still thumping in from the tree line. The crew chief was still strapped into his seat, suspended almost upside down in the wreck. As Bowers took his flying helmet off, he saw that he had been shot dead through the head.

Bowers found a door gunner close to one of the CH-21s. He told Bowers that his crew chief, Donald Braman, was wounded and still inside the helicopter. Bowers dressed Braman's shoulder, taking care to keep low as every time they spotted him, the guerrillas loosed off bursts in his direction.

Several of the ARVN company had been killed or wounded in the moments after they had jumped from the helicopters. The survivors were huddled with the CH-21 pilots in a shallow irrigation ditch. From time to time one of them would stick his rifle over the top and fire off a clip in the general direction of the western tree line. A brief burst of accurate return fire showed that Dung and his unseen comrades were still there, and maintaining their fire and camouflage discipline.

The ARVN company commander refused point blank to budge. He had called in artillery support, but the shells were falling harmlessly in the paddy between them and the tree line. The lieutenant acting as the artillery observer was too frightened to raise his head to see how he should correct the range. Bowers saw that they needed to add 100 metres, and then adjust the aim to send the shells down the length of the line of foxholes. The lieutenant refused to do so. Bowers asked the company commander to let him use the radio to direct the fire himself. The company commander refused. The American realized that they were unwilling to do anything that might force them out of the shelter of the ditch. A bullet knocked out the radio, and the ARVN squelched themselves deeper into the mud.

Swooping overhead, vann watched with frantic concern as his battle plan unravelled. The Viet Cong had dealt with the "helicopter-mobility" they had dreaded for so long: Vann looked down on the sagging, motionless rotors of the CH-21s and the smashed remnants of the Huey, and the cowering heliborne troops. There was no need for Dung and his comrades in the tree line to hide their presence from him now, and tracers flashed past his little aircraft.

But Vann still had his second trump card, the equally fearsome "armoured vehicle mobility", the company of 13 M-113 armoured personnel carriers, a mile away to the northwest. Two Americans, James Scanlon and Robert Mays, accompanied this unit and its aggressive commander, Captain Ly Tong Ba. The company had the brute firepower and sheer armoured presence to tip the balance of the battle. Indeed, it would be remarkable if it did not do so.

The M-113 had come into service in 1960, the first modern "battle taxi" designed to take infantry into combat. It was built of aircraft-grade aluminium, and weighed 10 tons, light for its size. It could carry two crewmen and eleven infantry cross-country, swim canals and rivers, and climb a 60-degree slope. The infantry could fire their BARs and rifles from it, and it was armed with a .50 calibre heavy machine gun. The two M-113 companies were the most effective combat units in the 7th Division. Between June and September 1962, they had killed 502 Viet Cong and taken 184 prisoners, at a cost of only four dead and nine wounded.

Nonetheless, Ba was reluctant to advance when Vann's urgent request that he "get his tracks over here as fast as he can" was passed on to him by the advisers. "I've got a problem, Topper Six," Scanlon radioed, using Vann's codename. "My counterpart won't move." Vann snapped back that this was an emergency: he had three helicopters down, wounded and dead Americans, and an ARVN company in danger of being overrun. "He says, 'I don't take orders from Americans'," Scanlon said.

Saigon politics, complex and corrupt, were intervening on the battlefield, as they so often did. Ba was a Buddhist, and his speedy, well-armoured M-113s with their infantry squads were well suited for use in a coup d'état. Neither of these things endeared him to President Diem, a Catholic who had narrowly survived an attempted coup by paratroops, and was just as concerned with military plots against him in Saigon as with fighting communists in the paddy fields. Ba was unwilling to move in an operation that was going wrong until he had covered himself against presidential disapproval by getting a direct order from the province chief, Major Lam Quang Tho. Tho was a close political ally of Diem, who had given him command of the armour at My Tho as insurance against a coup. Ba could not get Tho on the radio.

When Ba grudgingly began to move the carriers, they were delayed by having to cross a steep-sided canal. Water was not a problem for the amphibians, but their weight pulled them back as they tried to climb the far bank. The crews had to cut trees and foliage and pile it in front to give the tracks something to grip on. The first across pulled others through on steel cables, but it was a time-consuming business, and Ba and his crews did not hurry.

Another rescue mission was mounted for the helicopter crews. Vann asked his pilot to fly him low-level over the tree lines, to see if the enemy were still there in force. The non-com pilot agreed, though he thought it near suicidal, and asked to be relieved after the battle because he felt that such flying was commissioned officers' work. The Viet Cong held their fire. A CH-21 came in and set down behind the smashed Huey, whilst the gunships hosed and rocketed the tree lines. The guerrillas responded with the heavy whup-whup-whup of automatic weapons fire. The helicopter pilot radioed that he was taking multiple hits. He barely made it out before he was forced to land close to the M-113s. The Americans had lost five helicopters in a morning.

BY 12:00, HUMILIATION WAS STARING Vann in the face. Fear, though, was stalking Hoang. By now, the 7th Division troops who had been helicoptered to the north of Tan Thoi had come into contact with guerrillas of the 514th who were holding the dykes round the village. Hoang's men were in no danger of being overrun, even though they were one company against three. After a brief firefight, the ARVN had taken cover and settled in. When their American adviser, Captain Kenneth Good, went forward to try to get the stalled battalion moving, he was wounded and bled to death.

Nonetheless, Hoang's exit route from Tan Thoi to the north was blocked. He had ARVN and Civil Guards to his west and south as well. They might have had their heads down, but there was no chance of breaking through them without exposing his force to air and artillery, and a formidable force of armoured carriers was approaching his men from the west. The only unencumbered escape route from the battlefield was to the east from Bac, towards the Plain of Reeds. This was open ground, of paddy and swamp, and if the Viet Cong tried to cross it in daylight, the gunships and fighter-bombers would get them. They had nowhere to go till sunset.

At 13:45 Dung and the men with him in the western tree line watched the first of Ba's carriers clatter into the open, helicopter-strewn paddy in front of them. Hoang could not reinforce Dung's squad – the position in Tan Thoi was too fragile to risk sending men to Bac. The 261st men were on their own.

Hoang had already told them that it was suicide to break and run under the lash of the monster amphibians. They knew for themselves what had happened to the 502nd a few months before. They had seven hours before darkness came to save them. And they had nothing that could penetrate the man-eaters' armoured skin.

The M-113 was vulnerable to losing a track or breaking a track shoe: if the driver touched the brake or tried to steer when this happened, the whole machine was liable to roll over. The armour was relatively light, and these early models had petrol engines, so that the fuel lines caught fire easily if the skin was punctured. But the Viet Cong was still only lightly armed, without mines or RPGs, shoulder-held anti-tank rocket launchers.

Dung and his squad were at one end of the tree line overlooking the paddies, where the dyke was high, so that they looked down on the enemy. They had one .30 calibre machine-gun, and another was to their left, where the dyke pushed out into the fields a little, so that the two machine-gunners could catch the ARVNs between them in crossfire. There were about 75 men dug in along the dyke. An irrigation ditch wide enough for sampans to use ran down it. The company commander and Dung and the other squad leaders used it to move safely between the foxholes. A couple of men injured during the morning were brought out on sampans, and local volunteers took their place. Three of the wounded, though, were Party members, and they refused to go. Instead, they made up a mantra, and passed it from foxhole to foxhole, to chant repeatedly when the battle was at its worst: "It is better to die at your post. It is better to die ..."

It was a measure of their fear that, probably at Nguyen Bay's order, the guerrillas used up half a dozen of their valuable 60mm mortar shells in a forlorn attempt to stop the first carriers. The shells merely threw up arcs of water. If they were to live, they would have to stop the carriers with hand grenades and bullets.

They had never done so before, and Scanlon did not think they intended even to try. He thought they had already pulled out. He could see through to the south, where the Civil Guards were cooking chicken and rice for their lunch. It was all over, he thought, or would be as soon as they had picked up the helicopter crews and the wounded. Another air strike came in, the bomb loads falling into the deserted hamlet in red and black gouts of smoke.

After three-quarters of an hour, the last of the carriers crossed the canal. Mays was sitting atop the first one to make for the helicopters across the paddy. The Viet Cong fired their final three mortar shells at them. They splashed harmlessly, and Mays thought it was a sign of panic. As he jumped off the carrier to go to the wounded helicopter crewmen, incoming fire raced at him from the length of the tree line. He got into Braman's wrecked H-21, and found the boy was dead. So was the crew chief from the Huey. Mays himself was almost shot when his head was momentarily visible to a rifleman on the dyke. He hustled three of the pilots into his M-113, and then saw that the driver was dead, shot through the head. Bullets were bouncing off the hull. The aerial was shot away as he radioed Vann that he had three rescued pilots aboard, but two crewmen were dead.

Scanlon dismounted the infantry from another M-113 and began moving on the tree line. The BAR man with him was hit almost immediately. Scanlon could not make out the Viet Cong positions. The vegetation was dense enough to hide the muzzle flashes. He had the men remount the carrier, whose driver refused to advance and instead retreated back to the canal. The attack was going very wrong.

One of the nine men with Dung at the end of the dyke was a guerrilla named Duc. He gave an account of the battle in a letter supposedly written to his brother from safe sanctuary in the Plain of Reeds later in the month, and reprinted as propaganda in Hanoi. It was the noise of the "blind monsters", he said, that almost unnerved him and his companions.

"They had huge engines that send cold shivers down one's back," Duc wrote. "Thirteen of them swept down on us, in two lines. What a sweeping fire! The machine guns of the first tanks fired on us unrelentingly. What had we to oppose these steel monsters vomiting fire? All told nine men!"

Artillery and air attacks came in along the tree line. But the gunship and fighter-bomber pilots concentrated on the far side, nearest the hamlet, instead of the stretch overlooking the open paddy fields where the M-113s were manoeuvring. Waves of concussion shook the Viet Cong in their foxholes, and the air was rancid with smoke and flame, but it had been drilled into them that, if they broke, the enemy would have them all soon enough. "We clenched our teeth," said Duc. "Our withdrawal would leave the whole of our flank exposed. Rather risk our lives on the spot, now."

Hoang and Bay had dinned it in to them, too, that they concentrate their fire onto one machine at a time. Here they were helped by the overconfidence of an enemy who was used to fighting easy. The Viet Cong thought that the driver looked out through a slit, and Phuong, the .30 calibre machine-gunner in Dung's squad, hosed the front of the carriers trying to get a bullet through it. In fact, there was no slit. When the hatches were closed, they used a bullet-proof mirror system to see ahead. But the drivers had got used to pursuing a fleeing foe, driving with the hatch open and their heads sticking out above the armour.

The driver could "button up" and close the hatch if he chose to. The machine-gunners on the M-113 had no such option. They stood at their weapons with their chests and heads exposed above the armoured decks. The rationale behind this was that the heavy .50 calibre gun, with three times the destructive power of a .30 calibre, and the position of the gunner, riding up high behind the machine's snout, combined to make him near-inviolate. But the guerrillas along the high-sided dyke were firing down at the gunners, with a clear view of their heads and torsos. And they kept their nerve, and their accuracy.

"On my right was Huan, a marvellous sniper," Duc wrote. "In the thick of it, he screwed up his eyes a little, spent a long time taking aim, and said: 'Say your prayers, man!' He fired. The gunner in the tank on the right fell, his head shattered. The M-113 stopped, made a quick right about turn, and withdrew with a roar."

That, Duc noted, "dampened the ardour of the bandits." The power of a .50 calibre will swing the barrel upwards unless checked, and the lightly built Vietnamese had to brace themselves against the rim of the hatch to prevent this. The incoming fire, though, meant that they instinctively hunched lower into the hull. Their heavy bullets streamed high and harmless into the air, or chopped the tops off the palms and trees along the dyke.

With Mays's driver dead, and others hit, the surviving drivers buttoned up their hatches. They had little experience in using the mirrors to drive, however; their width and height of vision was much impaired, and they drove erratically.

The best manoeuvre for the carriers was to advance on the line of Viet Cong foxholes from the end where Dung's squad was dug in. That is what Mays wanted. It would greatly reduce the amount of firepower the Viet Cong could bring to bear. Instead of being open to fire from the whole length of the dyke, the carriers would only face Dung's little group. Once they had dealt with Phuong's machine-gun, they could bring the whole foxhole line under fire. The guerrillas would be driven out of the tree line into the open, fodder for the gunships and fighter-bombers.

A quirk of fate prevented Mays from putting this to Captain Ba, who was sitting atop his M-113. As he ducked down to the radio, Ba's carrier hit an obstacle in the paddy with enough of a jerk to swing the heavy barrel of the machine-gun onto his head. Ba slumped into the hull, half-concussed. For the next 20 minutes, the carrier company had no effective leadership.

Huan and the other marksmen took full advantage as the carriers milled around with the gunners on the .50 calibres in clear silhouette. The gunners were most often sergeants, commanders of the carrier crews and of the infantry aboard, and their loss was doubly demoralizing. The sergeant who took over Ba's carrier, whilst the captain recovered in the hull, was shot clean through the throat. As others were picked off, the drivers backed away. Vann could see what was happening from his spotter plane. He was frantic for Mays to get the carriers to button up and charge up onto the dyke, where the rifle squads could dismount and deal with the Viet Cong in their foxholes, starting with Dung's men. But Mays's aerial was gone, and the radios in the other M-113s were incompatible with the one in Vann's aircraft.

The M-113s returned for a third attack. One of them was a flamethrower, with a long fire tube mounted atop it in place of the machine gun. The Americans were sure that this signalled the end. The flamethrower had four 50-gallon fuel tanks, each topped by an air compressor. The effect was like napalm squeezed out of a tube at high velocity. A burning jet of jellied fuel could be thrown for 200 yards for 32 seconds. The machine closed within 100 yards of the tree line, and prepared to incinerate and asphyxiate the men in the foxholes. A stream of flame arced from the tube, but died out in the air after barely 20 yards. The crew had mixed in the wrong proportion of gelling chemicals, and it failed to burn properly.

Other carriers did not press home their attacks. The youth in the foxhole to Duc's left was a lad called Hap. He was not yet 18, and he had barely graduated to the main force from the self-defence unit in his village. As a boy, while minding buffaloes, he had hunted egrets with a slingshot. He had become a master of the art of stone-throwing. "He is not our best shot," Duc wrote, "but he has no equal with hand grenades." As a carrier closed to within 40 yards of their position, Hap hurled a grenade and the explosion lifted it and it retreated in a cloud of smoke.

There was another brief lull. "We showered so many compliments on Hap that he blushed with pleasure," Duc said. Fresh ammunition was brought along the irrigation ditch by sampan. Nguyen Bay ducked along it, urging them to stand firm.

The carriers came for them for a fourth time. Ba, half-recovered from his concussion, grouped eight carriers together and led them in an all-out assault. The firepower, each M-113 with a heavy machine-gun and a squad of men firing magazine after magazine from their BARs and rifles, was awesome. It flung boughs from severed trees high in the air, with red-hot rounds throwing up hissing steam in the mud, or setting small fires where the cut camouflage foliage had dried round the foxholes.

Despite this overwhelming firepower, the Viet Cong continued to show near-perfect discipline, concentrating their fire on the nearest carrier until they killed or wounded the gunner or one of the infantrymen, and the driver lost his nerve and stopped. The American advisers admired the tenacity and courage of their enemies, but their end again seemed near.

Phuong's .30 calibre was overheating when, with a sharp crash, it jammed solid. "We were left to break the attack with no resources," Duc said, "other than waiting for the enemy, ready to shower them with our hand grenades as they came within reach."

Ba's carrier and two others closed to within a few yards of the dyke. Dung and his squad looked directly at them. Within the next few moments, the 10-ton monsters would slither on their armoured bellies up onto the dyke over the foxholes, and the massacre would start.

Dung pulled himself up out of his foxhole. He was totally exposed, in muddy, faded cottons, without boots, a tiny figure in front of the inclined snout of the beast, sure-footed on its broad tracks, muzzle flashes stitching red streaks through the exhaust fumes and spent cordite. He ran and hurled a grenade that exploded on top of it. Inspired, others from his squad threw grenades. Bowers, peering from the ditch, saw two grenades burst above the carriers.

Nerve gone, Ba's driver backed up. The two other carriers followed. It was all over. Fourteen .50 calibre gunners were dead –

some carriers had lost two or more – and the survivors had no stomach for more. It was 14:30.

Dung was killed, either at the moment he decided the battle, or shortly after. "Three of us were killed and two wounded," Duc said. "Amid the rattle of gunfire, one of us took them to the rear. Only Phuong, Hap and I remained ...

"I succeeded in mowing down five of the enemy. I shouted for joy when one of my grenades exploded against the hull of the first carrier. The occupants bellowed with terror ... The machines, engines grumbling, released a last volley in our direction. A splinter hit me in the face. It did not matter. The enemy had been forced to retreat ..."

The young squad leader had achieved the impossible. "The whole battlefield was littered with enemy corpses amidst wrecks of planes and amphibious cars," the chronicler enthused. "Hard hit, the US officers hysterically shouted orders to their men to advance at the risk of their lives. But the puppet troops were scared to death by the dreadful sights of the shambles and infuriated by the US devils' pressure ..."

IT WAS NOT OVER YET. VANN STILL had the means to box in and destroy the enemy. The commander of the 7th Division, General Huynh Van Cao, had a battalion of paratroops in reserve. If they were dropped east of Bac, they would cut off the Viet Cong's only open escape route to the Plain of Reeds. Squeeze them between the paratroops and a fresh drive by the Civil Guard battalions supported by the carriers' heavy machine-guns, and they would surely be overrun.

It was not military competence, however, that had made Cao a general at 34. President Diem had marked him out because he was politically reliable, a well-bred Catholic from a mandarin family, useful insurance against coup d'états. If he dropped the paratroops where Vann wanted them, Cao would have more fighting on his hands. He did not want that. He wanted them dropped west of Bac, behind the Civil Guards and the carriers, and he wanted them to arrive close to dark, so that they would have no time to do anything other than secure a perimeter and settle down for the night.

Vann confronted him on the Tan Hiep airstrip. He demanded that Cao drop them to block the Viet Cong escape. Cao told him repeatedly that this was not prudent. Vann lost his temper. "Godammit, you want them to get away," he yelled. "You're afraid to fight. You know they'll sneak out this way and that's exactly what you want." Cao pulled rank on him. He was a general. Vann was a lieutenant colonel, and he had no American top brass to back him up.

Hoang knew from radio intercepts that the paratroops were coming. He did not know the position of the drop zone. The men of the 514th Company around Tan Thoi were still relatively fresh, for the ARVN had kept their heads down since Captain Good had been killed. Hoang ordered San Bich, the company commander, to be ready to deal with the paratroops when they came.

That was not until 18:05, and then, to Hoang's relief, the para-troops were so badly placed that his men started hitting them when they were still in the air. The paratroops had begun their jump from the seven C-123 transports, not at the start of the drop zone, but inexplicably at its end. They did not land safely behind the Civil Guards, but half a mile and more to the north, in front of the Viet Cong dug in round Tan Thoi. Nineteen of them were killed, and 33 wounded, including two of the Americans who had jumped with them.

It was soon dark. Hoang set 22:00 as the hour for escape, with an assembly point in Tan Thoi. The withdrawal was carried out in careful stages, using the canals and irrigation ditches linking the two hamlets. Dung's companions from the foxholes along the western tree line pulled back in the late afternoon. Sampans carried the wounded. Scouts confirmed that the way east to the safe havens of the Plain of Reeds was open.

Even now, had Vann been granted an aircraft to bathe the eastern paddies and swamp in the ghostly light of parachute flares, and called in air and artillery strikes, the guerrillas would have been mauled. Cao refused him. He allowed the artillery to fire no more than a token four shells an hour. The main-force men of the 261st were the first to leave, in a column carrying their dead and wounded, with the regionals following as a rearguard. They marched through the night, fording the streams, and by dawn were safe in camp among the reeds and swamps.

THE VICTORY WAS STUNNING – for 18 dead and 39 wounded, they had killed 80 and wounded over 100 in an enemy force four times their size – but it meant little in itself. Vietnam was a war of endless small engagements, and if Bac was large for the time, it would be dwarfed by others soon enough.

It was what happened in the immediate aftermath of the battle that gave Dung's action its historic importance. His self-sacrifice enabled his comrades to withdraw in good order, unmolested by the M-113s. It was thus the key to Viet Cong victory. And the proclamation of that victory, by the vanquished American advisers as much as by the victors, was in turn to escalate a civil war into a trial of strength between Hanoi and Washington. Dung created the moment of truth for Washington, the reality that the war was being lost, and that only an across-the-board increase in American involvement could save it. It was the moment, too, when Hanoi saw that the war was there for the winning, and committed itself to it. Dung was, in short, the catalyst for the Vietnam War as we know it today.

There were only a few Western correspondents in Saigon in 1963. But those working for the wire agencies had access to front pages around the world, and the most influential of

American newspapers, the *New York Times*, had its own man there.

The UPI correspondent, Neil Sheehan, made the dangerous night-drive down to the Tan Hiep airstrip as soon as he heard that five helicopters had been shot down. The Reuters bureau chief went with him. David Halberstam, the *Times*'s man, joined them the next day.

They witnessed the sickness in the ARVN command first-hand – they were almost killed in an artillery barrage mounted by General Cao in a fake "assault" on the long-departed guerrillas in Bac, designed to improve his martial image – and they saw the contempt and fury eating into Vann, a man whom they knew and respected.

Ap Bac was "a big picture that discredited the big picture" that the generals and diplomats were projecting, Sheehan said. "We exploited the battle as much as we dared for this reason, and when Vann, out of his anger and a shared interest, tacitly offered an alliance afterward, we entered it eagerly."

Vann was visibly angry, Halberstam said, and "spilled his gut". His face turned red, as it always did when his temper was high. He kicked the dirt and blurted out: "A miserable damn performance, just like always." The ARVN officers would not listen, he told Sheehan. "They make the same goddam mistakes over and over again in the same way." He told how Cao had arranged for the Viet Cong to escape, how he had deliberately landed the paratroops in the wrong place.

The helicopter pilots were scathing. "In this battle we had met the enemy and for the first time they stood and fought," Ostick said. "While I was OK, they did shoot down four of the ten CH-21s and they had gotten one of our five Hueys. So all in all the VC had a good day and the ARVN and the US had a very expensive day."

The pilots wrote a bitter little ditty, "The Battle of Bac", that they sang to the tune of "On Top of Ol' Smokey":

We were called into Tan Hiep
On January Two,
We'd never have gone there
If we'd only knew.

We were supporting the ARVN,
A group without guts,
Attacking a village
Of straw-covered huts.

The VC start shooting,
They fire a big blast,
We offload the ARVN,
They sit on their ass.

Four pilots are wounded,
Two crewmen are dead,
When it's all over
A good day for the Red.

All pilots take warning
When tree lines are near,
Let's land those darn copters
A mile in the rear.

THE MEN OF POWER thousands of miles away in Washington were aware within 24 hours that their Vietnam strategy was in deep trouble. The *Washington Post* put Sheehan's initial report, of a "major defeat" in which "communist guerrillas shot up a fleet of United States helicopters", on the front page. Halberstam wrote in the *New York Times* on 4 January of ARVN reluctance to fight. "The Vietnamese regulars lost the initiative from the first moment," he said, "and never showed much aggressiveness and consequently suffered heavier casualties." The headlines were brutal: "Costly

Viet Nam Battle Angers US Advisers", "Vietnamese Reds Win Major Clash". That stung the Joint Chiefs of Staff into asking CINCPAC, the Commander in Chief Pacific, for "an immediate report as to the veracity and full particulars if story accurate".

Later in the week, the correspondents were reporting that American advisers were questioning the whole American role in Vietnam. This, Halberstam wrote, was because "what happened at Bac goes far deeper than one battle, and is directly tied to the question of whether the Vietnamese are really interested in having American advisers and listening to them".

Sheehan twisted the knife further by attributing the death of Captain Good to the timidity of ARVN troops. "Vietnamese infantrymen refused direct orders to advance during Wednesday's battle at Bac, and an Army captain was killed while out front pleading with them to attack," he wrote. It was splashed in the *Washington Post* on 7 January under the headline "Vietnamese ignored US battle order".

Technically, the Americans had no right to give orders in combat. They were there solely to advise. Such niceties were swept aside in the growing storm. The battle progressed from news to the op-ed pages. Editorials said it was pointless to provide air support and artillery and carriers, no matter how good, if the men on the ground were not up to it. "Copters No Substitute for Men," the *New York Times* opined.

President Kennedy was in Palm Beach when he read Sheehan's story. He was so concerned that he asked his military aides to get him an immediate analysis of the battle. CINCPAC produced a bland assessment blaming "irresponsible newsmen" who filed "without careful checking of the facts". Vann would have none of this spin. He reported that friendly forces had failed "to ever make effective coordinated attacks against the Viet Cong". The operation, he wrote in his report, "must be counted a *failure*". He angrily underlined "failure".

To his alarm, Kennedy found that the *New York Times* moved on to attack the South Vietnamese government. It described it as "suspicious and dictatorial", stating that it cared only about "preserving itself in power", and that it "seriously hampers the spirit and effectiveness of the South Vietnamese forces". The paper called for democratic reform in Saigon. A cartoon by Bill Mauldin, famous for his acid draughtsmanship since the Second World War, showed a soldier in a helmet cowering eye-deep in a foxhole whilst an American adviser implored him: "When I say attack, don't just lean forward." To make it clear that he was attacking the Saigon government, and not just the ARVN, Mauldin marked the helmet "Vietnam".

The correspondent Richard Hughes, a veteran Asia watcher, realized Ap Bac was more than another battle. It was a drama with historic implications. "American officers must now begin to assert combat command over South Vietnamese troops in the field," he wrote in the London *Sunday Times*. This "major change" in policy, he said, was not going to be announced officially, and the Americans would maintain the fiction that they were only there to advise. But the "deepening combat commitment", he went on, "has long since passed the point at which active and more effective US direction could or should be shelved".

Ap Bac gave Washington a stark choice, he concluded: "either complete US withdrawal, or at least a ten-year local war to uphold a reactionary, isolated and unpopular regime."

There was, of course, a third option, and it was the one Kennedy took: the overthrow of that unsavoury government and the family of Ngo Dinh Diem.

By the summer, weakened by Viet Cong success in the field and growing hostility from Washington, Diem was tottering. His brother, Ngo Dinh Nhu, raided Buddhist pagodas, claiming that the monks were abetting the enemy, but arousing outrage when protesting monks doused themselves in petrol and set themselves alight. The Kennedy administration backed a coup by dissident officers. On 1 November 1963, Diem and his brother were seized, with Washington's tacit approval, and later murdered. "The US imperialists, terrified by Ap Bac and our victories," Hanoi claimed, "were forced to stage the coups that toppled Diem."

Three weeks later, Kennedy was assassinated in Dallas. By then, however, American prestige and purpose were so inextricably entangled in the Vietnam War that it was only a matter of time before US Marines landed and began combat operations. Squad leader Dung had hooked Washington body and soul into the war.

HE DID THE SAME FOR HANOI. Ap Bac had an electric effect on its allies. News agencies in Moscow and Beijing hailed a "great victory". In Castro's Cuba, a village was named "Ap Bac" in his honour. The *Liberation News* in Algiers devoted an entire issue to the battle.

In South Vietnam itself, a feast was held for the survivors deep in the fastnesses of the Plain of Reeds. "You can't imagine the amount of sugar cane, bananas, coconuts, cakes we were crammed with," Duc wrote. "Boatloads of them, from all over. Many mothers forced us to eat all they brought in ..." Dung and his men were given the title of the "Steel Squad". The commendation was confirmed by the president of the Liberation Front himself. "Just fancy that!" Duc wrote. "You can easily imagine my happiness to have been one of those at Ap Bac."

Skilful propaganda use was made of the battle. Demonstrations "against the death of husbands" were organized, where the "widows", real or otherwise, of dead ARVN troops, civil guards and self-defence corpsmen, gathered outside the My Tho city hospital. The Party central committee announced an "Ap Bac emulation" movement in March. Every three months, the Viet Cong units with the best record in "killing the bandits and winning merit" was awarded an Ap Bac "Steel Squad" banner.

Actions were aimed "directly at the heads of the American bandits, to cause the gang in Washington a splitting headache …"

The crucial factor, though, was the response in Hanoi. Ho Chi Minh and the leadership had been sceptical of the Viet Cong's ability to confront the ARVN in large-scale combat. They thought it would take several years of careful build-up before that stage was reached. In the meantime, they preached patience, and small-scale ambushes and assaults on relatively soft targets.

Ap Bac changed that. Le Duan, the Party secretary general, who had himself fought in the Delta in the French war, said that it heralded the "bankruptcy" of the Pentagon's "'heliborne' and 'armour-borne' tactics". It shattered the confidence of the ARVN in their modern equipment, and crippled American belief that "the puppet army could withstand our attacks". It showed three types of forces – main force, regional and local – successfully integrated under a single command. It proved that the Liberation Army "has come of age in seven-league boots …"

The Party central committee in Hanoi recognized the ability "of the revolution in the South to win ultimate victory: winning partial victories, advancing step by step, and advancing to a general offensive-general uprising". Though the political struggle continued, it concluded that "the most important, decisive matter in all cases is to continue to strengthen our forces – especially our military forces – in all regards".

It was decided to accelerate the pace of the war in the South. Hanoi appointed Tran Van Tra as commander of the liberation forces. Ho Chi Minh saw him before he left Hanoi. "Uncle Ho invited me to his house for dinner," General Tra wrote. "He handed me a box of cigars made in Cuba and said to me, 'I only have this gift – sent to me by comrade Fidel – to give to you. Take them with you and give them to the cadres in the south. Whenever you smoke them, remember my ardent interest – and that of our Cuban brothers – in the South."

Using the nom de guerre Anh Tu as commander of the liberation forces in the South, Tra trekked down the Ho Chi Minh Trail, the land route from North Vietnam through Laos and Cambodia to the South. A huge increase in materiel flowed with him as Hanoi increased its commitment to the Viet Cong in 1963. Five new main-force regiments were raised, equipped and began operations over the year.

New bases were set up in southern Laos, and the smuggling of arms by river and sea exploded. In 1961, only 317 tons of supplies had gone down the Ho Chi Minh Trail. Group 559, the Trail command, transported 165,000 weapons of all types in 1963, including mortars, recoilless rifles and 12.7mm anti-aircraft guns. Sea Infiltration Group 759, using camouflaged fishing junks, and starting pretty much from scrap, delivered 25 shiploads of 1,430 tons of weapons over the year to the Mekong Delta and the coastal provinces east of Saigon.

Hanoi and Washington were at each other's throats. Such was Dung's achievement.

WE MIGHT ADD THAT SOUTH VIETNAM now perfectly matched Clausewitz's five conditions for a successful people's war. These were:

that the war is "carried on in the heart of the country"

that it "cannot be decided by a single catastrophe"

that "the theatre of war embraces a considerable extent of country"

that "the national character is favourable to the measures"

and finally that "the country is of a broken and difficult nature,

either being mountainous, or by reasons of woods and marshes,

or from the peculiar mode of cultivation in use".

South Vietnam answered all of these, down to the mountains,

forests, swamps and rice paddies. The people's war was duly won, though Vann in particular delayed the victory.

Dung is commemorated by a whitewashed monument. It lies just to the east of the Ap Bac landing zone and the tree line where he died. A statue on a granite plinth shows Dung and members of his "Steel Squad" striding above an armoured personnel carrier. An inscription reads: "On 2 January 1963 a major battle happened at this site. It has brought about an echo all over the world." The site also displays a Huey helicopter, an M-113 and a 105mm howitzer. It is three miles north of Highway Four, a popular stopping point for tourist coaches.

The Viet Cong 514th Battalion was badly mauled by American troops on 2 May 1967 in what was called "Ap Bac II". The 3rd Battalion of the 60th Infantry, the "Wild Ones", came under heavy fire on an operation near Bac. The Viet Cong, trapped between M-113s and advancing infantry, were giving a good account of themselves from foxholes along a dyke when an American machine-gun team, seeing the lead man in their squad shot down, rushed the Viet Cong position. Without pausing, they ran along the length of the dyke, which had foxholes every five yards or so. They broke the 514th's nerve, as the ARVN had failed to do four years before. More than 200 Viet Cong were killed and wounded as they jumped out of their foxholes, for the loss of 15 Americans.

John Paul Vann was killed on 9 June 1972 when his helicopter struck a grove of trees near Kontum in the Central Highlands of South Vietnam. He had been replaced following his post-Ap Bac criticisms of the ARVN and the Diem regime in March 1963, and left the US Army. He returned to South Vietnam in March 1965, nominally as a civilian, in practice advising and often effectively commanding ARVN operations. He remained as perhaps the most effective and influential of Americans in Vietnam until his death. He was awarded a posthumous Medal of Freedom, the nation's highest civilian citation. He was the subject of *A Bright Shining*

Lie, a brilliant biography by Neil Sheehan, the UPI man at Ap Bac, and a film with the same title.

Commander Hai Hoang was killed during fierce fighting in the Minh Phung street area during the communist Tet Offensive in Saigon in 1968. He was commander of Long An province troops at the time. General Tran Van Tra survived to become the top Viet Cong officer at the Paris peace talks, and chairman of the Saigon military committee. He wrote that, as he entered Saigon in triumph in 1975, he was thinking of Hoang and Dung and of "the famous Ap Bac battle [when] we successfully countered the enemy's tactics of moving troops by helicopter and APCs for the first time".

7 · THE ONE-SHOT WONDER

Holding a bridge, like Horatius

"In every battle there arise moments of crisis, on which the result depends" (BOOK I, CHAPTER I). Such moments can take place, as seen here, before the main battle begins, and thus influence it more deeply.

THE RIVER ORNE, NORMANDY * 6 JUNE 1944

FIVE HOURS BEFORE H-HOUR – the moment at dawn on 6 June 1944 when the greatest seaborne invasion ever seen, before or since, broke on the beaches of Normandy – half a dozen plywood and canvas gliders wallowed in the wake of the bombers towing them to the French coast above the dark waters of the English Channel.

They carried 181 men, faces blacked, in paratroop smocks with field dressings attached, battledress trousers, heavy boots, and rimless airborne helmets, laden with magazine pouches, grenades, water bottles, fighting knives, spades and sub-machine-guns. They were chain-smoking and singing to keep up their spirits. In glider No. 6, a wiry young sergeant from south London, Charles "Wagger" Thornton, led his platoon in the hit song of the day, "Cow Cow Boogie".

The men had been isolated from the rest of the world for days past, to guard the extreme secrecy of their mission, living under canvas at a new glider base at Tarrant Rushton in Dorset. It was set in flat wheatlands, rare in the rolling English West Country, and its runways were long enough for the bomber-tugs to get airborne with 7 tons of loaded glider behind them.

They should have gone 24 hours earlier. They had kitted themselves out in full battledress on the afternoon of 4 June. It was wild and windy, and the rain violently lashed their tents. Off the coast, heavy seas were breaking beneath the low cloud. The Channel was too rough for the invasion fleet. The glider men were stood down. Some watched a film in camp, aptly called *Stormy Weather*, a black American musical with Lena Horne and the dancer Bill "Bojangles" Robinson. The officers joshed each other over bottles of Scotch.

It was still blowing hard early the next morning, 5 June. Buildings were "shaking and shuddering under a wind of almost hurricane proportions", recalled General Dwight D. Eisenhower, the supreme commander of the invasion forces, and the rain was "driving in horizontal streaks". To his astonishment, though, the meteorologist at the morning headquarters conference forecast a lull, to set in from the early hours of 6 June, with a window of perhaps 36 hours of good weather in the Channel.

Moon, tide and sunrise conditions – moonlight for the glider pilots, a spring low tide at dawn for the assault troops – would not be right again for a month. Eisenhower weighed the risk of bad weather against those of a further postponement of Operation Overlord, the Allied invasion of Nazi-occupied Western Europe. The Germans would get more time to prepare, and morale among his own highly wrought troops would be blunted. "The consequences of delay justified great risk," he said. He decided to go.

At noon the same day the glider troops were told Overlord was on. A padre came and held a short service. They had a light meal, fatless, to cut down on airsickness. They dressed for battle again. Trucks took them out to the Horsa gliders in the evening. At

22:20 they were given dixies of strong tea laced with rum. They blacked their faces with burnt cork, a final ritual. At 22:30 the glider pilots arrived, and they were ordered to board.

Horsas were low-tech machines, made of the cheapest materials. The fuselage parts were run up by woodworkers in a peacetime furniture factory, the cloth covering the wings stitched by seamstresses. They were, in the purest sense, disposable aircraft, abandoned at the end of a single one-way combat mission. They smelt of wood glue and aircraft dope – and, once they were in the air, of vomit, for they yawed and rolled behind their tugs with a stomach-turning motion. The men packed in tight behind the pilots.

Ten minutes before take-off, their commanding officer, Major John Howard, did the rounds to shake the platoon commanders' hands and wish them luck. He was a former stockbroker's runner and policeman who had come up through the ranks. His men were not career soldiers – they included a window cleaner, a labourer in a brickworks, a Cambridge undergraduate, a fruit-and-veg delivery man. Neither they, nor the major, had been in combat before. Howard found them "an amazing sight. The smaller chaps were visibly sagging at the knees under the amount of kit they had to carry." Each man with his equipment weighed 250 pounds, and "if you ever fell over", a lieutenant noted, "it was impossible to get up without help".

Shortly before the tugs started their engines, a soldier jumped out of a glider and ran off into the dark. He said at his later court martial that he had an unshedable premonition of death. The men who did go on this particular mission, a platoon to each glider, amounted to no more than a single company, "D" company of the 2nd Oxfordshire and Buckinghamshire Light Infantry, plus two platoons from "B" company, and some sappers with skills in explosives.

The tugs were Halifaxes, heavy night bombers. They were to

part from their tows off the coast, and fly on to drop their bomb loads on Caen, the major town inland from the Normandy beaches. The bombing raid was to divert attention. It was hoped that the Germans would mistake the gliders for low-flying or crashing aircraft from the bomber stream as they lost height and headed for their targets. Howard's glider with two others was to land near a bridge over the Caen Canal at Bénouville. The other three, including Wagger Thornton's, were to aim for a bridge over the River Orne a few hundred yards away, near the hamlet of Ranville.

THE FIRST HALIFAX–HORSA COMBINATION was airborne at 22:59 and 20 seconds. The glider reached flying speed first and lifted off a few seconds before the bomber. The other five followed at one-minute intervals. They climbed across Hampshire for 70 miles to reach the English coast at Bognor.

Here, they turned south and out to sea. They flew at 7,000 feet, without lights, the glider pilots maintaining position relative to the bombers' red-glowing exhausts. The night sky was hazy and streaked with moisture. Thornton sang in a light voice:

> Out on the plains down near Santa Fe
> I met a cowboy ridin' the range one day ...

They were making around 125mph, and there was time for contemplation. The men had been proud and excited when they had been told they were to be the first to set foot in Europe. "It was like being chosen for the England rugger team," said Lieutenant "Tod" Sweeney of 6 Platoon, "or walking out to open the innings for England at Lords." Now doubts set in.

They seemed a desperately ill-judged little force to be kickstarting an enterprise as colossal as the invasion of Hitler's *Festung Europa*, Fortress Europe. The Horsas were named after a Saxon warrior-prince, but they were unarmed and defenceless, gentle and bucolic creatures, like the Normandy dairy cattle towards whose pastures they were flying. The flimsy fuselage offered no protection against bullets and shrapnel, though the troops had been briefed to expect anti-aircraft guns at the bridges. The big plexiglass noses left the pilots vulnerable if they careered into trees, hedges or "Rommel's asparagus", the poles and metal stakes that the German field marshal had had driven into potential landing sites.

For all the weight of their kit, the men were scantily armed, carrying only rifles, light automatic weapons, grenades and small-calibre mortars, almost naked beside the heavy weapons and armour of Rommel's Army Group B that awaited them. Their unit, the "Ox and Bucks", was a fine and venerable English county regiment – it traced its history back to 1741, to the storming of Quebec, to Lexington and Bunker Hill, to the rout of Napoleon's Imperial Guard at Waterloo – but it was not known, at least for its first 200 years, as the sort of elite unit that planners would normally entrust with a vanguard mission of extreme delicacy and danger.

In Howard's lead glider, a 19-year-old private, Denis Edwards, felt insanity was afoot. "I was tense, strange, highly nervous," he said, "in a fantasy world … as if at any moment I'd wake up and find I was back in barracks." Everyone tried to laugh and sing. "Perhaps it was to show the others we weren't scared," he said, "but personally I was frightened to death." What they were carrying out – "a night-time airborne landing of such a small force in the midst of the German army" – struck him as "little more than a suicide mission".

The men kept singing, though, until the pilots picked up the white line of surf breaking on the Normandy beaches, and warned, "Enemy coast ahead."

A mile off the coast between the mouths of the Rivers Orne and Dives, at 00:07 on 6 June, the gliders prepared to cast off from

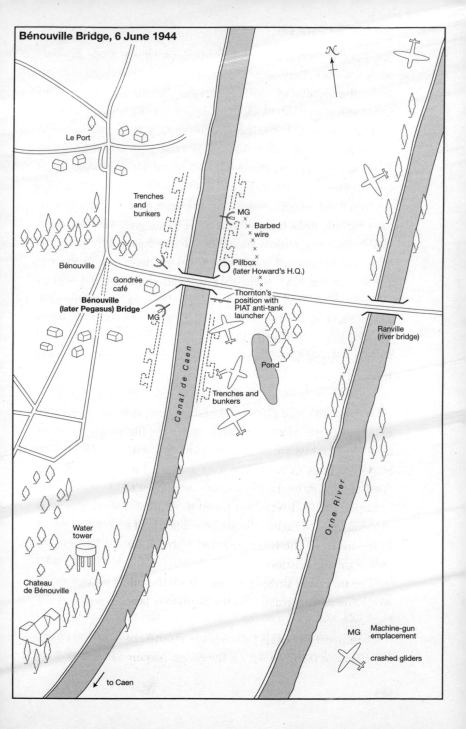

Bénouville Bridge, 6 June 1944

N

Le Port

Trenches and bunkers

MG

Barbed wire

Pillbox (later Howard's H.Q.)

Bénouville

Gondrée café

Bénouville (later Pegasus) Bridge

MG

Thornton's position with PIAT anti-tank launcher

Ranville (river bridge)

Pond

Canal de Caen

Trenches and bunkers

Orne River

Water tower

Chateau de Bénouville

MG   Machine-gun emplacement

crashed gliders

to Caen

the tugs. "There was a twang and jerk from the tow rope," Edwards said, "followed by almost total silence." The tugs flew on through thickening anti-aircraft fire to bomb Caen. The gliders slipped down in a darkness half-lit by the moon and its sheen on the sea and the rivers and the canal.

The three gliders destined for the canal bridge cast off correctly. Two picked out the river bridge, but one was taken astray by its tug, and disappeared in the dark. The little force had lost a sixth of its strength whilst it was still airborne.

The pilot of Howard's glider, Jim Wallwork, struggled with the heavy unpowered controls, "footballs of sweat" breaking on his face. "It was dark, with just enough luminosity to pick out the Orne and the Caen Canal running down to the sea," he said. "I saw the reflection of the waters in the canal, and then the bridge. Everything was so calm. I heard the wings whistling in the night ... After I had passed the bridge, I turned 90 degrees right. I'd already lost 3,000 feet. The glider was very loaded and it was flying very fast."

At 1,000 feet, the door was opened, and Howard gazed down "at those wonderful Normandy horses and cattle, grazing very quietly as if nothing was happening ..." As they got closer to the ground, they saw the trees flashing by at 90mph, and their guts churned.

Gliders did not "land", a word the pilots never used. They talked instead of "pranging", the slang for "crashing". The tricycle undercarriage usually disintegrated as the glider thumped into a field, and the co-pilot had a handle to jettison it altogether. The weight was then taken, at least in theory, by a skid that ran under the fuselage. Practice showed that the floor often collapsed under the strain, and the men's feet got trapped.

A drill was followed. As Wallwork prepared to crash-land, he shouted: "Brace for impact!" At this, Edwards said, "we linked our arms and raised our feet off the floor, and said a silent prayer".

It was in this strange fashion, arm-in-arm and with their boots in the air, as if in a rustic dance, that they arrived in Europe.

Wallwork could see the Bénouville bridge rushing towards him through the plexiglass, with barbed wire in front of it, and trees and a pond to his right. He was going too fast. The gliders had emergency chutes to slow them down. "We knew they were highly dangerous, never tested," he said, but he shouted at his co-pilot to stream it. It lifted the tail and banged the nose wheel down. The wheels were torn off. The darkness filled with a stream of brilliant sparks as the skid hit stony ground.

A sound like a giant canvas sheet being ripped apart gave way to a mighty crash like thunder. An ominous stillness followed. "God help me," Edwards thought. "We must all be dead."

The two pilots had been hurled through the windscreen and lay in the field ahead of the wreckage. They were the first Allied troops to touch French soil, and they were both unconscious.

IT SEEMED AN INAUSPICIOUS START to the liberation of half a continent. But upon its success rested the fate of Operation Overlord as a whole. The two bridges were the key to securing the eastern flank of the invasion.

Under the heading "INTENTION", Howard's top-secret orders stated that "Your task is to seize *intact* the brs [bridges] over R ORNE and canal at BENOUVILLE and RANVILLE and to hold them until relief by 7 Para Bn." The "METHOD" was to be "a *coup de main*", a swift and sudden blow, "depending largely on surprise, speed and dash for success".

It was spelled out that this was a do-or-die operation: "It is vital that the crossing places be held, and to do this you will secure a close br[idge]head on the WEST bank, in addition to guarding the brs. The immediate def[ence] of the brs and of the WEST bank of the canal must be held at all costs."

The extraordinary responsibility thrust on the tiny group of glider men had its origins in the nature of the invasion itself.

Bloody experience made the Overlord planners avoid a direct assault on a French seaport. Two years before, a largely Canadian force had been savaged during a raid on Dieppe. Every tank that was landed was lost, two-thirds of the 5,000 Canadians were killed or captured, and the RAF had the worst day in its history, losing 95 aircraft. To avoid a repetition, the heavily defended and well-garrisoned French Channel ports were bypassed, in favour of landings on open beaches.

It was planned to land 104,000 tons of equipment and 326,000 men in the first five days of the invasion. A long stretch of coastline was needed for a bridgehead large enough to absorb this build-up.

The Pas de Calais, the stretch of French coast around Calais in the narrows at the mouth of the Channel, was the obvious site. It offered the most direct route on to the German Reich itself. It had the best beaches. It was the closest part of the European mainland to the English coast, only 18 miles or so from Dover, clearly visible on a fine day. Hitler's V-weapons, the rockets he hoped would bring London to its knees, had their launch sites in the Pas de Calais, an added incentive to strike.

It was also where Field Marshal Rommel and other German generals in France expected the blow to fall. Hitler had a few intuitive flashes of battles further west, in Normandy, but he thought for the most part in terms of the Pas de Calais. In November 1943 he had ordered the defences to be reinforced, "for it is here that the enemy must and will attack, and it is here – unless all indications are misleading – that the decisive battle against the landing forces will be fought".

Rommel's Army Group B had two armies. The powerful and heavily armoured 15th Army, under a tough veteran of the Russian front, General Hans von Salmuth, was positioned for landings from the mouth of the Seine northeastwards to Calais and beyond.

The weaker 7th Army, with a higher proportion of foreign conscripts – Poles, Russians, Armenians – and men who had been wounded or suffered frostbite on the Eastern Front, under a less impressive general, Friedrich Dollmann, held the coast west of Rouen across Normandy to Brittany.

Aware of these perils, the Allied planners decided on landings on five beaches along a 50-mile stretch of 7th Army's territory on the Normandy coast, running westwards from the River Orne. The easternmost beach, at the mouth of the Orne, was codenamed Sword. Then, going west, came Juno and Gold, British and Canadian, like Sword, and then the American beaches, Omaha and Utah.

Both flanks of the invasion had to be protected. In the moments after the first landings, before self-propelled guns, tanks, trucks and heavy weapons were ashore in any numbers, the force was hugely vulnerable. The Germans had 11 armoured divisions in France, and 50 divisions of infantry, against the 5 the Allies were able to land on D-Day itself. German armour would create carnage if it broke through onto the beaches. In particular, the planners feared lest Rommel's 15th Army bring its weight to bear on the eastern flank, and start "rolling up" the beaches from Sword westwards.

To prevent this, the Allied plan called for paratroops to be dropped, at night, to secure the flanks before the seaborne landings began, with further paratroops reinforcing with drops and glider landings during the day.

In the west, on the right flank at the start of the Cotentin Peninsula, protecting Utah beach, 13,000 men of the 82nd All-American and 101st Screaming Eagle Airborne Divisions were to drop around Vierville and Sainte-Mère Église. In the east, on the left flank, 12,000 men of the British 6th Airborne Division would drop east of the River Orne, protecting Sword beach.

The first natural obstacle between the Orne and the 15th Army in the Pas de Calais was the River Dives, which runs roughly parallel to the Orne about 8 miles to the east. The British airborne troops were to prevent a 15th Army counterattack by destroying the bridges over the Dives, and holding the area through to the Orne. To do that with any hope of success, the lightly armed paratroops needed artillery and armoured support. That could only come from a link-up with the seaborne forces landing on Sword beach to the west of the Orne.

Only two bridges crossed the Orne, and the Caen Canal that ran almost alongside it, those at Bénouville and Ranville. Those bridges had to be seized intact, to deny them to an immediate German counterattack on the beaches, and to use to get the supplies and heavy weapons from the beaches to the airborne forces.

Paratroops, even when landed at night, can reasonably be expected to destroy a target. Capturing and holding one intact, the planners knew, particularly one that is primed for demolition, presents a different order of difficulty. The unit loses its shape and cohesion during the drop, and the enemy is alerted.

It was, ironically, the Germans who convinced General Richard "Windy" Gale, the big, bluff commander of 6th Airborne, to go for gliders. Gale remembered that the enemy had used them to great effect at Fort Eban Emael in Belgium in 1940, and at the Corinth Canal in Greece in 1941. A glider had the great merit of delivering a cohesive body of men – a platoon, with a range of skills, assault troops, sappers, medic, radio operator – to a single spot, ready for action as soon as it came to a halt. Gale planned for the gliders to go in first, three to a bridge. Pathfinder paratroops would then mark out the drop zones for the airborne troops, who would reinforce the bridge parties. The link-ups would be complete when the first troops arrived from the beaches, making their way 6 miles from Sword beach.

These commandos were not expected until at least 12 hours

after the gliders had landed. It was a long time to ask the glider men to hold out, as the vanguard in a battle all knew would be climactic. "In the East, the vastness of space will allow a loss of territory without suffering a mortal blow to Germany's chance for survival," Hitler said of it. "Not so in the West! If the enemy succeeds here, consequences of staggering proportions will follow within a short time." Overlord was an all-or-nothing effort for Eisenhower. "This operation," he said, "is not being planned with any alternatives."

No pain was spared to make the "bridge-prangers", as Gale called them, equal to their awesome task. They were selected as the cream of 6th Airborne during a special three-day exercise held for the purpose. They were moved to Devon, where a pair of bridges less than a mile apart cross the River Exe and the Exeter Canal. Aerial photographs of the real bridges in France were used to build replica machine-gun pits, bunkers and trenches. The owners of a café next to the Caen Canal bridge were members of the French Resistance, and a detailed picture was built up of the men of the German garrison. A scale model, detailing every tree and wisp of barbed wire, was changed each day as reconnaissance flights and Resistance reports detailed the changes the Germans were making under pressure from Rommel, knocking down build- ings to get better fields of fire, starting work on a new concrete bunker.

For the better part of a week, night and day, the men stormed the Exe bridges in every possible permutation. Platoons would be missing, to simulate lost glider-loads. Hand grenades disap- peared, ammunition was kept short, valves were taken from radio sets, as if broken or lost in the landings. Major Howard, and "Wagger" Thornton and other sergeants, were declared to be "casualties", so that the corporals and privates had to take command and think for themselves. For added realism, the bridges' "defenders" were dressed in German uniforms, shouted orders in German, and had German weapons, which the glider men became expert at using.

They were told to expect about 50 Germans to be stationed at the bridges. They knew they came from the 736th Grenadier Regiment of the 716th Infantry Division. The officers and NCOs were Germans, even if some of the men were foreign conscripts, and could be expected to fight hard. Surprise was essential, for the Germans were thought to have four 20mm light anti-aircraft guns and an anti-aircraft heavy machine-gun, which could wreak havoc on gliders.

The glider pilots flew 43 training missions. An early flight simulator was used, with cine film of the landing zones projected in a cockpit mock-up, but mainly it was a matter of flying by day and night, dropping the tug, and using a compass, altimeter and stop watch to try to land within 50 yards of the target.

When the exercises were finished, the men were given an advance on their pay. They celebrated with a pub crawl and some window-breaking in Exeter. Several were arrested – there had been a minor spat, too, when the men used their grenades to stun fish in the river for supper and the town council complained that they were fishing without a licence – but Howard was an ex-policeman and soon had them released.

In late May, they had moved to Tarrant Rushton. They were ready.

AFTER THE CRASH BY THE CAEN CANAL, Dennis Edwards heard bodies begin to unstrap themselves and move around the wreckage. Howard could see nothing. He thought he had been blinded until he realized that he had hit the top of the glider, and his crash helmet had come down over his eyes. They could hear the pilots moaning, but their training kicked in. Before helping anyone, they had to capture the bridge.

Edwards found his terror replaced by exhilaration. "I felt on top of the world," he said. "I remember thinking, 'You've had it, chum, no good worrying any more, the die's been cast.'"

As he smashed his way out, he found the big swing bridge in front of him, its high superstructure and counterweight unmistakable in the moonlight. Wallwork had landed them almost on it, in what the Overlord air commander called "one of the most outstanding flying achievements of the war". The two other gliders were within 500 yards. One had toppled into a marshy pond, drowning a lance corporal, Fred Greenhalgh, the first Allied casualty of D-Day.

Howard was already at the bridge, shouting, "Come on boys, this is it!" Lieutenant Den Brotheridge and others in the first platoon followed him. The garrison commander, Major Hans Schmidt, was entertaining his mistress in Ranville three miles away. The Germans thought that the bad weather in the Channel would rule out any invasion for at least the next two or three days. Some of the men, taking their cue direct from the major, were at a brothel in Bénouville. The others were asleep in their bunks by the bridge, the thumps and bangs in the pasture blending with the bombs falling on Caen and the anti-aircraft guns.

The two sentries on the bridge had little time to react. Private Helmut Romer had just about-turned at the end of the bridge when he saw a group of shouting, black-faced men in strange uniforms running at him. He had only a rifle for protection. He screamed: "*Fallschirmjaeger!*" – "Paratroops!" – and flung himself into a trench. The other sentry fumbled with a Very light pistol. He was shot as he pulled the trigger, and the flare went up above the bridge. Brotheridge threw a hand grenade into the machine-gun pit on the east side of the bridge. Return fire hit Brotheridge in the neck, and he fell back into the roadway.

The German NCOs fought. The foreign conscripts had no stomach for it. "They jumped to their feet and ran for their lives, scattering in all directions," said Edwards. "Relief, exhilaration, incredulity, I experienced all this on realizing that we had taken the bridge."

A German Feldwebel, Heinz Hickman, himself a paratrooper, was returning to his unit by car with four privates. He was about to turn left over the bridge at the T-junction in Bénouville when he heard the sharp rattle of British Sten guns. He went forward on foot to investigate. He recognized British uniforms, and he and his men started firing. He sprayed the bridge with his Schmeisser from 100 yards away until he ran out of ammunition. "I'm not a coward but at that moment I got frightened," he said. "If you see a Para platoon in full cry, they frighten the daylights out of you ... the way they charge, the way they fire, the way they ran across the bridge ... I gave the order to go back." He turned his car around and drove off.

Lieutenant Sandy Smith in the No. 3 glider had wrenched his knee in landing. He hobbled across the bridge and fired a burst from his Sten at a German who was throwing a stick grenade at him. The grenade exploded as the German fell back dead by the café on the west side of the bridge. The blast tore Smith's smock and trousers, and lacerated his right hand, but he led his platoon on to finish off the last resistance from the machine-gun positions and trenches. The second platoon commander, David Wood, took three bullets from a machine-pistol in the leg. "I regret to say there were no heroics," he said. "I simply fell down and couldn't get up." A medic gave him a shot of morphine, and dug his hip flask out of his pocket for a draught of Scotch.

Two men, Wally Parr with grenades, Charlie Gardner with a Sten, went through the German dugouts. "In with the grenade, bang the door shut, explosions," said Parr. "Smash it wide open again and Charlie finished them off. As we came back past the first dugout suddenly there was a moan or something from inside, and I pulled out a 77 phosphorous [grenade]. Took the cap off, gave it a twirl, undone the tape and jumped in and that went off."

The "poor buggers" had very little chance, Smith thought, because "We weren't taking prisoners or messing about."

The sappers checked for explosives. The bridge had been prepared for demolition, but Major Schmidt had chosen not to put the charges in place. He was worried that the Resistance or an accident might blow up the bridge prematurely. It had never crossed his mind that the Allies would choose it for their first assault.

A price was paid. Parr found Brotheridge lying in the road. "I put my hand under his head to lift him up," he said. "He just looked. His eyes sort of rolled back … a terrible waste. The first thing that went through my mind. What a terrible waste." One lieutenant was dead, and the other two wounded, but one of the bridges was taken, and in little more than five minutes.

THE NO. 6 GLIDER, WITH LIEUTENANT Dennis Fox and the songster Thornton aboard, landed 300 yards from the Ranville bridge. The No. 5 hit an air pocket on the approach and was half a mile short. The No. 4 landed eight miles away after the navigation error by the tug pilot.

"Apart from a herd of cows which panicked in front of us, we were quite alone," the pilot, Roy Howard, said. "Alone, in front of the whole invasion force which was not to land on the beaches 6 miles away until daybreak, and ahead of the main parachute drop by half an hour."

The German sentries had been alerted by the noise from the canal bridge. Fox had taken only a few steps when they opened fire with an MG 34 machine-gun. Fox went to ground. The impasse was broken by Sergeant Thornton. He was a quiet, self-effacing man "who'd as soon sweep the barrack room himself as order a soldier to do it," Fox said, "but in action he was absolutely first-class, and he virtually commanded the platoon. I was the figurehead …"

Thornton freed a 2-inch mortar from the glider, and got it going. "He put a mortar, slap down, a fabulous shot, right on the machine-gun," said Fox, "so we just rushed the bridge, all the chaps yelling ..." Lieutenant Sweeney arrived with the men from the second glider. "I went racing across the bridge with my heart in my mouth, eventually coming to a halt a bit disappointed," he said. "We were all worked up to kill the enemy, bayonet the enemy, or be blown up or something." No charges had been laid, and there was no explosion. Instead, they saw the enemy running away over the fields, and turned the MG 34 on them. These were the only shots the British fired.

At 00:26 Sweeney radioed the news to Major Howard. The codewords for the success at both bridges – "Ham" and "Jam" – were sent to 5th Para Brigade headquarters. Sweeney was ordered to secure the river bridge, whilst Fox and his platoon moved to the canal bridge, in anticipation of a German counterattack from Bénouville.

THE ORDERS HAD PREDICTED THAT taking the bridges would be the easier part of the mission. "Your difficulties will arise in holding off an enemy counterattack on the brs," they stated, "until you are relieved."

Noises were heard on the riverbank, and the response to the challenge – "V", to which the codeword for the response was "Victory" – seemed to be in German. The British opened fire. The next morning, they found the bodies of a patrol from the 21st Panzer Division, and a British paratrooper, one of the pathfinders who had marked the drop zones, and who had been captured.

A little later, an open staff car and a motorcycle escort approached the river bridge from the east, driving at speed from Ranville. Major Schmidt was returning to his men, after dropping his mistress off at her house. A Bren gunner killed the motorcyclist, sending him flying into the river. Sweeney riddled the car with his Sten. The driver crashed into a ditch. Empty wine bottles, plates, powder, lipstick, stockings and lingerie littered the wreck.

Schmidt was carried to the aid post. He told the medical officer that it was futile for the Allies to try to defeat the Germans, and then begged to be shot. "This I did," the MO, John Vaughan, said, "in the bottom, with a needle attached to a syringe of morphia." Vaughan amputated the driver's leg with a pair of scissors, but he had no blood for a transfusion, and the young man died.

At 00:50, the roar of aero engines billowed in the air as the men of 5th Para Brigade began to jump at low level from transports and converted bombers, searchlights and tracer fire racing across the silk canopies. High winds, navigation errors and difficulties in exiting the bombers scattered them over the fields and woodland. Some men stumbled through the parachute hatches early and fell in the sea, to be pulled under by their heavy loads, and the brigade major was hung up beneath the aircraft with his static line wrapped round his leg, the crew managing to pull him back aboard after 30 minutes on their way back to England. Paratroops did not begin arriving at the bridges in any numbers for 90 minutes.

THE MOMENT OF ABSOLUTE PERIL took place before then, at 01:30. Edwards was digging in – the ground was hard and he managed no more than a shallow scrape – when he heard sounds above the chinking noise of the entrenching tools. They were engines, and they came from the west, around Bénouville.

As they got nearer, he heard "an accompanying clanking, rattling and squealing". Tanks. "Obviously they were coming our way. It was terrifying for them to arrive so quickly, and we stopped digging ..." Sandy Smith remembered "feeling a sense of absolute terror, and saying 'My God, what the hell am I going to do with these tanks coming down the road?'"

The armoured engineer companies of the 716th Infantry Division, based at Bénouville and a mile or so away at Le Port, assembled half a dozen tanks, trucks, and a battery of 88mm guns for a counterattack. They set out for the canal bridge to find out what was happening. At the T-junction, the lead tank paused.

"We thought that was it, you know, no way were we going to stop a tank," said a corporal, Billy Gray. "It was about 20 yards away from us ..." Gray held his fire. Bren guns and Sten guns and hand grenades were useless against a tank. Worse, they would alert the crew to his position.

The single weapon that might stop it was a PIAT, an unloved weapon as clumsy as its name, Projector Infantry Anti-Tank. Each platoon was issued with a PIAT. All but one had suffered bent firing tubes or were lost in the debris in the crash-landings. The sole survivor was in the hands of Sergeant Thornton. He had just two shells or "bombs" to go with it, though it was so slow to reload that it was essentially a one-shot weapon anyway.

Back in 1942, the PIAT was one of the first infantry weapons able to project a high-explosive anti-tank or HEAT shell. It used a shaped charge to project a cone of copper or tin foil through armour at hypersonic speed. This was the so-called Neumann effect, named after a German engineer who discovered that TNT with a conical indentation could cut through steel plate that an ordinary charge would only dent.

The PIAT was based on a spring-loaded pre-war mortar, and was fired by a very heavy spring, which needed a pull of 200 pounds to set. If, as often happened, the first charge failed to re-set the spigot, the whole process had to be repeated. It was heavy, 32 pounds unloaded, and inaccurate at any distance.

American bazookas and the German Panzerschreck were making the anti-tank running by 1944. Their shells were rocket-propelled, making them much easier to use, but producing a violent gout of flame from the rear of the firing tube. The PIAT, with its spring mechanism, was free of this back blast and the tell-tale plume of smoke that gave away a position. It was well-suited to close combat in confined spaces, such as clearing a room or breaking through masonry in house-to-house fighting. It would have been in its element as a wall-buster at Stalingrad.

That was of no consolation to the unfortunate Thornton. He had to use it for its original purpose, to bust a tank, and it had earned a dreadful reputation. It had a rated range of 100 yards, at which its 3lb shell or "bomb" was theoretically able to pene-trate 4 inches of armour. In the field, British troops found that only a "perfect hit" – a bull's eye – would penetrate the frontal armour of newer German tanks even at lesser ranges. It was more successful against side and rear armour at very close range, provided the shell detonated. All too often, it did not.

"It's actually a load of rubbish, really," Thornton said. "The range is about 50 yards and no more. You're a dead loss if you try to go further. Even 50 yards is stretching it, very much so.

"Another thing is that you must never, never miss. If you do, you've had it, because by the time you reload it and cock it, which is a bloody chore on its own, you're done. It's indoctrinated into your brain that you mustn't miss." In any event, he only had two bombs with him.

He took up a position near the T-junction, lying under a pile of kit to hide himself and the weapon on its short bipod. "I was shaking like a bloody leaf," he said. "And sure enough, in about three minutes, this bloody great thing appears. It was more hearing it than seeing it, in the dark, and it turned out to be a Mark IV tank coming along pretty slowly."

The Panzer IV was conceived in the early 1930s by Heinz Guderian, a master of tank warfare. It was reliable and robust enough to survive in service in its various types until a final outing with the Syrian army against the Israelis in the Six Day War in

1967. It had a crew of five: commander, gunner, loader, driver, and radio operator-cum-hull machine-gunner. Its powerful 75mm gun gave it better penetrating power and longer range than the British and American tanks it had met and outclassed in North Africa. Its two machine guns, one mounted in the hull and the other on the turret, would also have made light work of Thornton, had he been spotted.

It had a single vulnerability that the sergeant could exploit. Its frontal armour was not well sloped. Hit a Panzer IV when it was square-on, dead ahead and at short range – the most perilous place, of course, for an anti-tank infantryman to find himself – and the shell might penetrate.

Thornton took a bomb, 16 inches long, brown with red and blue bands, edged with yellow, and the warning "TNT3" on it in black. The tank was less than 30 yards from him. It had turned at the T-junction and clattered towards the bridge.

"I told myself, 'You mustn't miss'," he said. "The lads behind me were only lightly armed. They wouldn't stand a chance if I missed and the whole operation would be over. Anyhow, although I was shaking, I took an aim, and bang, off it went. I hit him round about bang in the middle ... I was so excited and so shaking I had to move back a bit."

The bomb penetrated the armour. "Machine-gun clips inside the tank set off grenades which set off shells," said Thornton. "There was the most enormous explosion with bits and pieces flying everywhere."

Fox had to fling himself behind a wall to avoid the pyrotechnics. "You couldn't go far, because whizz-bang a bullet or shell went straight past you, but finally it died down and incredibly we heard this man crying out ..." The tank driver was lying beside the hulk, wounded in the legs. He was the commander of the 1st Panzer Engineer Company. A British soldier ran over and carried him to the aid post, but he died.

Three of the Horsa gliders that landed elite British troops in the hours before the D-Day landings lie (above, top) in a field by the Caen canal bridge in Normandy. The mission was to seize and hold the bridge (above). **"Wagger" Thornton**, a sergeant, prevented a German tank from retaking the bridge with a single projectile from a cumbersome and unloved PIAT anti-tank weapon (left). Had he missed, the left flank of the Allied invasion force would have been cut off. (*See page 188.*)

Zvika Greengold (left), a 21-year-old tank lieutenant, was at home when swarms of Syrian tanks slammed into the slender Israeli forces on the Golan Heights in October 1973. The Syrians seemed unstoppable by the time he hitch-hiked to his unit. Israeli tank commanders were particularly vulnerable (below). Greengold took command of a shot-up tank after dead crewmen had been removed from it. He became a one-man battle group, dubbed "Force Zvika", gaining and losing odd tanks in support. He held the Syrians for a night and much of the next morning. When he finally collapsed from exhaustion, he had destroyed at least 20 Syrian tanks, and probably twice that number, preventing them from breaking through before Israeli reinforcements arrived. (*See page 255.*)

Two Marines, on separate nights in October 1942, held the critical sector of a ridgeline on the perimeter of Henderson Field (above), the American airfield on Guadalcanal in the Solomons. They did so against Japanese attackers who outnumbered them many times. Lieutenant **Mitchell Paige** and Sergeant **John Basilone** (below, respectively third and fourth from left) later received Medals of Honor at a parade at Camp Balcombe, Australia. They changed the perception of the Pacific war, showing for the first time that the American fighting man could out-think and out-fight the enemy. The Japanese thought Guadalcanal to be "the decisive battle of the war". (*See page 276.*)

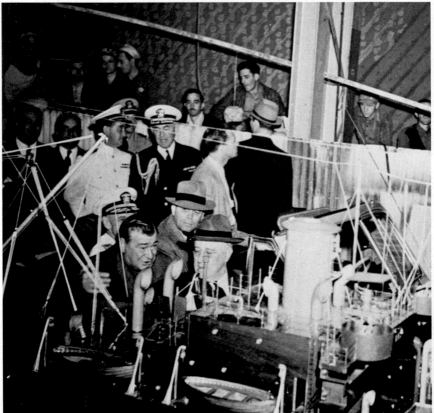

Andrew Higgins (opposite) was a small-time Louisiana boatbuilder with assets of $13,639 in 1938. Five years later, he had a workforce of 20,000, and nine out of ten of the US Navy's vessels were Higgins boats. He made amphibious warfare possible. Adolf Hitler called him "the new Noah". General Eisenhower, who relied utterly on Higgins boats in his strategy, said simply that Higgins was "the man who won the war for us". President Roosevelt visited his plant (opposite, below), to see boats being built that were used from Normandy to Borneo (above). (*See page 296.*)

The Indonesians who attacked a small British outpost in the Sarawak jungle in April 1965 outnumbered the defenders by more than ten to one. They had already overrun part of the position when **John Williams** (left), the paratroop sergeant major at the heart of British resistance, suffered severe head wounds and lost an eye. He fought on, though, and organized a counterattack that drove the attackers back through the wire. At dawn, the Indonesians broke off the attack. They never returned to the offensive. Williams "inspired his men with unbreakable fortitude", the citation for his medal recorded, and he proved to be the catalyst that ended *konfrontasi*, the undeclared war in Borneo. (*See page 327.*)

Forced to the surface by depth charges, the German submarine U-110 (opposite, below) wallows in the Atlantic swell in May 1941. Its captain, Fritz-Julius Lemp, seen here (above right) with Admiral Dönitz, was already a veteran, with a Knight's Cross and 19 ships to his credit. A Royal Navy lieutenant, **David Balme** (above) led a boarding party to U-110 from HMS *Bulldog*. He ignored the danger that the submarine would sink or that scuttling charges had been set. The code books and cipher machine he found helped the Allies win the U-boat war. King George VI personally congratulated Balme on what he called "the most significant event of the war at sea". Sixty years on, Balme held Lemp's hat (right), which he had found with the Enigma cipher machine aboard the U-boat, at a celebration of the victory in the North Atlantic. (*See page 333.*)

Julius Caesar arrived off the Kent coast in August 55 BC, with 10,000 legionaries aboard 80 transports. They looked at the hostile tribesmen lining the shore, and froze. "Our men were terrified," Caesar admitted, for they were non-swimmers and "lacked their usual dash and drive." Caesar faced a career-ruining humiliation. The **standard bearer** of the Tenth Legion saved him. He leapt into the water (above), charged forward and the others followed. He was rewarded with a mention in Caesar's *Gallic Wars*: the Roman Senate honoured Caesar himself with an unprecedented *supplicatio* or thanksgiving of 20 days. (*See page 213.*)

Masanobu Tsuji (left) was a little-loved eccentric – "that crazy man", his commanding officer said, "who lives in a filthy little room behind the stable" – who planned the Japanese invasion of Malaya. "I abstained from wine and tobacco, to say nothing of lust and appetite. My whole mind was concentrated on gaining the victory," he said. "I even became conceited, feeling that it depended on me whether we would win or lose the war ..." He made illegal and unauthorised flights over the British colony, saw its excellent paved roads, and decided that bicycles would give the invaders the speed and mobility they needed. Each division had 6,000 bicycles, each company a two-man puncture repair team. "Even the long-legged Englishmen could not escape our troops on bicycles," Tsuji said. "The assault on Malaya was made easy." (*See page 226.*)

The following tanks, Edwards observed, "were obviously not keen to chance their luck, and so with much revving of engines and general commotion they withdrew in disorder". They reported that the British were at the bridge in force with heavy anti-tank guns. The hulk continued to smoulder for the rest of the night, blocking the approaches to the bridge.

Groups of paratroops made their way to the bridges during the night. At dawn, the ground began to shake as a barrage of naval gunfire fell behind the distant beaches. As the landings got under way on Sword, heavier guns switched targets further inland towards Caen, and big shells shredded the air above the bridges. At 09:00, General Gale walked down the road from Ranville, with two brigadiers, confirming the arrival of 6th Airborne.

A counterattack by a German grenadier battalion at Bénou-ville was checked in a heavy firefight. A German fighter-bomber hit the canal bridge with a bomb, but it failed to explode and bounced off into the water. Snipers began to take a toll of men at the bridges, and German probes were becoming more determined, as the paratroops waited anxiously for the link-up with the seaborne forces. Lord Lovat's commandos of 1st Special Service Brigade had landed on Sword at 08:20. They had to destroy a coastal defence battery sited in a seaside casino before moving inland.

At about 13:00, Edwards was out of hand grenades and low on ammunition when he heard "a sound like banshees. A lad shouted, 'It's them, the commando!' ... We were English every one but those wild wailing bagpipes were like the sound of heaven." Lord Lovat appeared, in a white sweater and beret, carrying a walking stick. Beside him was his piper, Bill Millin.

"Everyone threw their rifles down, and kissed and hugged each other," said Thornton. "I saw men with tears rolling down their cheeks. Probably I was the same. Oh, dear, celebrations I shall never forget!"

Millin could hear shrapnel and bullets hitting the metal on

the bridge. Wounded men were being carried up from the canal banks to the aid post in the café. Lovat greeted Howard – "Pleased to meet you, old chap, sorry we're two and a half minutes late" – and then told Millin they were going to walk across the bridges. They came under sniper fire, but Millin started playing "Blue Bonnets Over the Border" as they crossed. The seaborne forces had linked up with the glider men. The operation had succeeded.

THORNTON'S SINGLE SHOT SAVED THE bridges. That is not in doubt. Had he missed, at a moment when the paratroop reinforcements were still scattered from the drop, the glider men would have been overrun.

His action has a dual significance. It denied use of the bridges to the Germans, and it enabled the British to use them to resupply and reinforce the 6th Airborne Division in its exposed position.

Even with the bridges in British hands, 6th Airborne suffered grievous casualties, a third of its force, 4,431 men, being listed as killed, wounded or missing. Without the bridge links, it would have been isolated on the east side of the Orne – and when the same fate overcame 1st Airborne at Arnhem a few months later, it was annihilated.

Had the Germans been free to counterattack westwards from the Pas de Calais, the landing forces would have been exposed directly to the full might of 15th Army. At best, Allied casualties would have been much greater. At worst – and all the Normandy evidence points to it being very much worse – the invasion would have failed.

The superiority of German tanks and tank gunnery was such that Allied tank crews nicknamed their own Sherman tanks "Ronsons" after the slogan of a famous cigarette lighter: "The Ronson lights first time every time." On 11 June, the 12th SS Panzer regiment destroyed 37 Shermans for the loss of just two Panzer IVs. A single German tank commander, SS-Unterscharfuehrer Willi Kretzschmar, destroyed 15 Allied tanks in fighting around Caen.

As it was, a regiment of the 21st Panzer division very nearly reached Sword beach on D-Day. The commander of the division's 125th Armoured Regiment, Colonel Hans von Luck, who survived the war, said that if the Orne bridges had been open to him, he would have joined the attack. He was confident that they would have broken out onto the beaches.

The PIAT round secured the bridges and the British flank. The elite German armour of 2nd Panzer, 1st SS Panzer and Panzer Lehr advanced slowly, bypassing the ruins of Caen, vulnerable to Allied air and sea power. When von Luck, stymied by the Orne, finally began to move, he was spotted by Allied aircraft, which called in naval gunfire heavy enough to halt him.

Thornton did not, of course, "win" the battle for Normandy. But he prevented it from being lost before the seaborne landings had even begun. Had he missed and Overlord failed, the results would have been as "staggering" as Hitler found the prospect of its success. Nazi Germany would still have been defeated. The strength of the Red Army and Anglo-American air power would have seen to that. The war in Europe would have lasted longer, with more destruction and loss of life, but the greatest consequence would have come when it was over.

All of Germany would have fallen to the Red Army, and perhaps Holland and Denmark, too, whilst Soviet influence was projected hundreds of miles further west. The whole balance of the post-war world would have been different.

AS TO WAGGER THORNTON, HE AND most of "D" Company became casualties in the fighting after D-day, an elite unit squandered in battles of attrition. Only 40 men returned unscathed to their barracks in September. Thornton was wounded in the leg and evacuated. He was awarded a Military Medal for "gaining the respect and complete confidence of the men of the Platoon by his enthusiasm, courage, disregard of personal safety and doing his job beyond the call of duty with conspicuous gallantry".

He soon shook off his wound and transferred to the 1st Airborne Division. He took part in the Arnhem operation, fighting at Arnhem bridge for four days before being taken prisoner. In civilian life, he worked for British Aerospace at Hamble, and retired before his death.

8 · THE BEARER OF THE EAGLE

A standard bearer saves the
reputation of Julius Caesar

Hesitation is punished harshly in war. One man, though,
may overcome it on behalf of a whole army, through
his "peculiar direction of mind, which conquers
every other fear by fear of wavering or doubting ...
[which] ... makes up resolution in strong minds"
(BOOK I, CHAPTER III).

THE KENT COAST NEAR DEAL　*　AUGUST–SEPTEMBER 55 BC

SHORTLY BEFORE MIDNIGHT ON 26 August 55 BC, a fleet of 80 transports sailed from Portus Itius in Gaul, today the Channel port of
Boulogne in northeast France. They carried 10,000 men of the
VII and X Legions, and their commander, Julius Caesar. A further
force of 500 cavalrymen and their horses were to join them later
on 18 "ships of burden".

It was late in the season. Winter set in early in these latitudes,
and the Channel gales were intimidating for troops with no
experience of the sea. Caesar nonetheless felt compelled to make
an expedition to Britain. As governor of Gaul, he had been
campaigning against Gallic and Germanic tribes since 58 BC,
extending Roman rule. The Britons, he complained, had "rendered

assistance to the enemy in nearly all my Gallic campaigns".

Fugitives from the Gallic Belgae, whom he had crushed in 57 BC, had fled to Belgic settlements in Britain, and the Veneti, who controlled the trade across the Channel, had been aided by the British tribes in their rebellion against the Romans in 56 BC. Caesar was already the first Roman to have crossed the Rhine into Germanic territory, having built a great wooden bridge over the mighty river in only ten days in June 56 BC. More fame, he would have noted, would attach to him as the first Roman to cross the sea to Britain, a place on the edge of the known world, but with a profitable enough trade in tin, hides and wool to be able to import Italian wine.

In *De bello gallico*, his classic account of his Gallic wars, Caesar claimed that, though it was impractical to start military operations at the end of August, "I thought it would be a great advantage merely to have visited the island", to see what kind of people lived there, and to "learn something about the country with its harbours and landing places". Ten thousand heavily armed legionaries were a lot of men to take on a mere "visit", though, and this was at the least an armed reconnaissance in force, on a big enough scale to turn into an invasion if circumstance allowed.

Caesar had first interrogated merchants who traded across the Channel. They naturally feared that this was a preliminary to the Romans slapping a tax on cargoes, and he "elicited nothing as to the size of the island, the names and strengths of the native tribes, their military and civil organization, or the harbours ..." He sent the tribune Caius Volusenus in a single warship to make a preliminary survey of the British coast, whilst he assembled the army in the Pas de Calais.

Volusenus was back in five days, scouting the Kent coast between Hythe and Sandwich, but not landing, since he "did not dare leave his ship and entrust himself to the barbarians". The

Britons were known to be bellicose. Warned of the impending invasion by merchants, ambassadors from some of the British tribes sailed to Boulogne to promise their submission. Caesar sent them back with his ally Commius, king of the Gallic Atrebates, to win over as many other tribes as possible.

The fleet of transports was made ready, together with some warships for the chief of staff, the officers of general rank, and auxiliary commanders. The two legions were embarked. Both had been with Caesar throughout the Gallic wars. The Legio X Equestria, named after its cavalry arm, was his favourite, from which he drew his bodyguards. Caesar hurried his preparations, pressed by fears that the weather in the Channel would turn. He left a garrison in the port, and sailed "at the third watch", around midnight. The legions had no baggage or heavy siege equipment, and the cavalry had not yet embarked.

Caesar was with the leading ships when they reached Britain at about 9 a.m. the following morning. "I ... saw the enemy forces standing under arms all along the heights," he wrote. He was off Dubris, or Dover, and its white cliffs were a formidable rampart. "Precipitous cliffs tower over the water, making it possible to fire from above directly onto the beaches," he said. It was "clearly no place to attempt a landing", so they rode at anchor until about 3:30 p.m. to await the rest of the fleet. He summoned his staff and company commanders, and warned them that, at sea, tactical demands change rapidly and that they must be ready to act at a moment's notice. The meeting broke up as the tide and wind turned favourable.

The fleet weighed anchor and sailed about eight miles up channel. They grounded slightly offshore from the gently shelving shingle beaches south of Deal. The British had followed the fleet along the coast, their cavalry and war chariots in the van with the main body close behind. They stood "ready to prevent our landing". Disembarkation was made "extraordinarily difficult" by the deep draught of the ships, which ran aground well offshore in several feet of water. The legionaries knew nothing of where they were, other than that, weighted with heavy armour, they had "to jump from the ships, stand firm in the surf, and fight at the same time". The enemy were perfectly familiar with the coast. They were unencumbered and "could hurl their weapons boldly from dry land or shallow water, and gallop their horses, which were trained to this kind of work".

"Our men," Caesar admitted, "were terrified." The ships' crews were familiar with the tideless Mediterranean, and the strong tides and treacherous sandbanks of the Kent coast were new to them, and their nervousness was picked up and magnified by the soldiers. The prospect of fighting on a strange shoreline further unsettled the legionaries, and Caesar noted with alarm that they "lacked that dash and drive that always characterized their land battles".

Their fears, compounded by the fact that most were non-swimmers, were well founded. Their armour would pull them under and drown them if they slipped, and their weapons were not adapted for fighting in the surf and shallows. Each legionary had a *galea*, a helmet, a round inverted bowl of iron with a ring on top to attach a plume during parades, with hinged cheek pieces and a neck protector at the back, heavy and awkward for a man trying to keep his balance on a sliding shingle shore. The *lorica segmentata*, the corselet of curved strips of metal fastened round the chest with leather thongs, added to the weight, as did the metal discs on the strips of leather that hung like a skirt from the thick *cingulum militare*, the belt. The hobnail and leather soles of the *caligae*, the boots, gave poor traction on water-slicked pebbles. Worse, the *gladius*, the short 22-inch sword with a two-edged blade, was designed for the stabbing and thrusting style of hand-to-hand fighting of classic legionary combat. Here, though, the water and the shingle made it difficult to get to grips with the enemy.

The men would not jump. Caesar tried to manoeuvre the warships to frighten the British. He had the oarsmen go astern of the transports, and then go full ahead on the British right flank. From here, they were to open fire with slings, arrows and artillery, light catapults firing metal and stone projectiles, and lead sling bullets. The Britons, so Caesar claimed, were "scared by the strange forms of warships, by the motion of the oars, and by the artillery, which they had never seen before." They halted.

But, with potentially fatal hesitation, the legionaries still baulked at jumping into the deep water. Some of the ships were 600 feet offshore, and the men would have to half-swim and half-wade under heavy fire from British missiles. Caesar faced failure and humiliation – both personally, for the news would reach his political enemies in Rome soon enough, and in terms of the prestige of Roman arms, with baleful consequences for Roman rule in Gaul – and he knew it.

He was saved by the *aquilifer*, the standard bearer, of Legio X. We do not know his name – Caesar recorded the deed, but did not think to identify a humble non-com by name – but we know much of what made him.

Each century, cohort and legion in the Roman army had its own standard. The century was a group of 80 men, despite its name, commanded by a centurion. The cohort was the basic fighting unit, made up of six centuries, or about 480 men and six centurions. The legion was formed from ten cohorts, the first being commanded by the *primipilus*, the "first javelin", the senior centurion of the legion. The *signifer*, the standard bearer of the century and cohort, was an experienced and respected man, an equivalent to a sergeant major, with a different and dangerous role. He carried the *signum*, the standard unique to each unit. It was a long and heavy pole, topped with insignia and symbols. It acted as a rallying point in combat, high enough for soldiers to see it in the clamour and confusion of combat, and to close on to consolidate the ranks if things went wrong. The *signifer* could also give simple visual commands through movements of the standard, and so he needed a good grasp of tactics.

The standard bearer stood in the first rank, and could only carry a small buckler, for his sword arm was encumbered with the heavy pole. He was triply vulnerable. He was unarmed. He was highly visible, deliberately so, because his whole purpose was to be seen, and to this end he wore an animal skin on his head. The standard itself, besides being an encumbrance, was a magnet for the enemy: to capture a standard was the high point of a victory, and a massive dishonour for the unit that lost it. The high casualty rate among standard bearers at times of intense combat, like the Gallic Wars, was reflected in the large numbers of *discentes signiferorum*, trainee standard bearers.

Our *aquilifer*, the "eagle bearer", bore the standard of the whole legion. The pride of the Xth was held in his rough hands, with its insignia and eagle made of pure silver, symbols of the power of Rome and the honour of the legion. The animal skin on his head was a lion skin. Only a veteran of proven courage and quality could be made *aquilifer* of a crack legion like the Xth, a man dedicated body and soul, for in pay standard bearers were no more than *duplicarii*, on double the 225 denarii a year pay of the common legionary. The lowest ranking centurion was paid 3,700 denarii, and the highest 15,000. There was a wide gulf between officers and even the most senior and highly decorated of NCOs.

Legio X had been raised by Caesar in 61 BC in Spain. It first saw action subduing hostile tribes in western Spain. The *aquilifer* in the Kent shallows was almost certainly with the legion from its foundation. It was one of the four legions that Caesar took with him to Gaul, and he would have fought with Caesar throughout the Gallic campaigns.

The legion saved Caesar at the Battle of the Sabis in what is now Flanders in 57 BC. Caesar attacked the Nervii, a group of

Belgic-French tribes, with six legions in light marching order. The baggage train followed, escorted by two freshly recruited legions. The Romans set up a camp on the north bank of the Sabis – the River Sambre. The cavalry crossed the river and skirmished with the Belgic cavalry, which retreated into woods. The experienced legions foraged for food and began building a camp and fortifications. The baggage train was two miles in the rear with its inexperienced escorts.

As they came in view, the Belgic force rushed out of the trees in formation and overwhelmed the Roman cavalry. They charged across the river, no more than three feet deep at this point, and charged up the hill at the legions making camp. The Romans had no time to get in formation. Many had no time even to get their helmets and shields. In the melee, they could not group by cohorts, but instead closed on the nearest standard they could see.

Four legions on the Roman left flank were fighting desperately to avoid being overrun by the barbarians. A gap in the line allowed the Nervii to flood into the camp. They began to outflank the two legions fighting on the Roman right from the rear. Almost all the centurions of Legio XII were killed or wounded. The *primipilus*, the senior centurion, had fallen. Several standard bearers had been killed, their standards seized by the enemy, and the soldiers were beginning to panic.

Caesar, himself taken by surprise at the attack, took a shield from a soldier and joined the XIIth. He shouted at them to spread out, because they had packed so tightly together that they could not swing their sword arms freely. His appearance calmed them, and he had the XIIth and VIIth join up and make a square formation to withstand the enemy's furious pressure.

Legio X crossed the river, smashed the enemy reserves, and seized the Belgic camp on the south bank of the river. From there, they saw the desperate position, re-crossed the river and retook the Roman camp. The battle now swung to the Romans, and the arrival of the legions that had guarded the baggage train enabled them to encircle the enemy. The Nervii were slaughtered, standing on the bodies of their dead comrades until they themselves were killed. The neighbouring tribes surrendered to Caesar, giving Rome control of most of modern Belgium.

There were other battles, from modern Switzerland and the Saône to Brittany, where Legio X earned Caesar's gratitude. That was as a legion. Now, in the shallows off the Kent coast, it was just one man from the Xth who did so. The *aquilifer* was physically and mentally strong, a man in whom the rank and file had absolute respect and confidence, one of their own but with martial qualities that set him apart, who was in short the character who has been the *sine qua non*, the vital ingredient, in crack units throughout history. Officers may direct the battlefield, but it is men who fight, and it is the first-rate sergeant, the *adjutant-chef*, the *Feldwebel*, who is the repository of their courage and their conscience.

"OUR MEN STILL HESITATED," Caesar recorded, "mainly because of the deep water." Eighty ships, packed with men, and not a movement. Only the champing of the horses and the barbarians on the shore. It was, he said, the "critical moment".

Then, the *aquilifer* of Legio X, "after calling on the gods to bless the legion through his act", poised himself on the bow of his ship. Caesar recorded the words he shouted: "Come on, men! Jump, unless you want to betray your standard to the enemy! I, at any rate, shall do my duty to my country and my commander."

With that, he "threw himself into the sea and started forward with the eagle".

This was the ultimate challenge to the troops watching from the transports. To lose a standard was shameful, to lose an eagle unthinkable. Punishment in the Roman army was brutal enough.

Cowardice by a unit might be dealt with by decimation, in which every tenth man in a cohort was randomly selected to be clubbed or beaten to death by the others. The *aquilifer*'s action, though, went beyond fear of retribution: it directly challenged the honour of every man who saw him with his lion skin and silver emblem splashing through the waves towards the barbarians on the shore.

It sank in. "The rest were not going to disgrace themselves," Caesar recorded. The men in the *aquilifer*'s ship, "cheering wildly", leapt down. As the men in the next ship saw them, they jumped too, and then the next after that, until the whole force was pouring ashore.

What happened now was, in the event, less important than the fact that, thanks to the *aquilifer*, it happened at all.

A bitter fight ensued, and Caesar soon realized that he was not going to master even the southeast corner of the island on the cheap. His men could not follow their appointed standards, because different shiploads became mixed up as they fought their way ashore, and "a good deal of confusion resulted". The British knew all the shallows. Standing on dry land, they watched the Romans jump from the ships in small parties, and galloped down and attacked them as they struggled through the surf. They surrounded them when they could, and attacked them from the flank. Caesar had the warships' boats and scouting ships filled with troops, so that help could be got to any point where his men seemed in difficulties.

After everyone had got ashore and formed up, the legions could at last charge. The enemy was hurled back. But Caesar could not pursue them for any distance. The cavalry transports had still not arrived. The natives recovered their nerve. They sent envoys to ask for peace, and returned Commius, whom they had thrown into prison after Caesar had sent him over from Gaul.

Late on 30 August, the fourth day after the landing, the 18 transports with cavalry on board sailed from Gaul in a gentle breeze. As they neared the Kent coast, a violent storm broke and the little fleet scattered. Some were driven back to Gaul but others shipped water in the breaking seas and were swept down the Channel, southwestwards past Dover. They managed to anchor, but as darkness fell, they stood out to sea and made back for Gaul.

It was a full moon that night. The Roman crews on the Kent coast were so ignorant of tidal waters that they failed to realize that lunar conditions would bring an abnormally high tide, made more dangerous by the gale-force winds. The warships, which had been beached, filled with water as they were caught by the rising tide. The transports were riding at anchor offshore. The seas were too high to get them under way, and they slammed into each other. Several ships broke up and sank. Others lost their anchors and cables, and their rigging was swept away.

Caesar was deeply concerned. He had no spare ships to get his legions back to Gaul, and he had no supplies to sustain them if he was forced to winter in Kent. The British chieftains saw that he was in trouble. They knew that he had no cavalry, was short of grain and ships, and had no heavy equipment to withstand a siege. They set out to "cut us off from food supplies" and to prolong the campaign until winter struck. Caesar realized the Britons were convinced that if they could wipe out his forces, the Romans would never again try to invade Britain. The British chieftains at his camp thus "renewed their vows of mutual loyalty, slipped away one by one, and secretly reassembled their forces from the countryside".

Timber and bronze were stripped from badly damaged ships to repair others as Caesar prepared to leave Britain as quickly as he could. He sent the VIIth Legion into the fields to harvest as much corn as possible. When sentries reported a large dust cloud where the legion had gone, Caesar feared that the "natives had hatched some new plot". He set out with cohorts of troops to find the VIIth in difficulties. The British had hidden in woods overnight, and attacked them whilst they were unarmed and busy reaping. A few were killed. Cavalry and war chariots were at work on the others.

He was fascinated to see British charioteers in action. They began by driving across the battlefield at speed, throwing javelins, letting the noise of the horses and the wheels inspire terror in the enemy. Then the warriors jumped from them, and prepared to fight on foot, as the chariot drivers withdrew and waited so that their masters could leap back onto them and retreat at speed if necessary. Caesar admired them: they combined the speed and mobility of cavalry with the tenacity and staying power of infantry. The charioteers' skill was great enough for them to stay in control of their horses even when at full gallop on steep slopes. The men from the VIIth were unnerved by these tactics. Caesar felt it was as well that he was intervening with reinforcements, and he led the men back to camp.

Commius sent over 30 horses. Caesar took advantage of cavalry to lead a sortie, overwhelming the enemy near the camp and burning all the buildings over a wide area. By now, all but 12 ships had been made reasonably seaworthy. The equinox was close and more storms were likely. As landsmen, the noise of the sea on the shingle of this coast must have chilled their senses. Two millennia later, in his great poem 'Dover Beach', Matthew Arnold wrote of this haunting sound:

> Its melancholy, long, withdrawing roar,
> Retreating to the breath
> Of the night-wing, down the vast edges drear
> And naked shingles of the world.

Caesar took advantage of some fair weather to set sail. The fleet left after midnight, to give the natives no warning, and returned safely to Gaul.

THE RESULTS OF THE *AQUILIFER'S* BOLD plunge into the Channel were felt most keenly in Rome itself. The landing in Britain that it ensured carried such high kudos that, when word of it reached the Senate, it decreed a *supplicatio* of 20 days in honour of Julius Caesar.

At times of great peril, these were supplications to avert the anger of the gods. With great victories, as here, they were solemn thanksgivings. All the temples of the city were opened, and the statues of the gods were placed in public for the people to offer up their thanks and prayers. They were most commonly held for three or five days. The first *supplicatio* of ten days had been decreed in honour of Pompey after his defeat of Mithridates on the Euphrates.

Pompey was, with Julius Caesar and the plutocrat Crassus, a member of the all-powerful "First Triumvirate" in Rome. Though Pompey was married to Caesar's daughter Julia, tensions and rivalries between the three were increasing, as each sought to emerge supreme. Caesar had been honoured with a 15-day *supplicatio* after Legio X had helped him defeat the Belgae.

The 20-day *supplicatio* after his British expedition was record-breaking. It further increased his prestige and power. As the commander of an army, he was not allowed to enter the territory of Rome itself – when he had last met his fellow triumvirs it had been at Lucca, across the frontier. But it was such celebrations as this that kept his name alive in the city.

Had Caesar's expedition been aborted off Kent, the humiliation would have ravaged his reputation. The *aquilifer* ensured that it did not. Caesar returned to Britain in 54 BC, the year when Julia died in childbirth, after which Caesar and Pompey drifted further apart. Crassus was killed in 53 BC. During the civil war against Pompey that broke out in 49 BC, Legio X remained faithful to Caesar. With the defeat of Pompey at Pharsalus the following year, Caesar was master of the Roman world.

If our *aquilifer* survived these few years, a pleasant retirement awaited him. Caesar disbanded the Xth in 45 BC. Its veterans were granted land around Narbonne, along the route of the Via Domitia, the first Roman road in Gaul, linking Italy and Spain, a place of vineyards and orchards. The Xth was reconstituted in 42 BC. It was last recorded at the beginning of the 5th century AD, serving near Vienna.

9 · THE BICYCLE BLITZKRIEG

The profound effect of pedal power

"It is ... not only the physical, but more frequently
the mental eye which is meant in *coup d'oeil*"
(BOOK I, CHAPTER II). Here, a single flash of insight
whilst flying over the jungle changed the
course of a campaign.

MALAYA * 8 DECEMBER 1941–31 JANUARY 1942

AT 07:00 ON 31 JANUARY 1942, the last two surviving pipers of the
Argyll and Sutherland Highlanders played a skirl as the Australians
and Gordon Highlanders who had been providing cover for the
retreat crossed the causeway linking the Malayan state of Johore
to Singapore Island. A few minutes later, they piped across the
final rearguard of Argylls to "Blue Bonnets over the Border". At
08:15 a team of sappers blew a 70-foot-wide gap in the causeway
with naval mines. Dust clouds roiled in the tropical air.

The British had lost Malaya.

In Johore Bahru, the city on the Malay side, a Japanese officer
called Masanobu Tsuji ran his eye over the gleaming white sultan's
palace. "Suddenly – look!" he wrote. "The Japanese flag was flut-
tering spiritedly in the sea breeze." Then he gazed south, at the
fine view across the water to Singapore, the British stronghold
which had dominated southeast Asia for over a hundred years. It

lay just over a kilometre away beyond the ruined causeway, "pawing the ground in its last moments".

The invasion had been planned to coincide with the attack on Pearl Harbor, though the first casualties, the crew of an RAF Catalina shot down by Japanese fighters, were killed over the South China Sea ten hours before the divebombers arrived over Hawaii. The first Japanese troops were landed before dawn on 8 December 1941, on the east coast on both sides of the Thai–Malayan border.

In scarcely 55 days, Tsuji exulted, the Japanese 25th Army had covered 1,100 kilometres, from the extreme north of Malaya to Johore. They had fought 95 large and small engagements and – a fact of importance – repaired more than 250 bridges. On an average day, they had fought two battles, fixed four or five bridges and advanced 20 kilometres. The speed of the assault, Tsuji claimed, was "unparalleled in the history of war".

The pace was the more remarkable for the lack of motor transport. The Japanese had less than a tenth as many trucks as the British, yet they had to move swiftly, for they were outnumbered in men, too, by two to one, and the British were waiting for further reinforcements to arrive from their big garrisons in the Middle East. Speed was of the very essence for the Japanese, and it was Tsuji who had provided it.

Tsuji was 39, the son of peasant farmers, many rungs below the samurai class, but clever enough to win a place at the Nagoya Yonen Gekko, a military preparatory school beneath the golden dolphins on the Nagoya Castle. He went on to military academy in Tokyo. He was short, even for the Japanese of the time, at 1.55 metres (5 feet 2 in), but with a fierce set to his head, and furious eyes behind owlish round glasses, whose thick lenses magnified the folds of his eyelids.

The cruelty in the gaze was part of the man. All his qualities, good and bad (and some were very bad) – his ingenuity, insights, courage, raging temper, disregard for authority, hatreds, racial contempt and patriotism – were exaggerated to a point close to lunacy. His bloodlust was given free rein after the Japanese invaded China. In 1937, as a captain, Tsuji had led a massacre of civilians in Shansi province as punishment for the refusal of the local warlord to cooperate with a Japanese campaign to liquidate Chinese communists.

Eccentric and ill-liked by his fellow soldiers in China – he was described by his commanding officer as "that crazy man who lives in a filthy little room behind the stable" – Tsuji was transferred to Taiwan at the beginning of 1941. He was given a meagre start-up fund of 20,000 yen, about US$5,000, and a monthly budget of 2,000 yen, or US$500, and put in charge of the scantily staffed Taiwan Army Research Department. His task was to look into the best ways of preparing Japanese troops for jungle warfare.

Like the Gurkhas, who came from the icy heights of Nepal, the Japanese were to win a formidable reputation as jungle fighters, but they also started from scratch. The Japanese had gained plenty of cold-weather combat experience by 1941 from their long campaigns in China and Manchuria, and in their short, sharp and unsuccessful border war with Soviet Russia. Now they were casting their eyes south, at the treasures of British Malaya and the Dutch East Indies, rich in oil, rubber, tin and tungsten. At that time Malaya was producing 40 percent of the world's rubber and 60 percent of its tin.

The task of preparing to fight here was so great and the time so limited that Tsuji called himself and his men the "Doro Nawa Unit", roughly equivalent to the "Stable Door Unit" in English, as in closing the door after the horse has bolted. He had just ten researchers to look into potential campaigns in the Pacific islands, against the Americans in the Philippines, the Dutch in the East Indies, the French in Indochina, the British in Malaya, Singapore,

Burma ... "They had not the faintest idea of where it would be best to turn their attention," he said of his men. "To make matters worse, they were completely devoid of data."

The Japanese knew how to organize troops and cavalry, and maintain mobility with horses, in temperatures of minus 20 °C. What would happen in unaccustomed heat and humidity? The jungles of southeast Asia were as dense as any on earth, covering the steep slopes of hills that rolled to the horizon in serried waves. Making progress through them drained body and soul. Other perils awaited: malaria, sunstroke, beriberi, snake and insect bites.

Tsuji gave each of his ten men a different region to study. "My appointed concern was Malaya," he said. "I was to study questions of military geography, equipment, tactics, and supplies – the whole organization of a campaign."

He tapped an old sea captain who had voyaged along the Malay coasts for tips on sea conditions, weather and suitable landing beaches. Mining-company engineers who had been in Malaya gave him details on terrain and transport. He talked to businessmen and bankers who knew Singapore. A Japanese resident sent aerial pictures of Singapore Island.

Men and horses would have to be transported "packed like sardines" into ships in temperatures of up to 49 °C, travel through heavy seas, and disembark on open beaches. How would they cope? Tsuji packed men "three to a mat", an area one metre by half a metre, on a ship and gave them a small water ration for a week, with their quarters battened down and airless to get the highest possible temperature. He found the troops could cope. Horses were a different matter. They would have to be replaced.

INTERNATIONAL TENSION WAS RISING. The Americans and British, concerned at Japanese aggression in China, were embargoing exports of oil, rubber and other strategic materials. Japan considered these to be hostile acts. The Imperial Conference in Tokyo, at the bidding of General Hideki Tojo, formally agreed on 6 September 1941 to set a secret deadline to go to war with the British and Americans if diplomacy was still fruitless in early October.

Tsuji was sent to French Indochina. Airfields would be needed there as a base for aircraft operating in any future campaign in Malaya. The Vichy French, their German masters being allies of the Japanese, were in no position to refuse.

Basing himself in Saigon, Tsuji went at his task of planning the campaign like a bull with its head down. The officer responsible for air operations was making slow progress. Tsuji waited until he was absent in Tokyo, and took an aircraft on a reconnaissance flight over the islands off the coasts of Vietnam and Cambodia. He found one suitable for airfields and started work. He did not bother to get authorization from the French. "I hurried two thousand coolies to Phuoquok Island," he said. "I kept the work secret even from Tokyo ..." He prepared two airfields for the aircraft that would protect the convoy of transports for the invasion of Malaya, and give air cover to the troops as they landed.

Tsuji sent a staff officer, Captain Asaeda, disguised as an agricultural engineer to spy on southern Thailand and Malaya. The young officer, chatting with Thais of all ranks, felt they would let Japanese troops cross Thailand without a fight. He found the Thai troops defending the coast had only a skirmish line, without pillboxes or even wire at the landing points. He reported that the airfields on the Thai side of the border were poor and crude compared with the RAF airfields at Kota Bharu and in Kedah.

Sitting cross-legged on a rush mat, maps spread out on the floor, Tsuji worked day and night on the plan of operations. "I abstained from wine and tobacco. I forgot instinctive desires and worldly passions, to say nothing of lust and appetite and even life and death. My whole mind was concentrated on gaining the victory," he said. "I even became conceited, feeling that it depended on me whether we would win or lose the war that would determine the destiny of the nation." Tsuji was armoured in vanity, prickly, tetchy, unable to take the slightest criticism, but in this case it was justified. This obscure planner, eccentric, disliked by many of his brother officers, was indeed to have a decisive impact on a campaign that changed history.

Tsuji was convinced that the British airfields must be overrun as soon as the Japanese landed. It was only in the air that the Japanese had a clear advantage, flying modern Zero fighters and bombers against antiquated fighters and biplane torpedo bombers. To make air superiority count, it was vital to have airfields much closer than Indochina, two hours' flying time away, and Asaeda's reconnaissance had shown that the Thai airfields were not up to the job.

To verify the terrain for himself, Tsuji determined to fly over Malaya. "Gambling with human life, one must risk one's own," he said. "There was nothing for it but to make a personal reconnaissance of the projected airfields." A young pilot, Captain Ikeda, arrived in Saigon in the evening of 19 October 1941. He had flown from Manchuria in a Mitsubishi Type 100 reconnaissance aircraft. Tsuji made a beeline for him. "Tomorrow I wish to go flying over the southern part of Thailand and northern Malaya," he said. "Can you do it?" Ikeda pondered for a moment – Tsuji did not have the rank to make such a request – but said he would.

Tsuji told him to start getting prepared immediately. He wanted to set out at 05:00 the next morning. "By way of precaution," he added, "have the Hi-no-Maru, the Rising Sun flag, painted over on the aircraft." It was the only indication that the trip was both illegal and unauthorized. The airfield was still dark when they arrived at the aircraft. Tsuji wore air force uniform, so that they would not appear to be spying for the army if they crashed. "At six o'clock, with the red sun behind us," Tsuji wrote, "we took off from Saigon …"

They crossed the Gulf of Siam at 6,400 metres. The weather deteriorated as they approached the Malay coast. He ordered the pilot to lose height. They went down through "clouds like silk wadding", the intense cold turning to a humid heat, so that sweat poured off them as the altimeter unwound through 2,000 to 500 metres, with no break in the cloud, until they came out over the sea at 300 metres. Tsuji could see seabirds skimming the waves as they broke on a beach, but the land was still covered in dense cloud. They circled and searched. Two and a half hours out from Saigon, Ikeda said they were at the limit of their fuel. They turned for home.

They tried again on 22 October. As they neared the coast, the Kelantan delta "shone in the sun, each branch of the river like a silver thread". They overflew Singora and Patani on the Thai coast, and the British torpedo bomber base at Kota Bahru on the Malay side of the frontier. The Type 100 had a top speed of 600kph, faster than any British aircraft in the region. Its Allied code name was "Dinah", and British and American airmen paid tribute to its elegant lines in song: "The Dinah with the nice linah".

As they flew on above Malaya, Tsuji had a moment of piercing insight. "Through a sea of trees, stretching as far as the eye could see," he wrote, "an asphalt road and a railway were visible running north and south. For about a kilometre on each side, the road was lined by rubber plantations. On this frontage alone would movement be possible for troops of all arms."

Even an army with superior numbers would find the road at the centre of its battlefront, with its flanks extending for not more than a kilometre to the right and left. "There was consequently no need to worry about the superior numbers of British troops," Tsuji told himself. The narrow front on which battles would be fought limited the number of troops who could be used effectively by either side.

He thought that a single good battalion could penetrate enemy defences and open up a line of advance. Units landed later could alternate with them as the troops in the vanguard became exhausted. In the rubber plantations and jungle, he said, the "authority of the naked sabre would be conclusive". This was terrain for infantry and combat at close quarters, offering "ideal fighting conditions for us".

They flew on, the only discordant noise in the peaceful sky the "sound of our own plane flying on its secret mission". The west coast was shut in with storm clouds and heavy rain. Ikeda lost height, and suddenly, through the rain, they saw a large airfield below them. It was the RAF base at Alor Star. "Fortunately for us, it appeared that because of the rain the British air force was resting," Tsuji said, and they gained height and continued south, seeing other airfields at Sungei Patani and at Taipeng, south-east of Penang.

To compare these developed airfields with the miserable Thai airstrips "was like comparing adults to children", Tsuji said. He realized that the only way to win was "by rushing in immediately to attack ... by any means whatever as soon as we made a landing, to seize the enemy airfields". At any sacrifice, the RAF airfields at Kota Bahru and Alor Star must be taken. The Japanese must advance to the left bank of the River Perak and "at one stroke seize the three bridges across it ..."

Below him, as he looked down from the Dinah, he could see the full length of the river, meandering like a silvery belt to the distant south. "It is impossible to ford this large stream, which can only be crossed by bridges or boat," he noted. "If the enemy destroyed the bridges, our advance would be held up for at least a week. This was the conclusion we reached in the plane." And the British would blow the bridges. That was certain.

He wanted to fly further south, but fuel was becoming critical. "End the recce. Turn back," he called out regretfully. They got back to Saigon at 11:10, having exceeded the Dinah's maximum certificated endurance by ten minutes. "The last drop of petrol was gone, and we landed with difficulty by gliding onto the airfield," he said. Five minutes later, and the Dinah would have crashed.

The British were to have good reason to rue the last fumes of petrol that got him home. He had carefully taken photographs on the trip, but the film or his camera technique was faulty, and none came out. No matter. "The image of everything I had seen was so strongly printed on the living retina of my eyes and on my mind that there was no need for photographs," he recollected after the war. "Even after all these years I can still see clearly everything that I saw on that flight."

He had seen the battlefield from the Dinah: the long strip of gleaming asphalt that ran down the spine of Malaya, for 1,100 kilometres, ever southward, from the Thai border to Singapore. Every bridge over it was a lock the British could snap shut with a few pounds of explosives. Tsuji, eccentric, a man whose thinking was done outside the box, found a key. The bicycle.

THE BRITISH HAD MEN IN PLENTY, more than 130,000 of them, in 13 brigades. Eight were from the British Indian Army, and three were British and two Australian. There were also two locally raised brigades. They had enough trucks and Bren-gun carriers to be partly dependent on them. The raw Indian and Australian troops lacked combat experience, though, and they had no tanks whatever, and were short of anti-tank guns.

Though their airfields had impressed Tsuji, the aircraft they flew were largely obsolete. The fighters were American Brewster Buffaloes, mostly fitted with reworked time-expired airline engines. Pilots of the Eagle Squadron, American volunteers flying for the RAF, described the Buffalo as "a delightful trainer" but said that it "should on no account be considered as a fighter". The Blenheim bombers had been relegated to training aircraft in Britain. The biplane Vildebeest torpedo bombers were yet more antiquated. British plans relied heavily on sending troop and air-force reinforcements to Singapore by sea. Enemy landings would be dealt with by sending Royal Navy battleships and cruisers.

The Japanese invasion force had 60,000 men in the three divisions of the 25th Army. The commander was General Tomoyuki Yamashita, a rotund but fierce figure who had recently been with a Japanese mission in Berlin. He sent his own spy to Malaya, Major Teruno Kunitake, who reported back that Tsuji had greatly underestimated the number of bridges that would have to be crossed. Yamashita could have had a fourth division but, even though outnumbered, thought it unnecessary and left it in Japan. Of the three others, the Imperial Guards Division had no combat experience. Tsuji dismissed them as "trained for elegant traditional ceremonies ... with no taste for field operations". The other two divisions, the 5th and 18th, though, were made up of warhardened veterans. Tsuji set great store by the 18th, a "thoroughly reliable fighting division", whose men included many former coal miners from northern Kyushu. They were "fond of rough work", and apt to "commit acts of violence and plunder", but for all that they were a strong and disciplined formation whom he thought "ideally suited for the capture of Singapore". The 25th Army also had a tank regiment, and three regiments of engineers, who proved very useful.

Tsuji's flights convinced him that three landings should be made, at Singora and Patani on the Thai side of the border, and at Kota Bahru in Malaya. Dozing off on his rush mat in Saigon in November, he had a dream about the invasion. He saw himself mingling with Thai troops and receiving a warm welcome from British soldiers as he crossed the border and made for the bridge on the River Perak. Then he woke up.

He had long since convinced himself that he was the "special one" of the campaign, blessed with rare insights by the gods. He decided to put his sleepy vision to use in what he called his "Dream Plan".

A "death-defying volunteer force" would masquerade as Thais in Thai army uniforms. When they landed at Singora, by "bribery or cajolery" they would win over Thai troops and be persuaded to advance at the head of the Japanese raiders. The next trick was to earn the warm welcome from the British he had dreamed of.

To do this, Tsuji said, "our troops should take refuge among Thai women by picking up café and dance-hall girls". They would then seize "twenty or thirty trucks or motor buses" and advance to the border. Here, "as if confused, with a simulated, sorrowful expression", they were to seek help from the British border guards, portraying themselves as a party of friendly Thai troops who had got lost after painting the town red with their busloads of whores. The troops were to be issued with Thai and British flags on landing.

The leading "revellers" were to "advance waving in one hand the Thai flag and in the other the Union Jack". They would then call out in English: "Japanese soldier is frightful … Hurrah for the English!" The border guards having been thrown off balance by this charm offensive, the troops would "thus break right through the frontier line".

Tsuji admitted that the subterfuge was a "breach of international good faith", but "for the sake of the conquest of Singapore, we had to disregard this aspect". In any event, he comforted himself, the issue would settle itself as soon as the Japanese had a military alliance with the Thais.

Ruses are common in surprise attacks. The Germans had started the Second World War with faked incidents on the Polish border. Few are as half-baked as Tsuji's, but it was taken seriously. Staff Officer Hayashi was despatched to Bangkok, returning with a Thai army uniform. The supply department ran up a thousand copies over the next two weeks. A unit was found that was willing to "brave almost certain death" wearing them – this was Major

Tadashi Ichikawa's battalion from the 5th Division. Thai-speaking Japanese were found. A clerk in the Japanese consulate in Singora was briefed on what to expect. A large sum of cash in Thai money was acquired for bribes.

Many snags appeared. What would happen if the Thai soldiers in Singora, far from welcoming the unexpected arrival of a Japanese invasion force, opened fire on it? Or if the British troops on the border were suspicious of the dawn revellers and their girls, and ignored the shouted compliments? One false step, Tsuji agreed, and Ichikawa's battalion would be trapped. It was clear that the proposer of "such a reckless plan" should take physical responsibility for it. "I resolved to do so," Tsuji wrote. "After persistent requests, I was given permission to take command of the detachment."

EVER WITH AN EYE FOR DETAIL, TSUJI prepared a booklet for the invasion troops. It gave practical hints on fighting in the tropics – "native settlements are nests of fleas, bedbugs and infectious disease ... avoid ordinary houses", "be most meticulous in the burning of anti-mosquito sticks", "be aware that humidity will steam up spectacles" – and in justifying the campaign for the troops it gave full rein to his own loathing for whites.

"Four hundred and fifty million Asians of the Far East live under the domination of less than eight hundred thousand whites ... six million Malayans by a few ten thousand British, thirteen million Filipinos by a few ten thousand Americans," the booklet said. "These white people may expect, from the moment they issue from their mothers' wombs, to be allotted a score or so of natives as their personal slaves. Is this really God's will?"

There were hints of the savageries that were to be done to white prisoners. Japan was involved in a "struggle between races", Tsuji wrote. "In the Japan of recent years ... we have unthinkingly come to accept Europeans as superior ... this is like spitting in our own eyes ... we must at the very least here in Asia beat these Westerners to submission, that they may change their arrogant and ill-mannered attitude ... with no thought of leniency to Europeans unless they be the Germans and Italians ..." In meeting the white enemy, "Regard yourself as an avenger come at last face to face with his father's murderer ... here before you is the man whose death will lighten your heart." Westerners, he assured, were "very superior people, very effeminate and very cowardly ..."

British intelligence did not get wind of the pamphlet, but it did learn of other worrying publications. A printing firm in Saigon was known to have won a contract to produce copies of a Japanese–Malayan pocket dictionary. It also had an order to print 50,000 maps of Malaya, overlaid with Japanese characters. Reports came in of the build-up of troops on Hainan Island, off the coast of northern Vietnam, and of aircraft in southern Vietnam. Japanese warships were observed in the South China Sea.

The last days of peace in British Malaya were sweet for the garrisons and administrators, and for the British businessmen and rubber planters and tin miners. In Singapore, they watched cricket on the Padang, the verdant grass square at the heart of the city. They went to the 1,300-seat cinema in the art deco Cathay Building – *How Green Was My Valley*, filmed in a Hollywood replica of a Welsh mining village, was the great hit of 1941 – and danced in the ballroom at Raffles Hotel, or drank *stengahs*, whiskies and soda, round the mighty pool of the Swimming Club. The soldiers' quarters were light and airy, and the officers' mess in the Tanglin barracks looked out onto a golf course and the orchids and bougainvillea of the Singapore botanic gardens. In Kuala Lumpur, always "KL", planters up from their estates dined in the "Spotted Dog", the Selangor Club, built in black and white "tropical Tudor" style.

On 30 November, a coded message was sent to General

Yamashita aboard his headquarters ship, the 10,000-ton *Ryujo Maru*, at Samah Harbour on Hainan. It read: "X-day 8 December. Proceed with plan." Tokyo had set the date for war with the British and Americans.

Two days later, two great capital ships of the Royal Navy, *Prince of Wales* and *Repulse*, arrived at Singapore with four fast escort destroyers. It was expected that they would savage any Japanese invasion fleet. That notwithstanding, on 3 December Yamashita vowed that he would try to capture Singapore on 11 February, the 2,600th anniversary of the coronation of Jimmu, the fabled first emperor of Japan.

As dawn broke the next morning, Yamashita's fleet left harbour for the open sea. Tsuji watched the 20 ships of the convoy from the bridge of the *Ryujo Maru* as a blood-red sun rose over a sea "shimmering with gold and silver waves".

THEY SAILED ON FOR TWO DAYS WITHOUT incident, on a diet of bean soup, pickled radish and buckets of boiled rice and barley, shared alike by officers and men. On the morning of 7 December, after passing Cape Cambodia, they had news that the RAF flying boat had been shot down. Tsuji thought it a "blood offering to the ground forces", though he feared that other aircraft would follow and the invasion be betrayed. But the weather worsened, with fog and dense cloud. As it grew dark, the fighter escorts turned back for the Phuquok airfields. Several of the pilots failed to find the island and flew on until they ran out of fuel and crashed into the sea.

The transports, rolling badly in the seas, picked up the coast shortly after midnight. The *Ryujo Maru* dropped anchor off Singora at 02:00 on 9 December. An element of farce crept in before they even reached the beaches. Staff Officer Hongo, at 76kg (12 stone) a heavyweight by Japanese standards of the day, fell on top of two other officers as he lowered himself into a landing boat, to gales of laughter from the troops. The boat ran towards the shore at Singora, closing on the street lights in the moments before dawn. As it grounded, Tsuji jumped. The wretched Hongo followed him, landing awkwardly and badly spraining his ankle. He had to be carried up the sandy beach on the shoulders of some soldiers.

As Tsuji advanced rapidly along the shore, he overtook a man pulling a rickshaw. "Hold on," he said, and caught hold of him and scanned his features. Tsuji was relieved that the man looked Japanese enough – identical but for a slightly swarthier colour – for the British to be fooled by Japanese troops in Thai uniforms. "There is still room for the Dream Plan," he told himself.

Tsuji had an interpreter and an orderly with him. The rickshaw driver directed them to the Japanese consulate. Tsuji pounded at the gate whilst a dog growled at him from the compound. At last, a corpulent man appeared, rubbing the sleep from his eyes. It was the consul, Katsuno. "Ah! The Japanese Army!" was all he said. He had the "odour of ripe persimmons" on his breath and he seemed to be suffering from a severe hangover.

Nothing had been prepared. A ludicrous blunder had been made by Major Osone, the officer sent to masquerade as a clerk in the consulate and to make arrangements for the Dream Plan. His letter of instructions had included a secret code for decipher-ing the telegram that would give him the time and date of the landing. Osone had burnt the letter too soon, without memoriz-ing the code, and had been unable to decipher the telegram when it came. He had therefore failed, Tsuji said angrily, to make the "last-minute arrangements with the Thai police and army".

That had to be put right. Four of them, Katsuno, Tsuji, the interpreter and the orderly, squashed themselves like sardines into Katsuno's small car and drove off along the dark road for the main Thai police station. The orderly was carrying a heavy cloth wrapper with 100,000 ticals, the old word for the Thai baht, worth a little over £9,000. It was the bribe money. They drove up to the large iron gate at the entrance to the police station. "Suddenly we heard a gunshot, and our headlight exploded," said Tsuji.

It was the first shot of the ground war in Malaya, and, said Tsuji, the "warning signal for the emancipation of East Asia". Given the war crimes already inflicted on the Chinese, and the further sadisms about to be inflicted in Malaya and the East Indies, "emancipation" is hardly the right word. But the shot was historic, certainly, and it sounded the death-knell for colonialism – as well as, almost, for Tsuji, the consul, the orderly and the interpreter.

Another bullet grazed Tsuji's right arm. The next passed between him and the consul. They abandoned the car and took cover in a drainage ditch. The interpreter kept shouting: "Don't shoot. It is the Japanese army. Ally with us and attack the British army."

In the darkness, the consul in his white suit became the principal target. More people joined in. Thirty or forty Thais were soon firing at random in the dark. "None of us wished for an immediate death," said Tsuji. They retreated along the ditch, dragging the consul with them.

The pack of Thai banknotes was still sitting intact on the back seat of the consul's bullet-ridden car. The orderly felt it to be his responsibility to retrieve it. "Mr Staff Officer," he said to Tsuji, "I will go and get it." Tsuji shouted at him to stop, as he crawled out of the ditch under heavy fire, but he "appeared as deaf as a gecko". He got to the car, grabbed the pack and crawled back to the ditch unscathed.

The foursome fell back 400 metres along the ditch. They came across a 5th Division battalion that had heard the shooting. It was commanded by a major who had graduated from military college with Tsuji ten years before. It was the first time they had met since then. They embraced. Tsuji was "quietly turning over in my mind the problem of the pacification of the Thai army ..."

He thought he had an answer. He assembled the battalion in a column of fours along the road. A large white flag that could be seen in the dark was hoisted at the head of the column. Buglers were also placed in the van. They marched off, white flag high, buglers playing. A machine-gun opened fire on them. They took cover at the side of the road. The Japanese "fighting spirit blazed up in us like fire," Tsuji said. They struck at the Thai rear and found themselves in a violent firefight – "which we wished to avoid" – with Thai military police.

Dawn was swift, and it was soon broad daylight. General Yamashita and the army HQ personnel had now arrived and were massing in coconut trees on the outskirts of the town. Other 5th Division troops were attached to Tsuji's force. They attacked and now overwhelmed the Thai military police. The firing stopped.

Tsuji took stock. Looking offshore, he saw 13 or 14 upturned landing boats, like "puffed-up globe fish which gurgle after being washed up by a big wave". The airstrip had been seized, but the Thai army was shelling it. The Japanese Zero fighters had to try to avoid the shells and deep pools of water from heavy overnight rain as they landed. Several somersaulted. The Thais continued resisting until noon. By then the local villagers, seeing which way the wind was blowing, were welcoming the Japanese with gifts of food.

Tsuji had to bow to reality, though. "It was obvious that the Dream Plan had broken down," he admitted, "and no longer had any prospect of success." He abandoned it. "Casting aside their Thai uniforms", his special troops "changed back into their own Japanese dress."

THIS WAS THE LAST MAJOR SETBACK. From then on, the invaders had luck, and skill and determination, on their side. And the bicycle.

Tsuji was certain that a lightly equipped, lightly supplied invasion would succeed. Japanese soldiers were used to fending for themselves in China. They could live off the locals as they advanced in Malaya. Their basic diet, rice and fish, was found in abundance. Provided the advance troops kept their teeth into the retreating British, not allowing them time to regroup, it would not matter if they were lightly armed. They had no need of massed artillery, because they were dependent on movement in place of traditional artillery barrages.

Speed and mobility were the key. Tsuji had seen that from the Dinah. The main roads led like arrows across the country and down the west coast to Singapore. It was there, dug in across the roads, that they would find the heavily motorized British, Australians and Indians. From the tarmac roads ran side roads into the rubber and oil-palm estates, with networks of dirt roads and paths on the plantations themselves. Mobile Japanese infantry, if held by motorized enemy units on the main axes, could readily outflank them through the estates and take or threaten them in the rear. Mobility meant the bicycle.

The 5th and 18th Divisions had made great use of cavalry and horses in China. Each had several thousand horses. They were used for hauling guns and supplies as well as serving with mounted cavalry and reconnaissance troops. Tsuji had found the climate in Malaya totally unsuitable for horses. So he replaced them with "a few trucks and many bicycles". Each infantry regiment was allotted 50 trucks for heavy machine-guns, regimental guns, heavy ordnance and ammunition. All officers and men, apart from a few on the trucks, used bicycles. Each division had around 6,000 bicycles.

Without bicycles, the invaders would have been so delayed by blown bridges that Tsuji estimated it would have taken a year to cover the 1,100 kilometres to Singapore. "With the infantry on bicycles, there were no traffic jams or delays," he said. "Wherever bridges were destroyed, the infantry continued the advance, wading across the rivers carrying their bikes on their shoulders, or crossing log bridges held on the shoulders of engineers standing in the stream. We could maintain hot pursuit without giving the enemy time to rest or reorganize. Even long-legged Englishmen couldn't escape our troops on bicycles."

The cyclists were often able to steal a march on the British, despite their motorcars and trucks, and seize a bridge in front of them, while Japanese aircraft strafed and bombed them from the air, blocking the road. "Their soldiers had to abandon their cars and trucks and continue the retreat on foot," Tsuji wrote. "They were continually driven off the road into the jungle, where their retreat was cut off and they were forced to surrender."

The biggest problem was the heat, which led to frequent punctures. Tsuji had a bicycle repair team of at least two men attached to every company. Each pair repaired an average of 20 bicycles a day. Sometimes, though, they kept a punctured bicycle going on its rims on the splendid paved roads that Tsuji so much admired. The metal made a low screeching noise that paid an unexpected bonus, as Tsuji observed: "Numbers of bicycles, some with tyres and some without, made a rattling noise like tanks. At night, when such bicycle units advanced, the enemy often retreated hurriedly, saying 'Here come the tanks!' 'It's tanks, tanks!'"

Winston Churchill was so devastated by the campaign that he flailed around for a scapegoat for so great a calamity. He blamed Japanese treachery, through the "secret infiltration of agents" and the setting up of "hidden reserves of bicycles for Japanese cyclists".

This was not so. "The truth is that Japanese bicycles, because of their cheapness, had become one of the principal exports for Japan to southeast Asia," Tsuji retorted. "As a result replacements and spares were easily available everywhere throughout Malaya." There were no prepared bicycle dumps. None were shipped in on the invasion boats. The invasion troops, the veteran Yoshiki Saito recalled, were told that no bicycles were allowed aboard ship because they were so plentiful in Malaya. Once ashore, Saito and his comrades converted themselves into a bicycle squad within a few hours by taking them from a village.

The Japanese looked, some thought, "like badly wrapped parcels" in their ill-fitting brown uniforms, with puttees, strange web-toed rubber boots and *boshis*, caps with a piece of cloth hanging at the back to protect the neck from the sun. They were combat-hardened, though, after years of fighting in China. Their equipment was excellent. The long samurai swords were not show weapons, but razor-sharp and fearsome. The Arisaka rifle was accurate to 1,000 metres. Their Zero fighter, and the Nell and Betty bombers, were superior to the antiquated RAF and RAAF aircraft stationed in Malaya.

The Nells and Bettys, flying from Saigon, attacked Singapore docks at 04:30 on 8 December. The street lights remained blazing throughout the raids but the sirens were silent. At dawn, two Indian divisions crossed the Thai border to meet the Japanese on the road south from Singora. They took heavy casualties and retreated. At dusk, *Prince of Wales* and *Repulse*, together with the escort destroyers, left Singapore to intercept the Japanese landings. The squadron, Z Force, had no air support.

The Japanese had tanks ashore the following day. They helped capture Kota Bahru not long after noon. Yamashita began a powerful drive to seize the important road and rail junction at Jitra. All but one of a squadron of Blenheim bombers was destroyed in a Japanese air raid on Butterworth airstrip as they prepared to take off to bomb Singora. The surviving RAF pilot, Squadron Leader Arthur Scarf, flew on alone, and was mortally wounded attacking Singora.

On 10 December, off Kuantan, Japanese bombers intercepted Force Z as the squadron steamed for the invasion sites. In less then 90 minutes, the two great capital ships were sunk. Churchill was in bed opening his despatch boxes when news came to him.

"I was thankful to be alone. In all the war I never received a more direct shock," he said. "As I turned over and twisted in bed the full horror of the news sunk in upon me."

Acknowledging the superiority of the Japanese aircraft operating in northern Malaya, an order was issued on 11 December that British fighters should only be used in defence of Singapore. The troops in Malaya no longer had any cover by air or by sea. The Japanese could strafe and bomb, and move troops in short hops by sea down the coast, almost at will. On 12 December, Penang was bombed.

The next day, the British northwestern front was in headlong retreat south of Jitra. Japanese aircraft, unopposed, strafed and bombed them as they fled.

No more than 500 Japanese had attacked the Jitra Line in pouring rain, which the British had spent six months building. The 11th Indian Division fled in panic. The bicycle-born attackers captured 50 field guns, 300 trucks and armoured cars, and huge quantities of food, ammunition and fuel. They lost 27 killed and 83 wounded, whilst taking 3,000 prisoners.

Alor Star, the airfield that Tsuji had so admired on his spy mission, was abandoned at breakfast time on 14 December. The Japanese found porridge, still warm, with the polished squadron silver on the table in the officers' mess. Bombs were still stacked neatly and a thousand drums of high-octane aviation fuel were found. By midday, the fuel was powering Japanese aircraft as the bombs were dropped on their previous owners. Yamashita moved his headquarters to Alor Star the next day. He held a dinner in the RAF mess to celebrate the opening of his campaign.

"The Japanese speed of movement, their ability to overcome obstacles," wrote Major General Kirby, "came as a complete surprise." Astonished, the British began slowly to realize that it was the bicycle that gave their pursuers their speed.

BICYCLES HAD BEEN USED BY ARMIES since the first "safety" models, with wheels of the same size, appeared after 1885. The 25th United States Infantry, an all-black infantry regiment with white officers, made epic bicycle journeys of up to a thousand miles in the 1890s. "Buffalo soldiers" stationed in Montana used them to cross roadless terrain at good speeds. Bicycle-mounted scouts and messengers were used in the Boer War, and medical corpsmen adapted them to carry the wounded in the First World War.

Ironically, Churchill himself had grasped the potential of the bicycle back in 1908. "The best of all methods of progression in Central Africa – however astonishing it may seem – is the bicycle," he had written in *My African Journey*. "From my own experience I should suppose that with a bicycle 25 to 30 miles a day could regularly be covered ... Though the tracks were only two feet wide, the bicycle skims along at a fine pace ..."

Experience in China made Tsuji aware of their virtues. They were swift but quiet, giving bicycle troops the ability to surprise and confuse the enemy with sudden and unexpected appearances. They took up very little room on invasion ships, and they needed no trucks once ashore. As beasts of burden, carrying men, or large loads of supplies of up to 180kg, they were superb. They did not need feeding. They used no precious petrol, and there was no need to forage around for hay and grass. They could cross almost any terrain, and, if necessary, they could be hoisted up and carried on the shoulder.

Nottingham- or Birmingham-made bicycles were most in demand, as Japanese bicycles were cheap and badly made. The chrome soon peeled off in the humid heat, and the steel frames rusted quickly. Mustapha Hassan, a Malayan nationalist in the town of Matang, said that anyone who could afford a British-made bicycle had bought one, so clear was their superiority over Japanese machines. The invading infantry thought so too.

When Japanese troops arrived in a town, they were soon seen

beating the few Chinese who refused to part with their posses-
sions. "Bicycles were simply snatched away or exchanged with
Japanese ones," Hassan said. "Japanese soldiers loved bicycles which
were made in England – especially the speedy Raleigh – to chase
after enemies they called *Inggerisu*, Englishmen. No one wanted
their Japanese-made bicycles in exchange, even when given free."

The Japanese looted torches, watches, fountain pens, chickens
and eggs, too, with a "tight smack to the face" of those who
resisted, but the bicycles were favourites. Tsuji himself, though,
preferred a car. "I took possession of a high-class car that the
enemy had abandoned," he purred with pleasure after a battle at
Gemas. "Churchill supplies", as the Japanese called equipment
abandoned by the British that they used, were an important factor
in oiling their advance.

Hassan recorded that only one bicycle in Matang escaped confiscation, despite being brand new. "Many a Japanese soldier
grabbed the new bicycle with a big grin, but when they measured
the distance between the seat and pedals, they gave it back with a
snigger and an '*Arigato*', thank-you," he said. "At 28 inches, it was
too high for the Japanese soldiers, who were by and large very
short."

Waves of cyclists, usually riding in groups of 40 or 50, three
or four abreast, were observed by Frederick Spencer Chapman
"talking and laughing just as if going to a football match".
Chapman, who was to survive as a "stay-behind" guerrilla behind
Japanese lines for three years of astonishing courage and resilience,
described Japanese soldiers "systematically searching the roadside
kampongs, estate buildings and factories for bicycles".

Each bicycle had the soldier's kit of up to 40kg attached to the
saddle. Each man would carry his own rifle or light machine-gun
slung over his shoulder. The soldiers rode for 20 hours a day at
times, with brief stops to eat the balls of rice and fish they carried
with them. The only special provision for cycling was a large

mackintosh cape with a hood. It covered the riders and their kit and allowed them to keep pedalling during tropical downpours. When they went into action, they left their bicycles with a guard. After it was over, he would round up local Malays or Chinese, and have them wheel the machines forward to rejoin them, with frequent blows and shouts of *"Kurrah!"* "Quick! Quick!".

THE CYCLISTS WERE AT PENANG, the island resort on the west coast, on 17 December. It had already been attacked by 85 divebombers. They had bombed and machine-gunned a crowded market. Some thought that the pilots had mistaken handcarts parked with their handles pointing skywards for anti-aircraft guns. Terror bombing was equally likely, though, for the Japanese advance was already marked by atrocities, including the mass murder of wounded prisoners. The hospital was overwhelmed with casualties, 126 of them dying in the first 24 hours. No anaesthetists were available, and amputations were carried out on patients who were conscious. The resident commissioner put the number of dead and wounded at 3,000. Cholera and typhoid were to follow.

Sixty of the 200 duty firemen were killed. As they struggled with the blaze – priority was given to the European quarters – they were convinced that Japanese pilots were targeting them. Japanese broadcasts taunted the British: "You English gentlemen! How do you like our bombing? Isn't it more of a tonic than your whisky soda?"

The European evacuation began on 16 December. They assembled at the famous "E and O", the Eastern and Oriental Hotel, and they crowded down to the docks, guarded by armed volunteers. As the ferries sailed, some feared that the manner of their going, abandoning their Chinese and Malay friends and servants, would neither be forgiven nor forgotten.

By mid-morning on 23 December, the British had withdrawn across the River Perak and had blown the concrete and steel

Iskandar bridge. The vital Slim River bridge fell to the Japanese intact on 7 January. The Argylls fought hard but were badly mauled. Two brigades of the Indian 11th Division were virtually wiped out. More than 3,000 prisoners, mostly Indian, were taken. Another haul of "Churchill supplies" gave the Japanese heavy artillery pieces, anti-aircraft guns, 550 trucks, 50 armoured cars, and large amounts of food, ammunition and medical supplies.

Central Malaya was lost. Kuala Lumpur was abandoned on 11 January. The last bridge was blown at 04:30. Troops of the Japanese 5th Division entered the deserted capital at 08:00.

Where the Allied troops disengaged from the Japanese advance units for long enough to set up ambushes, the cyclists were desperately vulnerable. A company under Captain Jack Duffy of the 2/30th Battalion of the Australian 8th Division set an ambush at the Gemencheh River bridge, a charmingly rustic wooden structure. The Australians had been able to get well clear of the Japanese vanguard, and they deliberately left most of the small bridges and culverts intact as they retreated over them, to lull Japanese suspicions.

The first cyclists passed the position where Duffy was hiding at 16:20 on 14 January. "The blithely chattering Japanese cyclists, riding four or five abreast," the Australian found, "resembled a picnic party rather than part of an advancing army, except that they carried arms." Duffy let 250 or 300 go past him. Then he gave the order to blow the bridge: "Japanese bodies, bicycles, timber, rocks and earth flew far and wide in a huge red flash leaving a gaping space where the bridge had been." Those who had gone past were dealt with by the rest of the battalion further down the road. Duffy had about 400 caught in his ambush area, and his Australians were on a high-banked cutting looking down on them, with Bren guns, Thompson sub-machine-guns, rifles and grenades. In most cases, the victims' weapons were still tied to their cross-bars. The Japanese admitted losing 70 killed and

57 wounded, though the actual figure was probably higher.

It was a victory, and it was followed by proof that the Japanese T-95 tanks were under-armoured. Having repaired the Gemencheh bridge with their usual speed – tanks were crossing it just six hours after it was blown – the Japanese armour caught up with the Australians. The Australian crews manning the two-pounder anti-tank guns found that their armour-piercing shot went straight through the Japanese machines, and switched to high explosive shells, which destroyed them.

The glad tidings of these two engagements mingled with the arrival of reinforcements to lift spirits for a while. The British plan had always been to reinforce from Australia or the Middle East by sea. On 13 January, the 53rd Brigade of Norfolks and Cambridgeshires disembarked at Singapore, part of the 18th East Anglian Division, which, had the Japanese advance not been so swift, might have held them. The ships also carried 51 crated Hurricane fighters, which were expected to end Japanese air superiority.

It was a false dawn. The Japanese continued to outflank and cut off the retreating Allied forces, by bicycle and by sea, using local fishing boats taken with the same insouciance as the bicycles. There were only 24 pilots for the Hurricanes, and they were less experienced than the Zero pilots. The last two brigades of the 18th Division landed in Singapore on 29 January, 96 hours after the final decision had been taken to abandon mainland Malaya.

Two days later, the Japanese were at the causeway.

Singapore was a prize indeed, the pivotal point of British domination in Asia. It was the great harbour on the steamship routes from Europe to the east, on to the north to Hong Kong and Shanghai, and south and east to the riches of the Dutch East Indies. It guarded the approaches to India from the east, and to Australia from the north. Singapore was at the heart of these great sea arteries, and of Royal Navy power in the Pacific. With

Gibraltar, Pearl Harbor and Malta, it was one of the world's four great harbour-fortresses. Its graving dock, the King George VI, was 1,000 feet long, 130 feet wide and 35 feet deep. The floating dock, towed out to Singapore in two pieces, was the same length, but 300 feet wide, and anchored in a depth of 70 feet.

The island had 29 garrison artillery pieces, five colossal 15-inch guns, six 9.2-inch, and eighteen 6-inch guns. All but two of the 15-inch guns were on full mountings, so that they could traverse to fire into Malaya as well as at ships out at sea. These were the world's greatest guns, backed by four airfields on the island. Singapore was impregnable from the sea. Not, though, from across the causeway, where Tsuji needed no field glasses as he ran his lusting eyes over it.

Its fall was a matter of time. The garrison surrendered on Sunday 15 February 1942. It was, Churchill said, "the worst disaster and largest capitulation in British history". Malaya had cost Yamashita 1,803 dead and 3,378 wounded. Singapore cost roughly the same again. British losses were some 7,500 killed, 10,000 wounded and 120,000 taken prisoner. Tsuji entered the city the next day. He had his camera with him, and the defeated troops asked him to take their photograph, in the hope that the international press would publish it, and their wives and mothers could see they were still alive.

TSUJI SUMMED UP THE CAMPAIGN: "Thanks to Britain's expensive money spent on the excellent paved roads, and to the cheap Japanese bicycles, the assault on Malaya was easy."

There were other factors, of course: poor generalship, the inexperience of raw troops, lack of armour and modern aircraft. But, as to the central issue, Tsuji was undoubtedly correct. The bicycle enabled the Japanese to keep the British off balance, with no chance to regroup and recover poise and nerve. It allowed the invaders to outflank the enemy constantly, so that the defenders' momentum was always back, towards Singapore, and their fear was always to be cut off.

In the short term, the tactic was a triumph. The long term was different. Tsuji was right that the Malayan campaign permanently undermined colonialism in south Asia. Nonetheless, on 5 September 1945, HMS *Kedah* led the Royal Navy back into Singapore. The British were back – if not with their pre-war self-confidence and status, lost irrecoverably. And that, too, was partly Tsuji's doing.

Like Sturmpionier Rubarth on the Meuse in 1940, Tsuji's variant of bicycle-borne Blitzkrieg made it appear that his side had found a new way of making war on the cheap. The Germans had told Yamashita a year before that it would take five divisions 18 months to conquer Singapore. In the end, the Japanese had done it in two months with three divisions. This stunning victory by troops who travelled light and lived off the land and "Churchill supplies" persuaded the Japanese to send further grossly under-supplied armies on other distant campaigns. After initial successes against ill-prepared enemies, the Japanese were often to be over-whelmed by starvation and the diseases stemming from malnutrition.

Less than a year after the fall of Singapore, more than 100,000 Japanese were dead in New Guinea, a place so devoid of food that they called it the "green desert". "There is nothing to eat. Everyone is in a weak and staggering state," a Japanese medical officer wrote a few days after arriving in New Guinea in November 1942. "Without food, having become thin and emaciated, the appearance of our fellow soldiers does not bear reflection. How could people at home understand this state of affairs? It must be seen to be believed." Tsuji himself was to witness the starvation of Japanese troops on Guadalcanal.

The Americans and Australians who mopped up the last Japanese resistance on the islands of the Pacific found many of the survivors to be "in the last stages of starvation", with evidence that some of them were practising cannibalism. Almost as many Japanese died of starvation as were killed by the Americans during the liberation of the Philippines in 1945.

Tsuji himself appears to have been a cannibal, dining on the livers of shot-down Allied pilots, though his taste for human flesh derived more from sadistic lunacy than hunger. In his booklet for troops, he had advised them to swallow the raw liver of any snake they killed: "There is no better medicine for strengthening the body." He was thought to have been responsible for atrocities against Chinese civilians in Singapore, and was also suspected of complicity in the murder of prisoners in the Philippines and elsewhere. He escaped execution after the war, and entered politics. Many years later, in April 1961, Masanobu Tsuji disappeared in Vietnam, in clouded circumstances.

10 · THE LOOSE CANNON OF
YOM KIPPUR

The hitchhiker who took on a division

The courage of one man can act as a multiplier of
strength in circumstances as desperate as those seen here,
for : "Courage is ... a feeling, like fear. The latter looks
to the physical preservation, courage to the moral
preservation. Courage is ... no mere counterpoise to
danger in order to neutralize the latter in its effects, but a
peculiar power in itself ..." (BOOK II, CHAPTER II).

THE GOLAN HEIGHTS, 6–7 OCTOBER 1973

THE ISRAELIS MANNING THE observation post high on the slopes of
Mount Hermon saw Syrian gunners start to remove the camouflage nets from their batteries along the Purple Line at 13:45. This
was the ceasefire line between Syria and Israel reached at the end
of the Six-Day War in 1967. It ran across the Golan Heights, a
high plateau of scattered basalt rocks, some the size of grey and
dusty oranges, others colossal boulders, and hills and *tels*, the
weathered stumps of long-extinct volcanoes, with tangles of
scrubby trees and bushes, and the ruins of villages abandoned
after the war.

A few memories of the old life survived, a minaret at Khusniye, slender, pocked with bullet marks, and Druze shepherds with their hardy flocks. But Kuneitra, the main town, was ghostly, its crumbling buildings festooned with wire by the Israeli garrison, and its streets cut by tank traps.

The array of aerials and dishes on the top of the Hermon observation post, and the sophisticated electronics protected behind steel shutters below, revealed the key importance of the Golan to the Israeli military. The plateau reached Lebanon and Jordan at its northern and southern extremities, but it marked the whole of Israel's border with Syria. It was never more than 24 kilometres from the Purple Line to the escarpment at the western edge of the plateau, and in places less than 16.

This thin strip of barren terrain was all the Syrians had to traverse before they reached the point where the land fell steeply from the Golan down to the River Jordan and the Sea of Galilee. Once over the Jordan bridges, no natural obstacles stood between an invader and the Israeli heartlands.

At 13:58 the observers saw five Syrian MiG fighters come in well below them – their post on the mountain was at an altitude of just over 2,000 metres – and make strafing runs with their cannon. A few moments later, incoming shells began bursting all along the Purple Line. The barrage was particularly intense at Kuneitra and Rafid, in the centre and south of the Golan. The Syrians had between 50 and 80 guns to the kilometre here. The Syrian gunners fired shells ranging in size from 85mm to 203mm onto the Israeli tank parks, camps, command posts and bunkers.

The barrage lifted after 55 minutes. By now, Syrian paratroops had landed on Mount Hermon and were attacking the 50-odd men in the Israeli observation post. Slap in the middle of the ceasefire strip just north of Kuneitra, in the United Nations observation post "Winter", an Australian observer watched in astonishment as 300 Syrian tanks rolled towards him. They were driving four abreast, in two columns each side of the road, and their turrets were open with the commanders standing proudly upright. "It wasn't like an attack," he said. "It was like a parade-ground demonstration."

As it approached his bunker, the column divided, and as it flowed past him, one column forked north of Kuneitra, and the other south. At least 700 Syrian tanks were in that first wave. Three hundred of them clattered past "Winter". Fifteen kilometres or so to the south, 400 tanks moved up the long and exposed road from Sheikh Miskin to Rafid. The Syrians had three infantry divisions in the line, totalling 40,000 men, with an independent armoured brigade attached to each of them. They had two armoured divisions in reserve.

Facing them were 200 Israeli infantrymen, hunkered down in ten strongpoints along the 65-kilometre front, and 177 Israeli tanks in two armoured brigades, one of them understrength. The northern sector, with a rocky hill line giving some natural protection, was held by the 7th Armoured Brigade. The southern sector, more open and difficult to defend, and facing Rashid, was held by the Barak Armoured Brigade. One of its commanders looked out from his turret at the approaching swarm, and said, "I never knew there were so many tanks in all the world."

It was now 14:50, on Saturday 6 October 1973. This was the Day of Atonement, Yom Kippur, the holiest of days in the Jewish calendar, chosen by the Arabs to launch their attack because the whole of Israel comes to a standstill. Sirens and radio broadcasts intruded into devotions and holidaymaking. They alerted Zvika Greengold, a 21-year-old tank lieutenant who was at home in Lohamei Haghetaot, a kibbutz in western Galilee. He was on leave, before starting a company commander's course. He was not currently attached to a unit, but he thought he might be able to help if he could get himself to Nafakh. Nafakh was little more than an underground command post in a compound with sandbagged bunkers. But it was the headquarters of the two defending Israeli armoured brigades, and it controlled the main route from the Golan into Israel.

Greengold flung on his uniform, and began hitchhiking for Nafakh.

HAMMER BLOWS WERE FALLING FAR to the south, too, where the Israelis had faced Egyptian armies across the Suez Canal since the Six-Day War. A thousand guns hidden by the sand dunes behind the west bank of the canal had opened a barrage in concert with the Syrians on the Golan. As it lifted, men started crossing the canal and clambering up the eastern bank with rope and bamboo ladders.

The violence of these attacks was infinitely magnified by surprise and shock. No one had expected them. Israel had been caught without its citizen army. Early warning was a necessity for the Israel Defence Forces, the IDF. It maintained small regular forces, bringing these up to full strength by mobilizing well-trained reservists from their civilian jobs. A sophisticated and well-oiled procedure existed for this, with codewords broadcast on radio programmes, buses driving pre-planned routes to collect and deliver reservists to their units, and tanks kept pre-fuelled and pre-armed.

Reservists did not appear instantaneously at the front, armed, equipped and ready to go. It took time, 24 hours at least, with most planning predicated on intelligence providing 48 hours warning of an attack.

On the Golan, particularly, that was vital. On the front with Egypt, *in extremis*, there was the huge and unpopulated space of the Sinai to trade for time. In the north, only a few kilometres of volcanic plateau separated the Syrians from the River Jordan.

The Arabs knew enough about Israeli planning to be able to stymie it. There had been some signs in May 1973 that an Egyptian

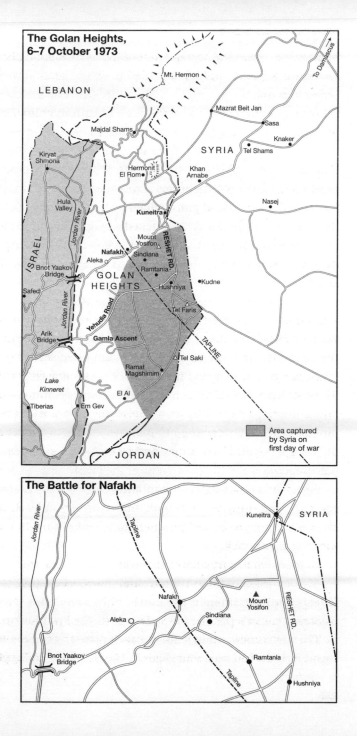

The Golan Heights, 6–7 October 1973

LEBANON

To Damascus →

Mt. Hermon

Mazrat Beit Jan

Majdal Shams

Sasa

Knaker

Kiryat Shmona

SYRIA

Tel Shams

Hermonit
El Rom

Khan Arnabe

Hula Valley

Nasej

Jordan River

Kuneitra

ISRAEL

Mount Yosifon

Nafakh

RESHET RD.

Aleka

Sindiana

Bnot Yaakov Bridge

Ramtania

GOLAN HEIGHTS

Kudne

Safed

Hushniya

Jordan River

Tel Faris

Yehudia Road

TAPLINE

Arik Bridge

Gamla Ascent

Tel Saki

Ramat Magshimim

Lake Kinneret

El Al

Tiberias

Em Gev

Area captured by Syria on first day of war

JORDAN

The Battle for Nafakh

Jordan River

Tapline

Kuneitra

SYRIA

Nafakh

Mount Yosifon

RESHET RD.

Aleka

Sindiana

Ramtania

Bnot Yaakov Bridge

Tapline

Hushniya

attack was imminent. Israeli intelligence dismissed this as brinkmanship, but a partial mobilization was ordered, at considerable cost and disruption to civilian life. Other, later omens – notably a meeting of the leaders of the front-line states, Egypt, Syria and Jordan, in Cairo on 12 September – were ignored.

The Israeli Air Force shot down 12 Syrian aircraft the following day, for the loss of a single IAF Mirage. The Syrians had scrambled MiG-21s after IAF Phantoms and Mirage IIIs penetrated their airspace to photograph arms deliveries by Soviet ships. It was known that a big arms build-up was taking place, though the Israelis were not aware of the numbers of SA-6 SAMs (surface-to-air missiles) that Moscow was providing to Damascus, or how effective they were. The Syrians had wanted to fire their new SAMs during the 13 September slaughter. The Soviet advisers retained control of the launchers, and refused to fire them. The secret of the SAMs was maintained, and the Syrian build-up on the Golan was concealed beneath a smokescreen of angry rhetoric.

An annual exercise was held by the Egyptians each autumn. This hid their movements, whilst their diplomats continued talks with the United Nations and the Americans on peace proposals, and the Cairo and Damascus press invented a rift between Sadat and Assad, their respective presidents. On 28 September, Syrian-paid Saiqua gunmen hijacked a train at the Czech-Austrian border, taking Jewish hostages. Israeli attention focused on Austria. Golda Meir, the premier, flew to Vienna, not returning to Israel until late on 3 October. The incident provided further cover for Arab military activity, too, for Damascus might simply be taking precautions against Israeli retaliation.

The Egyptian planners misled their own side as well as the enemy. The highest-ranking prisoner to be taken during the war, a colonel, told his IAF interrogators that the first he knew of the assault was shortly after 13:30 on the day itself, when his commanding officer, a lieutenant general, rose from his prayers to say that the war would begin in a few minutes. Syrian company commanders were given an hour's advance warning.

It was not until 2 October that S-hour – *sifr* is the Arabic for zero – was set for 14:00 hours on 6 October. The Syrians had wanted to start in the early morning, so that they could attack out of the rising sun, with the whole day to seize the Golan. The Egyptians wanted the late afternoon, so that they would have the moonlit darkness for getting their men and armour across the canal. The compromise, as things evolved, was one of the few bits of luck that came Israel's way on the first day. It robbed the Syrian tanks of almost seven hours of daylight.

Tell-tales of the coming attack were there, though, and Israeli intelligence and the general staff were to have a rough ride when it was over. Photographs taken above the Golan on 20 September had shown three Syrian infantry divisions and attached tank brigades in the front line. More mechanized units and infantry were in a second line. IDF intelligence estimated that the Syrians had 670 tanks and 100 artillery batteries on the Golan. Given the thin Israeli forces on the plateau, these numbers were highly alarming.

The more so, as Yitzhak Hofi, the major general commanding in the north, pointed out, there was no space-for-time option on the Golan. By 2 October, intelligence was adding 130 tanks and 20 batteries to its estimates. Three days later, it put Syrian strength at 900 tanks and 140 batteries. That was frightening even for the ultra-cool defence minister, General Moshe Dayan. Leave was cancelled on the Golan. An emergency stand-to was ordered, and the remainder of the 7th Armoured Brigade, which had been stationed at Beersheba in southern Israel, was ordered to move to the Golan to act as a reserve at Nafakh.

On the eve of Yom Kippur, the IDF was put on its highest state of alert, Gimel C. But that was only the small standing army. The reserves were looking forward to spending Yom Kippur, the holiest day of the year, in the bosoms of their family, at their devotions, or on the beach with the sea still warm enough to swim in.

AS THEY SWEPT OVER THE CEASEFIRE line on 6 October, the Syrian tanks, self-propelled guns and armoured personnel carriers carrying infantry equipped with anti-tank Sagger missiles and RPG-7s simply ignored the Israeli infantry in their bunkers.

An anti-tank ditch, 5 metres wide, 3 metres deep, with the spoil heaped into a bank of almost 2 metres, was the first obstacle. There were minefields on both sides of the ditch, in belts 3 metres wide, with a mine every metre. The Syrians had MT-55 bridge-laying tanks and PT-55 mine rollers to deal with these. The Israelis excelled at long-range gunnery, and their artillerymen began to pick off the Syrian mine-clearers at ranges of 2,000 metres. As one bridge-layer went up in flames, though, another took its place.

The sheer scale of the armour loosed on the Golan swamped even the most recent intelligence estimates. Each of the three attacking infantry divisions had an integrated armoured brigade of 180 T-54s and T-55s. They were backed by two armoured divisions, each armed with 230 of the most modern T-62s that the Russians had then allowed to be exported, equipped with the powerful 115mm main gun. Add in a further 400 tanks in independent brigades, and the Syrians had 1,400 tanks available. Against that, the Israelis had 177 on the Golan.

The Israelis' exceptional tank handling skills and their air power gave them confidence in coping with an 8:1 ratio, at least in sectors where this was not exceeded. At the breakthrough points, though, the Syrian advantage was often 15:1. Or worse. No armour on earth could survive such odds – unless it had absolute air superiority on its side.

That was the next great shock. In the 1967 war, the IAF had played havoc with enemy armour. Only three weeks before, it had shot down a dozen Syrian MiGs. The IAF had electronic counter-measures that had dealt easily with the radar-guided SA-2 and SA-3 missiles, familiar to the Americans from Vietnam. Now, though, the Syrians were able to use their new SA-6 missiles, effective against aircraft flying at medium and high altitude. The earlier missiles were command-guided throughout their flight. The SA-6 homed in on heat reflected from the target aircraft, and the radar that guided it in the early stage of its flight operated over a much wider bandwidth, using separate frequencies during search, acquisition, tracking and guidance. The high-heat-intensity flares that American pilots had dropped as decoys on operations in Vietnam were ineffective against the SA-6s. The Soviets had come up with a counter-countermeasure.

Israeli fighter-bombers tried to avoid the SA-6s with a low-level, high-speed approach over Jordan, popping up over the Golan plateau to attack the Syrian tanks from the flank before turning away west of Mount Hermon. But this put them within range of the equally deadly Soviet ZSU-23 radar-controlled anti-aircraft guns.

It took three days of intense research, in Israel and the United States, to evolve techniques to counter the missiles. IAF warning radars were modified to provide a squeal in the pilot's earphone when an SA-6 launch threatened him. A violent evasive manoeuvre, turning the side of the aircraft towards the incoming missile, sharpening its turning angle, could cause the SAM to lose its lock. The "split-S" was used by pairs of aircraft, the lead plane diving sharply into and across the missile's path, whilst the other dived across the vapour trail.

Before then, Israeli aircraft were vulnerable as never before. At one stage, they were losing three in every five aircraft they sent to the Golan. The tanks had lost their air cover. They had to live off their wits.

The tanks based at Nafakh were mainly British-designed Centurions, one of the best tanks of all time. It had an all-welded steel hull and a cast turret, and its armour was excellent. Averaged out, every Israeli tank on the Golan was hit one and a half times. Though 250 were knocked out, all but a 100 returned to combat after being patched up. The Centurion had a four-man crew: driver, gunner, radio operator and commander. It fired APDS (armour-piercing discarding sabot), a shell with a hard, high-density core, in a soft, low-density jacket. The jacket fell away after leaving the barrel, leaving the smaller projectile able to move at super-velocity. It was the world's first main battle tank to have a gun that was stabilized in both elevation and azimuth. The fuel tank was well protected. The Centurion Sho'ts were British Mark IIIs and Mark Vs re-gunned with 105mm guns. The Sho't Kal was also re-engined with a V12 diesel engine.

The Syrian T-54 and T-55 had 100mm rifled guns. They had a low silhouette and exceptional long-range endurance, but the external fuel tanks were very vulnerable, and the armour protection was poor. The gunner had only a limited ability to depress the main gun, which hindered him in firing in defilade from high ground, forcing the tank to expose itself to engage targets. The turret, with a distinctive half-egg shape, had good ballistic qualities, but it was cramped and tiring for the crew, leading to a low rate of fire. The T-62 was more formidable. It had the world's first smoothbore tank gun, giving greater velocity than Western guns.

The Centurion was slightly higher than the Syrians' Soviet tanks, at 2.94 metres to 2.32 metres. But this was an advantage in the rolling terrain of the Golan, where the Israeli tanks were able to take up much safer firing positions than the enemy. This was because Centurions were able to position themselves hull down (i.e. with the hull concealed) on rear-facing slopes with only the turret and gun projecting above the hilltop or rise. The Soviet-built tanks could not depress their guns enough to do this. The whole hull was visible when they fired.

The Syrians, however, had another surprise – as unpleasant

for Israeli tank crews as the SA-6 had proved for the fighter-bomber pilots. The Sagger was a wire-guided anti-tank missile with a shaped-charge warhead. It was carried in a fibreglass "suitcase", and launched from a rail attached to the lid of the case. As the wire unreeled behind the missile, it was guided by a control box with a sight and a control stick. It could penetrate over 400mm of armour, though it could not engage targets at less than 500 metres or more than 3,000 metres. As it flew it gave off a cloud of grey smoke and a loud roar, but was slow, taking 25 seconds to maximum range, a long and dangerous wait for the operator, who had to track both the missile and the target simultaneously. Saggers had three-man teams, the gunner carrying the suitcase with the control box, and the assistant gunners carrying a missile each. One of them was also an RPG-7 gunner. The Syrians had hundreds of these general-purpose grenade launchers.

ZVIKA GREENGOLD GOT TO NAFAKH in the late afternoon of 6 October, a "cheeky-looking young boy" with blond hair and freckles. There was no reserve tank for him to take, but three Centurions damaged in the fighting were brought in for repair. The Barak Brigade was already in critical difficulty in the line south of Nafakh. The strategists had expected the enemy to concentrate his strength to break through the "Kuneitra Gap", a valley that led through the hills north of Kuneitra. Tank ramps had been built on the hills overlooking the valley, from which the Centurions showed only their turrets and guns as they fired on the fully exposed Syrian armour below them. The 7th Armoured Brigade tanks were in these strong defensive positions in the northern part of the line. They were hard-pressed but holding.

The Syrian main effort did not comply with the predictions. Instead, it was developing towards and to the south of Nafakh, where the Barak's commander, Colonel Yitzhak Ben-Shoham, had just two tank battalions, with 77 machines. One thrust was beginning to cut the Golan in two down the main road from Kuneitra to Nafakh. This road led on to the Bnet Yakov bridge over the Jordan. The tanks of the Syrian 7th Division charging in from Rafid were dividing. Some headed for Nafakh along the route of the Tapline, an oil pipeline. Others were threatening to break through to the Arik bridge at the point where the Jordan reaches the Sea of Galilee, and others to El Al on the southerly road at the tip of the Sea of Galilee.

A dust cloud marked the Syrian advance. A Barak tank crew saw three tanks emerge from it. "All three were hit by our first shells," the commander said. "I aimed at a fourth tank that appeared, and after the first shot saw its turret flying into the air. We thought it was the end of the battle. But it was just the beginning. Out of the curtain of dust emerged dozens more tanks, tank-bulldozers and armoured personnel carriers. We divided the attackers among us and picked them off one after another ... but before we could catch our breath, another wave moved towards us."

The lead Syrian tanks were caught in intense fire. In one stretch, 13 were destroyed, in a parade-ground straight line, their guns all pointing forward, knocked out without firing a shot. The Syrians handled their tanks erratically. At times, they stopped for no apparent reason. Their gunnery was poor. They made little or no use of manoeuvre. They had none of the sense of positional advantage so precious to the Israelis. But there were many of them, and they did not yet hesitate to engage in combat with the Centurions, even when these were hull down and destruction was the only likely outcome.

And numbers told. Once through the defences, they were able to fan out into line abreast, forcing the Israelis to withdraw or be outflanked. No longer hull down in prepared positions, and now short of ammunition, Israeli losses began to escalate as they were caught up in a fighting retreat. One company was reduced to a platoon of three tanks. The company commander was dead, his second-in-command was wounded, and the survivors were collecting ammunition from destroyed machines.

The shot-up tanks removed to Nafakh were evidence that the Barak Brigade was being overwhelmed. Greengold helped with the removal of the dead crewmen and the bloodstains. Tank commanders preferred to fight with their heads outside the turret, for better vision, and they were consequently decapitated in enough numbers for orders to be given that they carry dog tags round their ankles to make identification easier. Any crew whose commander's headless body had collapsed into the hull were deeply traumatized, of course, and might be withdrawn from combat. The tank itself, however, remained operational once the blood had been washed with diesel fuel, which did away with the smell.

The damaged tanks were operational again by 21:00. Lieutenant Colonel Yisraeli, the Barak's second-in-command, told Greengold to take two of them. "You'll be known as Zvika Force," he said. "Get moving along the Tapline." This was a narrow asphalt road inside a high chain-link fence that had been built to secure the oil pipeline buried alongside it against sabotage attempts. The pipeline ran for 1,900 kilometres from Saudi Arabia to Lebanon, running south–north through the Golan across the axis of the Syrian advance. A report that "Zvika Force" was going into action was heard across the southern Golan tank force. "It was very encouraging," a crewman said. "A sign that reinforcements had arrived. We thought, here comes Zvika Force to our rescue." He had no idea that it comprised the newly arrived hitchhiker and two hastily repaired tanks.

Greengold himself did not yet realize how dangerous things were. "The situation wasn't clear," he said. "We thought our tanks had blocked the Syrians, that overnight they would mop up the area." From what he heard over the brigade radio, and from his own assessment, the task did not seem too difficult.

It was dark, but he had been on exercises on the Tapline and he knew the terrain, and there was moonlight. The road ran straight but it had frequent dips and rises that a tank commander could use for cover, and that were particularly suited for Centurions. He ran into a convoy led by a jeep after about 5 kilometres. The officer in the jeep said that he had seen many Syrian tanks at the Hushniya crossroads further on. There were no IDF tanks: anything out there was hostile.

A little further on, he saw the outline of a tank as he headed a rise. "I fired and he burst into flames," he said. "There was a terrific flash so I backed away fast. Then I found the radio wasn't working. I moved to the other tank and changed places with the commander." He found three Syrian tanks on a slope and destroyed them.

Taking up a new position, hull down, he saw a swarm of "cat's eyes", the small running lights the Syrians put on their tanks. A column of about 30 tanks and trucks was advancing along the road. He let the lead tank come within 20 metres before destroying it. He stalked the others for some time, using the terrain to fire and move back into cover, with the added advantage of knowing that any tank he saw was hostile, whereas the Syrians could not be sure who he was in the brief moments he exposed the Centurion.

He was alone, facing a Syrian *Schwerpunkt* (focal point of attack), with enemy tanks to the front and right. He fired at them, destroying a number, moving backwards all the time. "They began a search with lights," he said. "I destroyed a few more." He kept to rear slopes where possible, with only gun and turret visible, changing position constantly through the chain fence, dragging a long length of it behind him. He did not remember how many tanks he hit before the Syrians disappeared, perhaps convinced by his movement that they were fighting a larger force. His kills reached double figures in his first hour of combat.

A terrible picture emerged as he listened to the radio net in the lulls. It was filling with desperate reports, of terrifying numbers of Syrian tanks, of lack of fuel and ammunition. Repeated pleas for reinforcements were turned down. There were no reserves. It dawned on him that his was the only tank between the Syrians and Nafakh. "A feeling of helplessness overtook everyone, including the commander, because he had no reserve forces," Greengold said.

Colonel Ben-Shoham contacted him, assuming that Zvika Force was at least of company strength. "He asked over the radio how many tanks I had left," Greengold said. He was aware that the Syrians would be scanning the radio frequencies, and that it was dangerous to admit that he was alone. He replied: "My situation isn't good and I can't tell you how many."

To his intense relief, Greengold was told at 22:10 that ten tanks from a "rapid reaction" reserve battalion under Lieutenant Colonel Uzi Mor were coming along the Tapline road to join him. They were the first reservists to reach the Golan. Mor spoke with Greengold, and they moved off, Greengold moving parallel to the column of tanks on the asphalt. As they went down a deep dip in the road, the first eight tanks were ambushed by waiting Syrian tanks and infantry with RPGs. Mor's tank was hit and he was thrown out of it, badly wounded, losing his left arm and his sight. His crew managed to carry him back up the slope. Other men who jumped out of their burning tanks were taken prisoner by the enemy infantry.

Greengold's tank was hit. His gunner's clothing caught fire, and the two of them got jammed in the turret as the gunner tried to scramble out. Greengold ducked back into the hull to let him go. There was an explosion in the tank. Greengold was wounded in the face, and his uniform caught fire. He jumped out and rolled in the roadside ditch to put out the flames. He thought the tank was about to explode, and he forced his way over the chain-link fence and hid among the boulders with his gunner and loader. The driver had been killed.

They went back up the hill, yelling: "Don't shoot. We're Israelis, we're Jews, don't shoot!" Other wounded men and the dead were put on two of the three of Mor's tanks that had not been hit. Greengold climbed on the rear deck of the third tank. The cool night air revived him. He began to feel the pain from his wounds, but he also knew that he could and should keep fighting. He signalled to the tank commander to take off his headphones. "My name is Zvika," he said. "I've been fighting here all night. I know the area. Let me take your tank." The other man was a reservist. He looked at Greengold, bloodied and burnt, and gave him his helmet and got down from the tank.

Greengold ducked into the hull and introduced himself to the crew: "I'm Zvika. I've been fighting here since the beginning of the night. I'm your commander now." The two other tanks left with the casualties. Greengold was alone on the Tapline once more. He announced himself as "Zvika Force" over the radio to Ben-Shoham. The colonel wanted to know how many tanks he had between the Syrians and Nafakh. Greengold again declined to give any details. But he did say, "We need a general here." It was his way of indicating the scale of the catastrophe he was facing. Ben-Shoham had an inkling of what he meant, and advised him to get into a safe position and only fire if he saw tanks moving up towards Nafakh. He was all there was to stop the 51st Syrian Armoured Brigade.

IT WAS 02:00 ON SUNDAY 7 OCTOBER. As he waited for reinforcements, Greengold thought of his parents. His kibbutz was named after and founded by Ghetto Fighters from the Second World War. His parents were among these Holocaust survivors, and he felt that he now stood between his people and oblivion, as they had.

It was a powerful emotion: with their backs to Galilee, and not far beyond that, the sea, Israeli motivation in the desperate hours in the southern Golan had formidable force. The Syrian inroads were so great, and the Israelis stretched so thin, that the senior officers had effectively lost control of the battle. They did not know where the enemy was. They did not even know what "Zvika Force" was.

A few tanks joined together in a small battle group – Zvika Force was a one-man battle group – and fought as best they could. "You have a choice – to succumb to shock or to become a tiger," a platoon leader was quoted in Abraham Rabinovich's classic account, *The Yom Kippur War*. "It became clear in the first hour that the battle had been left to the company and platoon commanders and individual tank commanders. The adrenalin rush was tremendous. Orders from some officer in the rear didn't matter much. We were alone and we made the decisions." It is a ghastly irony, but perhaps the last tank crews to have shown such flair and flexibility of thought in desperate and outnumbered defence had been the Panzer crews, against T-34s rather than T-54s and T-62s, on the Eastern Front in 1944 and 1945.

Against all tactical sense, Syrian armour halted for long periods in the early hours of 7 October. The most likely explanation lay in the compromise start time agreed with the Egyptians of 14:00. The Syrians had wanted to attack at dawn, and, to the great good fortune of their enemy, the change seems to have disrupted them. Even though individual Israeli crews were clearly superior, despite lacking the enemy's night-vision equipment, the Syrians had broken through in the southern Golan in such numbers that the Arik bridge over the Jordan was at their mercy. They had only to keep rolling. They did not. They waited for sunrise, a pause made more remarkable since captured maps and interrogations of prisoners confirmed that the Syrian planners (and their Soviet advisers) were wholly aware of the need to clear the Golan before Israeli reserves had a chance to appear in numbers. Greengold had some quiet moments before 05:00.

It was still dark when Ben-Shoham sent his deputy, Lieutenant Colonel David Yisraeli, from Nafakh to command the reservist-manned tanks that had joined Greengold. The group was still called "Zvika Force" on the radio net. As it grew light, Yisraeli led them forward. They saw tanks coming towards them. The Syrians had begun moving again, towards Nafakh. Ben-Shoham himself arrived. His brigade had virtually ceased to exist; the only way he would count now was as a front-line fighter.

The Syrians were forced back nearly two kilometres, the Israeli tanks taking turns to refuel and rearm. Greengold's crew, one of them still dressed in civvies, saw him for the first time in daylight when they dismounted. His face and his blond hair were red and black with soot and blood, his uniform ripped and burnt. He was exhausted, and had come close to fainting during the night. He had not eaten. The crew would not let him help them load the shells. One of them gave him an apple.

At 07:00, four Skyhawks came in low over the southern Golan from the southwest. The ground forces looked up with horror as each of the four exploded in the air. Another four were circling the Sea of Galilee, waiting to follow. The flight leader told them to stay low to avoid the SAMs, and to "hit anything you see". The other pilots realized that meant there were no more friendlies there. As they swept in over Ramat Magshimim, they saw large numbers of tanks parked in formation. Two of the Skyhawks were hit and exploded in mid-air. A shoulder-launched Strela missile exploded near the tail of the third aircraft, setting off engine-fire alerts on the control panel, though the pilot was able to get back to the Ramat David air base. Eight Skyhawks, six destroyed, one damaged. It was as desperate in the air as on the ground.

As fresh Syrian tanks massed towards Nafakh, Ben-Shoham, Yisraeli and Greengold moved cross-country to intercept, leaving the rest of Zvika Force on the Tapline. Yisraeli's tank ran out of shells, and attacked firing its machine-gun, but was hit and Yisraeli was killed. Greengold lost sight of Ben-Shoham in the terrain, though he heard him call for support: "I'm in the lead alone. Close up on my right and left."

A kilometre or two from Nafakh, Greengold came on Ben-Shoham's tank lying on its side. The colonel had been exposed in the turret of his tank when it passed a knocked-out Syrian tank. A Syrian crewman opened fire with the machine-gun and killed him. Ben-Shoham's driver, traumatized, had lost control of the tank and it had rolled off the road.

Greengold fired on Syrian tanks outside the perimeter of Nafakh camp and drove into the compound. He yelled at the command bunker that it was safe to come out. Headquarters staff emerged and jumped into trucks and half-tracks. The divisional commander, Major General Rafael Eitan, drove off in a jeep to set up a new command post in an open field a few kilometres to the north.

With Ben-Shoham dead, tank commanders began to radio Greengold for orders. He passed them on to the brigade intelligence officer, Major Zurich, who was at Camp Aleka, a few kilometres further down the road from Kuneitra, towards the Bnot Yakov bridge over the Jordan. As he set off for Aleka himself, Greengold heard gasps and panting from the driver, a reservist torn from home and finally overcome by the stress of Greengold's frantic war-making. The driver climbed out of the tank, silent, and sat down with the wounded in a half-track. Greengold radioed Zurich and had him send up a volunteer driver.

The replacement driver was a youngster whose driving skill was in inverse proportion to his enthusiasm. The tank lurched away from Nafakh, past burning tanks and wounded men shuffling to the rear, until it stopped at a roadblock outside Aleka. Zurich was waiting there, and Greengold collapsed into his arms as he stumbled down from the tank. "I can't any more," he said. Ninety percent of the Barak Brigade's officers were dead or wounded. Major Zurich was the last remaining brigade officer with field rank.

They put Greengold in a jeep and drove him to hospital.

GREENGOLD THOUGHT ALL WAS LOST. "I got out of the tank feeling that the Israeli army had reached the end of its road and the Golan wouldn't stand fast. I felt defeated and broken ... the helplessness of inadequate force and inability to help our weak points," he said. "One thing that stayed with me after this war was the feeling of being alone – not in a room, but in a war – with one tank."

In hospital, lapsing in and out of consciousness, he kept muttering, "What a mess, what a mess." When he finally awoke, he was astonished to see his girlfriend at his bedside. She was from a kibbutz in the Jordan valley. He was sure that the Syrians would have come down from the Golan and seized the valley by now. "How did you get here?" he asked.

In fact, the tide had begun to turn at about the time he collapsed. At 06:00 on Sunday morning, the Israelis had picked up a radio transmission from the commander of a Syrian unit. "I see the whole of Galilee in front of me. Request permission to proceed." The reply was terse: "Negative." By the early afternoon, a Syrian brigade was on the Yehudia road less than ten kilometres from the Sea of Galilee. Another was 1,200 metres from El Al.

That was the high water mark of the Syrian advance. By the late evening on Sunday, the Israelis estimated that they had destroyed 400 Syrian tanks. The first reservists of the 679th Armoured Brigade had arrived. Replacement crews were being flown in by helicopters. They were organized into three-tank platoons, integrated into the communications net, and sent down the Tapline. By nightfall, the 679th had cleared the area around Nafakh and blunted another thrust by the Syrian 7th Division.

The Israelis started pushing the Syrians back on Monday. By Wednesday 10 October they had forced them back over the Purple Line. Before they stopped, on 14 October, the Israelis had driven into Syria and were able to shell the outskirts of Damascus. In the south, in another extraordinary reversal of fortune, the Israelis had crossed the Suez Canal, cut the last road linking Cairo and Suez, and trapped the Egyptian 3rd Army east of the canal. A cease-fire came into effect on 22 October. Organized fighting had ceased on all fronts by 26 October.

"THERE ARE MEN, ALIVE AND DEAD, who did wonderful things we don't even know about," Greengold said of his experience. "The men on the line did exceptional things and I pale by comparison."

Officers who were in the battle put it rather higher than that. They said that, but for Zvika Force, the Syrians would have driven up the Tapline on Saturday night and taken Nafakh. They would have seized the divisional and brigade headquarters, rendering the Israelis leaderless, and gained control of the key crossroads on the road from Kuneitra to the Jordan bridges. Zvika Force thereby saved the Golan – and Zvika Force was Zvika Greengold.

Ninety percent of the Barak Brigade officers were killed or wounded. Not one company commander survived the first battles. Only one company second-in-command and two platoon commanders were still in the field on 11 October. But the retreating Syrians left 867 tanks behind them on the Golan. Greengold destroyed at least 20 of them, and possibly more than twice that. He recovered from his wounds, and began a successful career in business. He was only one of six recipients during the war of the Medal of Valour, Israel's highest award for gallantry.

11 · BLOOD FOR ELEANOR!

Two sergeants and the turn of the tide

Long campaigns may have a tipping point in a particular combat, visible only in hindsight. Heroism is a constant thread in combat, for "blood is always the price of battle, and slaughter its character …" What makes it remarkable here is that the first subtle but fundamental shift in fortune between the adversaries resulted: "In one point of space and time all action is here pressed together …" (BOOK III, CHAPTER I).

GUADALCANAL, THE SOLOMON ISLANDS ✳ 23–25 OCTOBER 1942

GUADALCANAL WAS THE TURNING point of the Pacific war. It was the first major Allied offensive against the Empire of Japan, and the first strategic victory to be won on land. It followed the humiliations in Malaya, Singapore, Guam, Wake Island, the Bataan Peninsula and Corregidor. It did more than stop the rot. It introduced Japanese infantry to defeat. It showed that the American fighting man could out-fight and out-think them in close combat, displaying initiative and fierce resolution, qualities submerged by defeat before Guadalcanal.

Guadalcanal is the main island of the southern Solomons, a string of volcanic islands on the outer limit of the drowned portion of the ancient Australian continent, a part of the circum-Pacific Ring of Fire.

The Japanese occupied the islands in May 1942, and had begun building a base and an airfield on Guadalcanal to protect the big Japanese base at Rabaul on New Guinea. It would also threaten Allied supply lines to Australia, and act as a staging area for further offensives against Fiji, New Caledonia and Samoa.

Sixteen thousand Allied troops, most of them United States Marines, landed on 7 August 1942. They overwhelmed the out-numbered Japanese on Guadalcanal, and secured the half-built Japanese airfield without difficulty, renaming it Henderson Field. The 886 Japanese navy men in the naval and seaplane bases on the other islands resisted fiercely, and were killed almost to the last man. The Marines lost 122 men. It was an early indication of the suicidal character of Japanese courage.

Henderson Field was the key to the islands. The Japanese were ready to sacrifice large numbers of aircraft, ships and men to get it back.

In heavy air fighting, the Americans lost 14 carrier aircraft during the landings. Concerned at this, and at the vulnerability of their carrier, the *Saratoga*, to further Japanese air attacks, the carrier task force was withdrawn on the evening of 8 August. With the loss of air cover, the transports also pulled out, even though less than half the supplies and heavy equipment needed by the Marines ashore had been landed. The Allied warships screening the transports were attacked by a Japanese force, and three American cruisers and an Australian cruiser were sunk.

The 11,000 Marines on Guadalcanal formed a defensive perimeter around the airfield. They used captured Japanese equipment to get it ready for operations on 18 August. Guadalcanal is as beautiful as any tropical island, with white beaches spreading out beneath the shade of coconut palms, splashes of orchids and parrots against the green of the rain forest, and peaks towering to 7,500 feet, ascending from jungle to slopes grassy with ferns and mosses. But it had snakes, too, and scorpions and crocodiles, and a humidity that rotted boots and soured skin, and mud and dysentery and malaria. The Marines lived in pup tents in the mud, with rats and lizards, always wet, many with infected sores on their feet, and all were short of food. The Japanese and Korean construction workers who remained beyond the perimeter foraged for coconuts. The Japanese called the island Gadaruka-naru. *Ga* means "hunger", among other things, and they were soon referring to Guadalcanal as "Hunger Island".

When the Marines sent out a 25-man patrol, led by a lieutenant colonel, to see if the Japanese were willing to surrender, the Japanese responded by annihilating the entire party. Thereafter, aggressive Marine patrolling steadily reduced the number of surviving Japanese. Grumman F-4 fighters and Dauntless dive-bombers flew in to Henderson. They were known as the "Cactus Air Force" after the codename for Guadalcanal. They fought daily air battles with Japanese fighters and bombers.

The Japanese began landing fresh troops in an attempt to retake the island. The first 917 men of Colonel Ichiki's 28th Infantry Regiment landed from destroyers on 19 August. They underestimated Marine strength. They attacked the Marine perimeter at Alligator Creek on the coast in the early hours of 21 August. By nightfall, all but 128 of them were dead, their colonel with them. The survivors returned to Taivu Point, a Japanese naval outpost, about 20 miles from Henderson Field.

Troop transports were found to be too slow and vulnerable to aircraft flying from Henderson. The Japanese thus began sending in troops by destroyers, fast enough to make the run down "the Slot" to Guadalcanal and back in a single night. The Americans called this the "Tokyo Express" and the Japanese themselves "Rat

Transport". In five nights from 29 August, light cruisers and destroyers managed to land almost 5,000 troops at Taivu Point. A further 1,000 were landed from a barge convoy. They came ashore light, though, with no heavy artillery, and limited food and ammunition. These forces were under the command of General Kawaguchi, who planned to "rout and annihilate the enemy in the vicinity of the airfield".

The key to the defence of Henderson Field was a thousand-yard-long coral ridge just to the south. It was named after Lieutenant Colonel Merritt A. Edson, a battalion commander, whose Marines defended it from furious frontal attacks by 3,000 of Kawaguchi's troops for two nights from 12 September. When Kawaguchi pulled back, he had lost 850 killed at a cost to the Marines of 100 dead.

General Hyakutake at Rabaul sent news of the defeat to Imperial general headquarters in Tokyo. Here, the senior army and navy command staffs decided that Guadalcanal could "develop into the decisive battle of the war".

This elevated the island into a trial of strength between the giants. Hyakutake, with Tokyo's blessing, ordered a pause in the Japanese campaign in New Guinea until the "Guadalcanal matter" was settled. He needed as many troops as he could get, and troops were switched to go to Guadalcanal. The Americans, too, increased the stakes by sending a further 4,000 Marines to the island, though losing the carrier *Wasp*. Both sides fed fresh aircraft into their bases. There were daily dogfights between aircraft from Henderson and Japanese fighters and bombers from Rabaul. Tokyo Express runs by destroyers on four nights in mid-September brought in more men, ammunition and supplies.

On the night of 11 October a force of three Japanese cruisers and two destroyers tried to get close enough to bombard Henderson Field. An American task force intercepted them and sank a cruiser and a destroyer for the loss of a destroyer. Two nights later, the Japanese sent two battleships, *Kongo* and *Haruna*, which fired salvoes of fragmentation shells. Many aircraft were destroyed, fuel dumps were set on fire, and aircrew killed. The Cactus Air Force remained in being, however.

FURTHER JAPANESE TROOPS REACHED the island. On 23 October they were ready for a frontal assault on the Henderson airfield perimeter. A crucial central sector of the ridge line was held by the platoon of Gunnery Sergeant John Basilone, a machine-gun platoon sergeant in support of Company C of the 7th Marines.

He was a pre-war regular, known as "Manila John" after his fond reminiscences of the Philippines, one of ten children from an Italian immigrant family from a poor area of Raritan, New Jersey, that better-off locals called Goosepatch. He was no scholar – he listed his hobby as "chewing gum" in his eighth-grade yearbook – and he liked to play truant from school to swim at "Bare Ass Beach" on the Raritan River. After working as a golf caddie, and a laundry driver's assistant, he left home in 1934 and joined the army. He came back after his stint in the army in Manila, and was working as a labourer when he enlisted in the Marines in July 1940.

In rain-filled darkness, the first violent assault began at 21:30 with intense firing and grenades amid Japanese cries of "*Banzai!*" and in English "Die! Die!". The machine-gun pit on Basilone's right was overrun. His own machine-guns were running low on ammunition. The sergeant knew that the Japanese who had broken through on the right were between him and the ammunition dump. If his gun teams were not resupplied, they would also be swept away.

He took off his mud-clogged boots, stripped off his webbing, and ran leaping for 150 yards down the trail. He came back with six belts of ammunition festooned around his chest, a load of 130 pounds. Heavy machine-guns were the key to survival, and he went to the abandoned gun pits to his right. He found the two machine-guns there to be jammed. He ran back to his own position, took one of his guns and ordered a gun crew to follow him. Though it weakened his own position, it was a crucial decision in re-establishing a cohesive line.

The Marines began cutting down a second assault wave of Japanese, the men with grenades and rifles with fixed bayonets, the officers with revolvers and double-edged samurai swords. Basilone lay in one of the gun pits, and repaired and loaded its machine-gun. Japanese bodies began to pile up in front of the pits. At one point they blocked the line of fire, and Basilone had his gun crews throw the bodies back to clear the field. He made several more trips of desperate peril to the dump for ammunition.

Eight separate waves of Japanese crashed into Basilone's position that night. His platoon fired more than 25,000 rounds. Before dawn, the Japanese withdrew, leaving bodies thick on the ground at their intended breakthrough point. Basilone checked on his wounded. "He was barefoot, and his eyes were red as fire," one of them, Nash Phillips, recollected. "His face was dirty black from gunfire and lack of sleep. His shirt sleeves were rolled up to his shoulders. He had a .45 tucked into the waistband of his trousers."

Basilone and his men are thought to have killed 300 enemy in the course of the five-hour battle. Twelve of his own men were killed, and two others wounded. His machine-guns were pivotal to the battalion's defence. The Japanese failure at their chosen break-through point ruined the assault.

THEY WERE BACK IN THE EARLY hours of 25 October. It was now the turn of another platoon sergeant of 7th Marines, Mitchell "Mitch" Paige, the son of Serb immigrants from Charleroi, Pennsylvania. He and his platoon of 33 Marine riflemen from the 1st Battalion were on a knoll on the ridge. The army's newly arrived 164th

Infantry Regiment was holding the rest of the line. The grounds in front of Paige's men sloped gently down into the jungle. They had been on alert since nightfall. The Japanese had sent two infantry regiments, the 29th and the 16th, against them.

At about 02:00 Paige sensed movement right along the line, and deep in the jungle to his left. Pieces of equipment jingled. Soft voices hissed as the Japanese squad leaders gave their final orders. Small coloured lights flicked on and off, like fireflies in the intense darkness.

These were the Japanese assembly signals. The assault force numbered some 5,600 infantry of the 2nd Division, but they were near exhaustion. They had had to march a 15-mile trail to get to their start lines, through terrain so difficult that they were forced to crouch beneath branches for much of it. Each man carried an artillery shell or a piece of a field gun as well as his own gear. Cooking was not allowed, for fear the fires would alert American pilots. Food was shorter, and disease more prevalent, than for the Marines. Kawaguchi had wished to postpone the assault, but Masanobu Tsuji had come on to Guadalcanal from his triumphs in Malaya and Bataan, and had schemed with Rabaul and Tokyo to have it go ahead. Despite that, Tsuji was struck with "an omen of doom" and his "bones felt cold" just before the attack went in. Every man was ordered to "fight desperately and fulfil his duty in repayment of His Majesty's favour".

Paige crawled round his position. He told his men not to fire until the enemy were almost on them, as the muzzle flashes would give away the American positions, and the Marines were greatly outnumbered. In front of their foxholes they had strung pieces of wire, on which they had hung blackened rations cans with empty cartridge cases, to give warning of an enemy approach.

The crew of the number-two machine-gun, men with Marine nicknames, "Big Stoop" Gaston and "Muscles" Leiphart, whispered to Paige that there was rustling in the undergrowth very near to them. He told them to hold their fire. He saw a corporal, "Moose" Stanberry, nervously arrange and rearrange grenades in a row in front of him. The hisses came closer. Paige pulled the pin out of a grenade, and held the lever ready to throw. He heard others do the same. Then a can rattled, there was a shriek and grenades began to go off.

Japanese rifles and machine-guns fired blind as the first wave of Japanese came out of the jungle flanking Gaston's machine-gun pit. Stansberry pulled out grenade pins with his teeth and lobbed them down the slope. The Japanese were screaming "*Banzai!*" and calling, in English, "Blood for the Emperor!" Stansberry replied with a tribute to President Roosevelt's wife: "Blood for Eleanor!"

Paige saw Japanese racing towards Leiphart, who was kneeling, and seemed already hit. The sergeant shot two of them but a third ran Leiphart through with his bayonet, with such force that he lifted him high in the air. Paige took careful aim and shot him.

The other machine-gunner, Gaston, was flat on his back. "A Japanese officer was hacking at him with a two-handed Samurai sword and grunting with the exertion," Paige said. "One of his legs was badly cut from the blows … The Japanese officer raised his sword for the killing thrust and Gaston, with maniac strength, snaked his good leg up and caught his man under the chin with his boondocker [boot], a violent blow that broke the Japanese's neck."

On the left flank, one of the machine-gun crew was killed and the second wounded in the head. "Stansberry, who had been near me, was hit in the shoulder," Paige recollected. "The last time I saw him he was still firing his Tommy gun with ferocity and shouting, 'Charge! Charge! Blood for Eleanor!'"

A "seemingly endless wall" of Japanese were still coming up the slope. Paige estimated that 75 Japanese were crashing through his platoon, most on the left flank. One of them lunged at Paige with a fixed bayonet, but the American put his hand up, and the bayonet hit between his little finger and ring finger, enough to let him parry it off. "As he went by me," Paige said, "he dropped dead on the ground."

The first wave of Japanese began to melt back down the slope. Navy corpsmen moved forward to treat the wounded. Paige fixed a jammed machine-gun, at the cost of a finger nail, found the spare-parts kit, and changed the belt feed pawl. As with Basilone, he used the time between attacks to made sure weapons were functioning.

Some Japanese had climbed to the top of tall trees overlooking the platoon position. They fired down from them, with the men in the foxholes on the crest of the ridge highly vulnerable. Two of them were wounded and helped out of the line by corpsmen. Paige was getting ready to feed a new belt of ammunition into the repaired gun when he felt a sharp blow and pain in his left hand. "I fell back momentarily and flapped my arm and stared angrily at the gun," he said. It had been wrecked by a burst from a Japanese Nambu light machine-gun.

A second wave now crashed into the position. The machine-gunner on the left flank, already wounded, withdrew after all his supporting riflemen were killed or wounded. Paige saw men from Fox Company to his left pulling out and retreating from the crest. He fired a shot at them, shouting to them to hold the line. The Japanese were swarming into the Fox position in great numbers, armed with three heavy and six light machine-guns, sub-machine-guns and mortars. Paige was shocked – "Dear God, Major Conoley and his small command post are just over the crest." Taking Gaston's machine-gun, "I swung it around toward our own lines, as there was nothing between my gun and the crest but enemy soldiers."

He fired a full belt of ammunition into the backs of the crouching enemy, praying they would not get over the crest to the command post. He found out later from a Marine captain that it was thought that the Japanese were firing his gun, and that he was dead, along with all his men.

By 05:00 the enemy were all over the ridge. "It appeared they were going to roll up the entire battalion front," Paige said. "I continued to trigger bursts until the barrel began to steam. In front of me was a large pile of dead bodies." He tried to convince the Japanese that the Americans were still on the ridge in strength. "I ran around the ridge from gun to gun trying to keep them firing, but at each emplacement I found dead bodies," he said. "I knew then I must be all alone."

He kept stumbling into Japanese in the dark. They seemed not to know that they were in almost complete control of the knoll. He found two Marines with a big water-cooled machine-gun. He grabbed the gun, and ordered them and some other Marines to fix bayonets and form a skirmish line. They still had 1905-vintage 16-inch bayonets, with the front edge sharpened for its whole length, and the back edge for 5 inches from the tip.

It began to get light. Paige knew that once the Japanese could see the grip they had got on the ridge, they would send in a further wave to consolidate. He saw a group of Japanese on the ridge just above Major Conoley's command post. He fired a full belt of 250 rounds into them. He then spotted other Japanese heading for one of his platoon's machine-guns, abandoned, the crew dead or wounded. He raced for the gun. He drew sniper and mortar fire, but reached the gun and jumped into the gun pit, just 25 yards away from a Japanese infantryman, who started firing at him.

"I turned the gun on the enemy and immediately realized it was not loaded," he said. He scooped up a partially loaded belt lying on the ground. He was fumbling and trying to load it when a "very strange feeling" came over him. He was trying to pull back the bolt handle to cock the gun, but he found he could not move. "Even so," he said, "I could feel a warm sensation between my chin and my Adam's apple. Then all of a sudden I fell forward over the gun, loaded it and swung it at the enemy gunner, the precise moment he had fired his full thirty-round magazine at me." He thought later about the mystery and "somehow I knew that the 'Man Above' also knew what happened". By God's grace he shot the Japanese.

He found three more belts of ammunition and fired them. All Japanese fire concentrated on him, as his was the only automatic weapon still firing at them. When he ran out of ammunition, he "glowed with pride" when three of his platoon voluntarily crossed the fierce field of fire to resupply him. The first was hit in the stomach as he arrived, and the second was knocked over by a shot in the groin. The third, Bob Jonjock, had already been wounded. Just as he jumped into the gun pit, to help reload, Paige saw "a piece of flesh fly off his neck". Jonjock had been hit again.

Paige was afraid he would bleed to death, and shouted at him: "Get the hell back, Jonjock!" He refused to go: "No. I'm staying with you." The sergeant hit him hard enough to knock him over, and convinced him to obey the order.

Major Conoley rounded up a force of wiremen, runners, cooks and even mess boys. He led a counterattack into the Fox Company position. They counted 98 dead on the spur by actual body count.

The "beautiful charge" inspired Paige to lead one of his own, at about 05:30, as the dawn was breaking. He yelled out in Japanese for the enemy to stand up: "*Tate! – tah-teh, tah-the!*" Then he shouted to hurry: "*Isoge! – ee-soh-geh!*" At once about 30 Japanese popped up. One of them looked "quizzically" at Paige through field glasses. Paige fired a long burst, and they "just peeled off like grass under a mowing machine".

At that point, he turned around and said he was going to charge. "I want every one of you to be right behind me," he told his men. He threw the last two remaining belts of ammunition over his shoulder, and unclamped the heavy machine-gun from its tripod and cradled it in his arms. It weighed 80 pounds, and its water jacket was searing hot, but he did not notice. He fed in a belt, and started down the slope. There were Japanese there, hidden in the tall grass, and he raked the grass. He noticed an officer of field rank among them, who had emptied his revolver, and was reaching for his sword. He was only four or five feet away and Paige ran into him and knocked him flat.

His skirmishers followed him, giving the rebel yell, "shrieking and cat-calling like little boys imitating Marines", sounding as if they were a thousand strong, instead of a handful. They followed Paige all the way down to the start of the jungle, from where the Japanese had started out four hours before. "There we found nothing left to shoot at," he said. "The battle was over."

The jungle was so quiet that, but for the presence of so many bodies, it might all have "only been a bad dream of death". Paige sat with a captain, who had joined the skirmishers, and who kept slapping him on the back and saying, "Tremendous, tremendous!" There was blood coming through the captain's dungarees. He had a bullet hole in the right leg.

There were hundreds of enemy dead lying in the grass, along the ridge and on the slope to the jungle. "We dragged as many as we could into the jungle, out of the sun," he said. A corpsman smeared Paige's left arm with ointment, and cleaned the bayonet gash and the bullet damage to his left hand. As he left, the corpsman said, "You know, you have some pretty neat creases in your helmet."

THE JAPANESE 29TH HAD LOST 553 killed and missing, and 479 wounded among its 2,554 men. The losses of the 19th were not detailed, but American burial parties handled 975 bodies in their sector. All the men in Paige's platoon were either killed or wounded during the night. Tsuji went back down the trail to report on the destruction of the 2nd Division, its commander and most of his officers dead on the battlefield. He passed a terribly wounded battalion commander and some of his starving men. When he fed them with his own rice, they "opened their mouths like baby sparrows" when the chopsticks came towards them.

No further frontal assaults were made, so the actions on 23 and 25 October were decisive. This was not for lack of Japanese effort. The 38th Infantry Division was boarded on transports with fresh supplies and equipment as reinforcements for the island. A task force with two battleships was also despatched to shell Henderson Field and put the Cactus Air Force out of commission, thus helping the infantry to overrun the field.

On 13 November, amid darkness and rain squalls, the naval battle of Guadalcanal erupted when the Americans engaged the Japanese task force. It was a confused, close-quarters fight, a "barroom brawl after the lights had been shot out", with the Japanese battleship *Hiei* passing 20 feet from the American destroyer *Laffey,* unable to depress her guns sufficiently to hit her. The Japanese battleships had loaded their guns with fragmentation shells, intended for the aircraft and Marines at Henderson, and the time lag as they switched to armour-piercing shells saved the American ships from even greater losses.

The main engagement lasted for 40 brutal minutes, in Ironbottom Sound between Savo Island and Guadalcanal. Marines watched from ashore: "Star shells rose, terrible and red ... giant tracers flashed across the night in orange arches ... the sea seemed a sheet of polished obsidian on which the warships seemed to have been dropped." The inability to take out Henderson Field was critical, for, after the clash of warships, bombers flying from the island played havoc with the troop transports. The Japanese lost two battleships, a cruiser and three destroyers to the American losses of two cruisers and seven destroyers. But 11 Japanese transports were lost, and only 2,000 troops got to the island, not enough to mount a new assault on the perimeter.

Slowly, the remaining Japanese were ground down, and the Marines pushed their perimeter out beyond artillery range of the airfield. The Japanese evacuated the last of their troops on 7 February 1943. Two days later, after more than six months of combat, the Americans were able to signal: "Tokyo Express no longer has terminus on Guadalcanal."

The Japanese themselves consider Guadalcanal, not Midway, to be the real turning point of the Pacific War. Basilone and Paige, by ensuring the survival of Henderson Field, mired the Japanese in a war of attrition. The weight of American industry, logistics and manpower was certain to overwhelm the Japanese in time. The bitter fighting at Guadalcanal was the first evidence of this, and of the quality of American troops where it most mattered in close-range combat, at sergeant level.

BOTH BASILONE AND PAIGE WERE awarded the Medal of Honour. Paige went on to have a distinguished career in the Marines, retiring as a colonel. He died in 2003. Basilone was brought home, put on a war-bond tour with Hollywood starlets, and then assigned to guard duty at the Washington Navy Yard. He pined to return to his unit, though, and he turned down lucrative boxing and film contracts to "stay with my boys". On 19 February 1945, on the black volcanic sands of Iwo Jima, he was killed after destroying an enemy blockhouse. He was posthumously awarded the Navy Cross.

12 · KILLED COLD-DEDE AND CASTEN OVER-BORDES

An unknown predecessor of Drake defeats an earlier armada

An action taken in an instant, as here, can sway a battle, for "when surprise is successful in a high degree, confusion and broken courage in the enemy's ranks are the consequence" (BOOK III, CHAPTER IX).

THE ENGLISH CHANNEL OFF WINCHELSEA * 29 AUGUST 1350

AT THE TIME OF VESPERS, IN THE early evening of 29 August 1350, the Castilian fleet was sighted in the Channel off Winchelsea. It was under the command of Don Carlos de la Cerda, a soldier of fortune from a branch of the Castilian royal family. It was returning to the Basque coast of Spain from the mouth of the River Sluys in Zeeland, and it was laden with spoils seized earlier from English ships as well as Flemish merchandise.

Three weeks earlier, at Rotherhithe, King Edward III had said that he would attack the Spaniards as they sailed for home. The English fleet was assembled at New Winchelsea, just to the west of Rye in Sussex. The old town had been overwhelmed by the sea in a series of great storms in the century before, and was lost beneath the waters of Rye Bay. The new town was one of the major ports of the kingdom, and the head of the Cinque Ports, the alliance of Kent and Sussex ports formed for protection against frequent raids by the French.

The king had gone there by land, with his wife Queen Philippa and her ladies, and his sons, the Black Prince and John of Gaunt. The ladies were placed in a convent. Many nobles had come, to fight with the fleet, and for entertainment: the magnificent wine cellars beneath the broad streets allowed for feasting in style whilst they awaited the Spaniards. Prayers were offered up in the great church of St Thomas the Martyr. Edward went aboard his flagship on 28 August.

On its outward voyage to Flanders, the Spaniards had captured English trading ships, and had thrown the crews overboard. They were allied to the French, and piracy and raids on coastal towns by ships from both countries had done much damage to English trade. Ships laden with wool were plundered as they sailed from English ports, whilst ships inbound from Bordeaux with wine were targeted so frequently that convoys were used on the trade routes to Gascony, large fleets of merchantmen being escorted by royal ships filled with men-at-arms.

The trade in wool and wine was a vital source of royal revenue. Edward had claimed the French crown and declared war against Philip VI of France in 1337, thereby starting the Hundred Years' War. He had defeated the French navy at Sluys in 1340, and had conquered much of Normandy and beaten the French army at Crécy in 1346. His ambitions were expensive, and the dent in customs revenue caused by piracy was a serious worry. Particular damage was done by the Genoese sea captain Julius Boccanera, known as Barbenoire or Blackbeard, who had been made admiral of the Castilian fleet and created Earl of Parma by the king of Castile. His squadron of 30 Genoese galleys had ravaged English shipping, and he had sailed them out to sea to escape capture when the English had destroyed a French armada at Sluys in

1340. Winchelsea itself had been sacked several times by the French, despite the walls and heavily fortified gates built to repel them.

It was to right these wrongs, and to further his campaigns against the French and their allies, that Edward lay at anchor at Winchelsea awaiting Cerda. Intelligence of this had reached Cerda in Flanders. He delayed sailing. The boats known as *tarets* in his fleet were rowed by oarsmen like galleys, and were swift and deadly in combat. Carpenters fitted out the Spanish merchantmen with high wooden castles fore and aft, above the clutter of the decks, from which crossbowmen could fire down on the enemy ships. The Spanish had provided themselves with "all sorts of warlike ammunition", the chronicler Froissart recorded, including "bolts for crossbows, cannon, bars of forged iron, and large stones". Cerda had also recruited mercenaries, mainly crossbowmen, from the taverns in the ports of Flanders.

He had the northeasterly wind in his favour as he ran down-Channel. He could easily have avoided the English by keeping closer to the French coast. Instead, Froissart recorded, he "disdained to sail by". The ships sailed close enough to be seen clearly from the shore at Winchelsea, and Froissart recorded that it was a "fine sight to see their forty vessels of such a size, and so beautifully under sail".

The English fleet was waiting at anchor. The king was sitting on the deck of his flagship, the *Thomas*, with his knights and nobles. His minstrels were playing German airs, and they were listening to the singing of the sweet-voiced Sir John Chandos. When the lookouts at the mastheads reported the enemy in sight, the king and his company drank to each other's health. The trumpet sounded. The anchors were weighed, and the fleet stood out to sea. Queen Philippa and her ladies and other spectators watched from the sea cliffs at a spot since called the "Look-out".

Edward's force was put at 50 ships and pinnaces. They were

merchant ships, in the days before a standing fleet, and were arrested for royal service by sergeants-at-arms with writs from the king, some from ports up the east coast from the Thames to the Humber, others from the southwest, as well as those from the Cinque Ports, which were obliged to provide ships for 15 days annually to form the backbone of the fleet. The *Thomas*, the king's ship, was a cog, oak built with a single mast and a square sail, caulked with tarred mosses, a sturdy seagoing trader, beamy and deep-hulled, with fore and stern castles added to turn her into a warship. Most of the other English ships were also cogs, with names as sturdy and workmanlike as themselves: the *John*, the *Edmund*, the *Michael*, the *Welfare*.

With the wind from astern of his ships, Cerda had the advantage of the weather. His *tarets*, too, were low-lying and more manoeuvrable than the high-sided cogs, able to ram them and hole them below the waterline. Edward directed the *Thomas* into the Spanish line. She was hit by a Spaniard with such force that the castles of both ships crashed into one another, and the *Thomas* was holed. As she took on water and began to sink, she was probably hit again, because she started to break up. To save themselves, the king and his crew grappled and boarded an enemy ship as the *Thomas* foundered. They killed or threw the enemy crew overboard.

The "fight was hot". The Black Prince's ship was also holed, in several places, and he and his men abandoned it and captured another shortly before it sank. Cerda's crossbowmen "did much execution", and the higher-built Spaniards were able to damage the lighter English ships by dropping heavy stones and iron bars on them. The conflict went on into the twilight of the hot August day.

The nature of combat at sea was caught by the poet Chaucer, writing a few decades later:

> And from the top doun come the grete stones
> In goeth the grapenel, so ful of crokes
> Among the ropes renne the sherynge-hokes.
> In with the polax preseth he and he
> Behynde the mast begynnyth he to fle,
> And out ageyn, and dryveth hym overbord ...

(Great stones were hurled down from the tops. The grapnel went across, with its "crokes" or "sherynge-hokes" – its hooks and the shearing-hooks used to cut the rigging – whilst a man with a "polax", a battleaxe, drives the enemy to jump overboard.)

One of the largest of the English vessels, *La Salle du Roi*, which carried the king's household, was commanded by the experienced Fleming Robert of Namur. A big Spaniard attacked her and grappled her, locking her alongside with grapple irons, and began to drag her off. The crew called for help, but were either not heard, or the other English ships were too pressed themselves to help her. *La Salle du Roi* was about to be taken, as the battle reached its decisive point, when a squire of Robert of Namur, called Halking or Hannequin, jumped on board the Spaniard.

Almost in the same movement, Halking slashed the mainsail halyards and the mainstays with his sword. The mast tottered for a few instants without its stays, and then crashed with lethal force onto the deck. The sail collapsed, trapping crew members under it, and the heavy yard stunned others as it smashed down with the sail. The Spaniard drifted out of control. Other crewmen followed Halking aboard and seized the ship, throwing the survivors overboard.

This proved the turning point of the battle. The Spaniards made to break off the engagement, but the English grappled with them. In the words of the poet Laurence Minot, writing shortly after the battle, the "archers of England full egerly shootes" and their arrows "hittes through the hard steel full hertly", striking through the Spaniards' armour. After the English boarded boat after boat, following Halking's example, their crews were "killed cold-dede and casten over-bordes".

Inspired by Halking, writes Minot:

> Then was hed-ropes hewen, that held up the mastes;
> There was contek [fighting] full keen and cracking
>   of shippes!
> Grete cogges of kemp [war] crashes in sonder!
> Many cabane [cabins] cleved, cables destroyed,
> Knightes and keen men killed ...

As the enemy crewmen "lepen in waters", there the "fissches to fede", the English laughed and cheered:

> All our lordes on loud laughen at ones!

By nightfall, when the battle ended, as many as 24 Spanish ships had been captured or sunk. The survivors sailed on down-Channel for Spain. The known English losses were two. Since these were the two largest ships – the *Thomas* and the Black Prince's ship – it is likely that a few others were sunk. The engagement, which became known as the Battle of *Les Espagnols en Mer* ("the Spanish at Sea"), was a rousing victory.

What became of Halking, we do not know. His master, Robert of Namur, was made a Knight of the Garter, and granted a pension of 300 livres a year by Edward III, and it is clear that *La Salle du Roi* and its crew were critical to the victory. It was at Robert of Namur's insistence that Froissart wrote his famous *Chronicles*, so the account of Halking's decisive action was based on a first-hand report. In medieval combat, at sea as on land, the personal prowess of individual knights and squires could influence the outcome of a battle, though rarely as decisively as here. It was a singular and most uncommon honour for a chronicler to mention as lowly a participant as a squire in the account of a battle.

13 · "TRULY, THIS MAN IS THE NEW NOAH"

The maker of the amphibious assault

Industry is a vital arm of war, for any army is "in a state of necessary dependence on the sources from which it draws its subsistence" (BOOK V, CHAPTER XV).
In this exceptional case, a small-time manufacturer made possible a new form of warfare.

THE MEDITERRANEAN, NORMANDY AND THE PACIFIC ∗ 1942–5

A GERMAN PARATROOP OFFICER, Colonel Frederick van der Heydte, climbed the church steeple at Sainte-Marie-du-Monte in Normandy after dawn on 6 June 1944, and looked out across the pastures towards the sand and shingle and the sea. "All along the beach were these small boats," he recollected with horror, "hundreds of them, each disgorging thirty or forty armed men."

The boats were built by a bull-necked, hard-drinking civilian from New Orleans called Andrew Jackson Higgins. Years later, General Eisenhower, supreme commander on D-Day, summed up Higgins with pithy brevity: "The man who won the war for us."

Eisenhower was not one to exaggerate. He could have chosen one of the great military men he knew; indeed, he might have qualified himself. It says much for his insight into modern warfare that he selected a civilian, acknowledging how much the outcome depended on sheer industrial production. Here, he might be expected to plump for one of the war's icons. The Spitfire, say, the masterpiece of the dying English aircraft designer R.J. Mitchell, who poured the last of his strength into perfecting the fighter that, after his death, helped save his country from German invasion in the Battle of Britain. Or the T-34, the fruit of engineer Tsyganov's design team in Kharkov. This was perhaps the best tank ever built in its combination of armour, mobility and fire-power, which, added to ease of manufacture and maintenance, enabled it to play a key part in turning the tide on the Eastern Front.

Yet Eisenhower chose for his extraordinary plaudit a man who made the most ordinary of boats – humble, workaday, wooden vessels with a top speed of 12 knots and the unromantic name of LCVP, for landing craft vehicle, personnel. "If Higgins had not designed and built those LCVPs, we never could have landed on an open beach," Eisenhower told the historian Stephen Ambrose. "The whole strategy of the war would have been different."

The phrase "designed and built" is key to this eulogy. The LCVP was, flesh and blood, Higgins's creature. He foresaw the need for it, and anticipated how it would be used, and carried the project through from concept and drawing board to trials and mass manufacture. He raised the finance for it, paid for proto-types out of his own pocket, and fought naval bureaucracy tooth and nail to get it accepted. He built it in the boatyards of his own company, Higgins Industries, with his own labour force of 20,000 men and women.

He had in plenty, then, the production genius that made America the "arsenal of democracy". But there is more to Higgins than that. The Spitfire and the T-34 were fine examples of their type, but they did not change the nature of the war. The LCVP did, and it did so in both the war against Hitler, and the war against Japan. In September 1943, to take a single month, it made it possible for the Americans to land at Salerno in Italy to fight the Germans, and for the Americans and Australians to assault the Japanese half a world away at Lae in New Guinea.

By then, the US Navy had just over 14,000 vessels of all types. Ninety-two percent of them, or 12,964 craft, were Higgins-designed, and the bulk were Higgins-built. This came from a man who five years before had net assets of $13,639 – and not a single Navy contract.

The Marines and commandos and assault troops who landed from LCVPs onto the bloody beaches of the Mediterranean, Normandy and the Pacific paid him a compliment as handsome in its way as Eisenhower's. They never called them LCVPs. They were simply "Higgins boats".

THE EVENTS IN A FRENCH PORT ONE morning in the high summer of 1942 are the yardstick by which Higgins's importance is best judged. A slaughter took place whose repetition, on a yet grislier scale, Higgins prevented.

In the early hours of 19 August, a force of 6,100 troops was aboard a fleet of 250 ships crossing the English Channel from Portsmouth for a raid on Dieppe. Five thousand of them were Canadians, champing for action after months of training in England. "Don't worry, boys," their commanding officer, Major General J.H. Roberts reassured them. "It'll be a piece of cake." Their objective was to seize and hold a major port for a short period. The exercise was a rehearsal for the eventual full-scale invasion of German-held northern Europe.

A seaborne invasion puts immense strain on ship-to-shore movements. Prodigious inputs are needed to sustain the invaders. Tanks, bulldozers and construction equipment, artillery, trucks, rations, explosives, bridging equipment, runway surfacing, ammunition, medicines, operating theatres, fuel, spare parts must all be landed onto a hostile coast from the supply ships that have carried them across the sea. They must be got ashore quickly, too, so that enough men and weapons are in place to resist the inevitable and furious enemy counterattacks.

Pre-Higgins, this meant that at least one major port – and, in an enterprise as vast as D-Day, two or better three – had to be captured. Only then were freighters and troopships able to moor alongside quays to unload their cargoes directly on land with their own or dockyard cranes. Without an existing port, conventional wisdom had it, it was impossible to offload the necessary bulk at sufficient speed. A reason for the failure of the last major landings, at Gallipoli in 1915, was the time it took to transfer even the modest equipment needed by non-mechanized infantry from freighters to lighters and then to shore.

Dieppe had been an important fishing port before the war, with commercial docks and a cross-Channel ferry service to Newhaven in Sussex. It was the type of port that would need to be taken and held in a conventional invasion. The raid was expected to give valuable lessons in assaulting such a target. Landings by commandos were planned to the east and west of the town, to take out heavy coastal guns and batteries. The main landings involved a frontal assault by infantry backed by tanks on the beaches by the harbour entrance. An esplanade where tourists took the sea air in peacetime, lined with holiday hotels and a casino, lay between the beaches and the town.

The Germans were perfectly aware of the strategic importance of the French and Belgian Channel ports, of course, and they had formidable defences in place. Dieppe lies on the estuary of the River Arques, with high chalk cliffs on either side. Eight 75mm guns were sited on headlands overlooking the town. Two batteries of 150mm heavy coastal guns covered the approaches to the harbour and the sweep of beaches and inner harbour. Artillery pieces and machine-guns were dug into caves high in the chalk cliffs. The beaches and positions overlooking them were festooned with machine-gun posts, pillboxes, barbed wire, concrete walls and field batteries. The casino on the front had been turned into a strongpoint. The town was garrisoned by the 571st Infantry Regiment of the 302nd Division. These were not front-line troops, but they were trained, and more than adequate for fixed defences.

Weather forecasts for the Channel were made by the Germans each evening with special stress given to the possibility of invasion. Light winds from the south were expected for the night of 18–19 August, with moonset at 23:20 and a morning mist with high water at 04:03 and sunrise at 05:10. "These conditions," the report concluded, "make an enemy landing appear possible in the Eastern sector of the Channel during the night." A strict night watch was ordered for German troops along the coast, with a warning from headquarters that the optimum time for invasion was a few minutes before dawn.

As bad luck had it, the 571st was aware well before then that something was afoot out at sea. At 03:47, the lead ships in the fleet sailing from Portsmouth ran into a small convoy of Dutch merchantmen being escorted by E-boats, fast German torpedo boats. Star shells and an exchange of tracer fire briefly shattered the night. "We tried to settle down again," said Bert Pittaway, a Canadian sergeant, "but in every mind was the awful thought that now the German defences would be waiting for us."

Indeed they were. The 571st was alerted by the German naval HQ west that an enemy surface force had been spotted 20 kilometres off Dieppe. Five minutes later, the army command confirmed: "Troops have intensified their lookout. Army and air authorities have been advised."

A 15-minute delay in the landings denied the leading boats the cover of the pre-dawn half-light. The southerly breeze blew the smoke dropped along the shoreline by British aircraft back out to sea. The boats came out of the smokescreen into brilliant sunshine as they closed into the beaches. No mass air attacks had preceded the landings to soften up the defences. The Germans found this failure "mystifying", but the planners had feared that an early bombing strike would rob the raid of surprise, not knowing that this would already have been blown by the freak encounter with the E-boats.

The men were thus exposed in clear daylight to a fully alert enemy. The result was a massacre. Shelling by four destroyers and low-level strafing runs by five squadrons of Hurricanes had no impact on the well-protected defenders. The first assault waves of infantry and engineers were smashed by enfilading fire on the beaches. The following waves broke on the remains of the first. Tank tracks lost their traction and spun on the deep shingle. A few tanks clattered onto the area of the promenade, swept by fire from the 100-foot-high cliffs, but none broke into the town. A handful of infantry got through, soon to be cut off, but the reserves in the ships offshore were sent in to be slaughtered before the extent of the disaster was realized.

The signal to withdraw – "Vanquish 11:00 hours" – was sent to all the assault forces at 09:40. It was the sign for further horrific casualties among the naval officers and ratings in the boats, as well as to the raiders desperately fighting their way back to them.

Survivors who got off and returned to Newhaven brought tales of horror with them.

"THE SMOKE WAS SPOTTY AND THE last 30 yards was in the clear," a survivor from the Royal Regiment of Canada said of the initial assault. "The German ack-ack and machine-guns on the cliff were deafening. The ramp went down and the first infantrymen poured out. They plunged into about two feet of water and the machine-gun bullets laced into them. Bodies piled up on the ramp. Some men staggered to the beach. Looking out the open bow, I saw 60 to 70 bodies, men cut down before they could fire a shot.

"A dozen Canadians were running along the beach towards the 12-foot high seawall. Some fired as they ran. Some had no helmets. Some were wounded, their uniforms torn and bloodied. One by one they were hit and rolled down the slope to the sea."

The war correspondent Ross Munro, seeing the Royals "lying sprawled on the green grass and the brown earth", said he had never witnessed such carnage on any other front. "There was one young lad crouching six feet away from me," he wrote. "He had made several vain attempts to rush down the ramp to the beach but each time a hail of fire had driven him back. He had been wounded in the arm but was determined to try again. He lunged forward and a streak of red-white tracer slashed through his stomach. I'll never forget his cry as he collapsed on the blood-soaked deck: 'Christ, we gotta beat them, we gotta beat them!' ..."

Only one party of Royals got off the beach. Twenty officers and men led by their commanding officer, Lieutenant Colonel D.E. Catto, cut through the wire at the end of the seawall. They reached the cliff top and cleared two houses. They were cut off by machine-gun fire covering the gap in the wire. After the raiding force withdrew, they surrendered.

The regiment had started the day with 554 men. It was all but wiped out in five hours. One in two of its officers and men died on the beach or later from their wounds. Only 65 Royals got back to England. Of these, just 22 were not wounded.

This damage was inflicted by just 60 well-placed infantry of the 571st with some Luftwaffe anti-aircraft gunners. At no time were they reinforced. It was terrifying evidence of the superiority of the defenders in a prepared seaport over a seaborne invasion force.

Two miles west of Dieppe, the men of the South Saskatchewan

Regiment were held up at a bridge crossing the River Scie. It was 200 yards long, as much causeway as bridge, with no protecting balustrades and exposed for all its length to a large concrete fort on the hill across the river. The river was in spate from summer rain and the only way to cross it was to swim or to take the bridge. "I saw the first men trying to cross," a survivor said. "Bullets pinged off the road. In a minute or two, what had been a smooth concrete road was gashed with craters and pockmarked with bullet holes. Our men were mown down."

The Saskatchewans' commanding officer, Lieutenant Colonel Cecil Merritt, strode up the road, wiping sweat from his forehead. It was a hot day. "Now men," he said, "we're going to get across. Follow me. Don't bunch up ... Here we go!" With that, erect and with his helmet hanging from his wrist, he walked forward. "As I watched him lead his men through that thundering barrage, I felt a quiver run up and down my spine," a survivor recalled. "I'd never seen anything like it."

It came to nothing. The Saskatchewans were joined by the Queen's Own Cameron Highlanders of Canada. Their commanding officer was killed as they landed, their bagpipes playing against the whine of German shells and the sharp rattle of machine-guns. Merritt took several of the positions commanding the bridge in a series of attacks. But the high ground was still in German hands when the regiments were ordered to withdraw, taking heavy casualties. Merritt led a courageous rearguard that prevented the Canadians from being overrun as they made for the beaches. Many of those who embarked were wounded. The Saskatchewans had 68 percent casualties among their 523 men, the Cameronians 53 percent of 503. All this in a single morning.

The Calgary Regiment with its Churchill tanks landed ten minutes late, on a beach where, deprived of armoured support, 200 soldiers already lay dead and wounded. Of the 30 tanks, carried by a new type of craft, the LCT, landing craft tank, two were swamped between ship and shore and only half got beyond the beaches. Many bogged down in the sand and deep shingle, or were stopped by the seawall. Some got round the ends of the wall onto the esplanade, but neither the tanks nor assault engineers managed to clear the concrete obstacles that prevented the armour from getting into the streets of the town. The tanks nonetheless gave the infantry some cover behind their hulls, and continued firing on German gun positions until the enemy brought up heavy guns and knocked them out one by one. Not a single tank was evacuated.

Men of the Royal Hamilton Light Infantry landed on the beach in front of the casino and the esplanade. The commanding officer, Lieutenant Colonel Robert Labatt, watched spellbound on a ridge of shingle as a solitary soldier crawled forward under the wire from a group pinned down by a pillbox on the corner of the casino. The man ducked below the pillbox, took a grenade from his belt, and tossed it through the gun slit. Smoke and flame spewed from the pillbox. The man, grinning, beckoned his comrades on. None could. In those few instants, they had all been killed or wounded.

A captain and a section of RHLI broke into the casino. They stalked German snipers through the once-elegant, high-ceilinged gaming rooms, down parquet-floored corridors, past balconies and French windows. Four Germans were killed by grenades as they ran down a wide circular staircase, and a Canadian bayoneted a sniper. The first two floors were eventually held by over a hundred Canadians – infantry, engineers and signallers – with German snipers still ranging round the third floor and the roof. Some RHLI got into the town, lashed by machine-guns and snipers, with hand-to-hand fighting in buildings they broke into. Little more than a third of the regiment's 582 men got back to England.

Overhead, the RAF was having its worst day of the war. It lost

119 aircraft, including 64 Spitfires and 20 Hurricanes, though it protected the men on the beaches from attacks by Luftwaffe bombers and fighters.

The Essex Scottish landed close to the two long moles at the harbour entrance. The whole beach was enfiladed by big guns on the headlands, and by anti-tank guns, machine-guns and field guns hidden in caves in the chalk that could be run out to fire and then withdrawn in the face of counter-fire. Hotels along the promenade housed sandbagged machine-gun nests and snipers. The half-demolished casino had concrete pillboxes amid the ruins. A fortified tobacco factory and a tank hull-down in concrete defences on the harbour mole cut down the Canadians.

They were pinned down along a seawall when a company sergeant major, Cornelius Stapleton, blew a gap in the barbed wire with a Bangalore torpedo and charged in a furious zigzag for 200 yards across the broad boulevard and promenade with an echoing battle cry. He was followed by about 15 men, whilst the men at the seawall fired incendiary grenades, setting buildings aflame to give some smoke cover. The tobacco factory was swept by flames as Stapleton broke into the building next to it. A party of German infantry were mown down as they jumped from their trucks on the boulevard, and others were killed in the burning buildings. Ammunition almost spent, Stapleton's group raced back across the corpse-strewn esplanade to the seawall.

They had been gone for no more than half an hour, but they had unwittingly sown a fatal confusion. Not long after they had set out, a little after 06:00, the Essex Scottish commanding officer, Colonel Jasperson, had used the only working radio to say: "Twelve of our men in the buildings. Have not heard from them for some time." The message was intercepted by General Roberts's head-quarters staff aboard the destroyer *Calpe*. This suggested that the Canadians had crossed the esplanade and got into buildings in the town. At 06:15 Labatt reported that the RHLI were at the casino. At 06:20 a garbled message was received from the naval beach master with the Royals: "Impossible land troops." The vital words "any more" preceding "troops" were missing.

Roberts was thus fooled on two counts. He thought that the Essex Scottish and the RHLI were making much better progress than they were. And he thought that the Royals, in reality being slaughtered on the beach, were still in their boats offshore. He therefore ordered in his reserve battalion, Les Fusiliers Mont-Royal. They took fire all the way to the beach, and landed badly strung out on the extreme right of the battle, on a broad beach exposed by the ebbing tide to heavy fire from the headland above. As he jumped onto the shingle, the commanding officer, Lieutenant Colonel Dollard Ménard, made for a concrete pillbox a hundred yards up the beach. "I think I had taken three steps when the first one hit me," he said. "You say a bullet or a piece of shrapnel hits you but the word isn't right. They slam you the way a sledgehammer slams you. There's no sharp pain at first. It jars you so much you're not sure exactly where you've been hit, or what with ..."

Some 200 of his men reached the base of the cliff and huddled under the overhang on its face. Of the 584 FMR men who were landed, only one in five returned to England that afternoon.

The final reserve was 40 Commando of the Royal Marines. The lead landing craft was exposed to such heavy fire that the commander, Lieutenant Colonel Joseph Phillips, put on a pair of white gloves to semaphore that the following boats should not attempt to land. He was hit and killed, and none of the commandos who landed got more than a few feet up the beach, but his action saved the others.

THESE AWFUL SCENES CONTRASTED with the cool and calm of the Germans who were inflicting them.

Army HQ had regular and accurate updates from Dieppe: "06:40: enemy continues to land ... destroyers making smoke along the coast ... up to now 12 tanks have landed, of which one is on fire ... 08:40: situation is becoming clearer. The local reserve of the 302nd is already counterattacking. The heights on the two sides of Dieppe are entirely in our hands ... 09:03: enemy is in flight, apparently to the foot of the cliffs ... The 302nd signals that the enemy has lost 500 men killed and prisoner. Battery 8132 had fallen into enemy hands, but has been retaken. It is firing again with two guns ... 12:10: wireless intercepts confirm that the enemy is retiring ... 12:15: the enemy gives up. He is completely beaten to the east of Dieppe and is being repelled to the west and in the woods and on the cliffs, and it is now only a question of time ..."

By then, Field Marshal von Runstedt had strong detachments of the 10th Armoured Division with tanks and artillery in place. He ordered them to go forward immediately at 12:15: "Every weapon available must now contribute to the total destruction of the enemy," he signalled. "All fronts on which the enemy has landed must now be cleared up in the shortest possible time."

At 12:33 the 81st Army Corps signalled: "The enemy force landed to the east of Dieppe has been destroyed. At Dieppe itself the situation has been cleared up. Small centres of resistance remain. Estimate of prisoners taken is about 1,000 ..."

In the late afternoon, Major General Zeitler, the army chief of staff, had visited the scene and reported: "Prisoners make a good impression, young, fresh, intelligent." The dead were "everywhere, especially in front of our heavy gun positions. In front of one machine-gun post which flanked the narrow strip of beach between the sea and the cliffs, there are piles of dead (more than 100 only in this spot), much booty in equipment and infantry weapons." Making no distinction between Canadian and British, he concluded: "The British fought well ..."

The beaches, with their burnt-out transports and knocked-out tanks, and funnels and masts sticking out of the water, reminded

Zeitler of Dunkirk. He noted that shops had reopened as early as midday in most of Dieppe.

Of the 4,963 Canadians who had embarked at Portsmouth, only 2,210 returned to England, 378 of them wounded. For years after, on 19 August, a small box arrived in the post for General Roberts, its contents a piece of stale cake, a cruel reminder of his assurance at the pre-raid briefing.

IT WAS UNFAIR TO LAY THE BLAME on Roberts. His men died because that is the fate of soldiers, "young, fresh, intelligent" though the Germans found them, who come from the sea to fight a well-prepared enemy defending a target as prime and predictable as Dieppe.

The finest units in an army noted for its courage were destroyed, and by the common-or-garden garrison in place. A German armoured division arrived in the afternoon – "its powerful aspect", Zeitler noted, "made a great impression on the populace" – but it was not needed. On the central beach, a company's worth of German infantry and gunners repulsed an attack by three battalions.

The raid showed with brutal clarity what would result if the Allies continued with their plan to open the invasion of mainland Europe with the capture of a port. It would be a bloodbath, on an unimaginable scale, and it might well fail.

Yes, but how could ports be bypassed? How could a landing be made on open beaches? How could the insatiable demand for ship-to-shore movement be satisfied? The answer, Eisenhower and his planners found, was the Higgins boat.

"Those boats could go right up on the beach," said a coxswain, Milton Cooper, who handled one when the US Marines landed at Guadalcanal. "You'd run her wide open, the faster the better. You'd get her up on the beach, and the men would jump out. You'd never shut her off, just put her in reverse. She had a tunnel built in her hull, so the prop wouldn't get stuck in the sand."

After they landed the assault troops, Higgins boats brought in supplies, ferrying between the transports and the shore, sometimes for days at a time, the crews at Makin in the Gilbert Islands sleeping on their cargo and living on coffee and food lowered to them on lines from the big ships. On their return journeys, they brought out the wounded.

Without the boats, there could have been no landings. Without Higgins – and, as Eisenhower grasped, it is this that sets him apart from other manufacturers – there would have been no boats.

HIGGINS WAS BORN IN NEBRASKA in 1886, one of ten in an Irish-American family, a tempestuous and hard-grafting boy. His wartime strengths were laid down as a teenager. He ran grass-cutting and newspaper-delivery services, hiring older boys as employees, and eventually selling out to an adult. He built himself an iceboat, sailing at up to 60 miles an hour on frozen lakes, showing skill and ingenuity as a boat designer and builder. He had his first experience of amphibious training as a Nebraska militia volunteer on manoeuvres across the Platte River, stimulating a lifelong interest in military strategy. He spent summers working in Wyoming logging camps, which gave him an interest in the timber industry.

At 20 he moved from Nebraska, at first to Alabama. "I came south," he said later, "because I loved boats and forestry." He bought a farm and timberland near Mobile. A hurricane wiped out his lumber business, and he pawned his mandolin to stay afloat before moving to New Orleans in 1910. There he began a timber business, importing hardwoods and exporting southern pine and cypress, shipping on his own account after buying an old schooner, later lost in a great storm. He bought a large tract of timberland near Natchez, Mississippi, that was going cheap because the streams running through it were shallow and it was difficult to log. He built himself a workboat with a shallow draught and the propeller mounted in a tunnel to prevent damage when the boat grounded. In a weak market for timber, he found himself with an over-supply of mahogany, the ideal boat-building wood. He had a self-taught genius for making small boats, and this became his main enterprise.

By 1926 Higgins was working with the US Army Corps of Engineers on shallow-draught boats, gaining experience in engines, clutches, gearboxes and heavy-duty transmissions. His boats proved themselves the following year in rescue work after the great floods on the Ohio and Mississippi Rivers. A Dutch order for 20 of his tunnel-propeller boats soon after confirmed that boatbuilding was a better prospect than the timber business. Cavitation was a particular problem with tunnel boats: the water in the tunnel was aerated by the propeller, and the bubbles meant that the propeller had less water to bite on, so that performance dropped off. Steady improvements meant that his boats were making over 10 knots, a good speed for a tunnel boat.

Floating debris and logs were constant hazards on delivery trips to the swollen Arkansas River. Higgins began building a new bow design, based on a film he had seen on blue whales. He used the line of the whale's jaw and the forward part of its belly to create a rounded "spoonbill" bow. This proved capable of dealing with debris. Its propeller protected by the tunnel, the boat was often able to power its way over logs and branches.

Boat speed was also improved. In 1930, Higgins's boat *And How III* took 3 hours off the 90-hour record from New Orleans to St Louis (a distance of over 1,200 miles along the meandering and often difficult and shallow waters of the Mississippi) set 60 years before in the famous steamboat race between the *Robert E. Lee* and the *Natchez*. A year later, his son lowered the record to 72 hours in his speedboat *Dixie Greyhound*. Prohibition rum runners were duly impressed by such performance, particularly when allied to good cargo-carrying capacity and a draught shallow enough for them to be able to navigate little-used creeks and estuaries.

A spell of voluntary bankruptcy early in the Depression ended when the market for sturdy workboats picked up. Local demand came from trappers and oil prospectors in the Louisiana swamps, and, further afield, from companies drilling for oil or providing transport services in South America. These boats had to cope with streams choked with fallen trees, water hyacinth and sandbanks. They had to be able to run aground, and then get off astern again. They needed to carry a good load, of equipment and people, and they had to be tough and reliable, for they operated miles away from harbours and boatyards.

Higgins made the rounded spoonbill bow from a curved piece of pine, which acted like a bumper on a car, absorbing the impact of hitting a sandbank or a log, and helping the boat climb over it. A happy error on the moulding floor, which distorted the amidships and stern hull shapes, was found to solve the cavitation problem. This distortion meant that the boat now pushed water away from the bow, but drew water in from amidships to the stern, giving the propeller bite and helping manoeuvrability. A speed of 17 knots was reached, and the hull shape was found ideal for retracting astern off a bank or beach, and then turning swiftly to go forward again. Delighted, Higgins named the design after Archimedes' great cry of discovery, Eureka.

The Coast Guard's naval architect was deeply impressed by a demonstration Higgins laid on for him of a boat he had built for the Biological Survey Agency. This could maintain full speed in a foot of water with three men and a 60-gallon fuel tank on board. The boat was run "through shallow water, over sandbars and full speed up a seaplane ramp", the architect reported, reversing off, and going on to hop over 3-foot-diameter logs, 5-gallon containers and clumps of water hyacinth.

The customer Higgins wanted, though, but which did not

want him, was the US Navy. As early as 1935, Higgins was fore-seeing the need for fleets of Eurekas, taking the military to war and sustaining them after they were landed. The standard launches the Navy was foisting on the Marines were ponderous – heavy, slow, and liable to broach in surf. They heeled when they were beached, and were difficult to retract, often damaging their propellers in the process.

The Marines wanted a specialist beach landing craft, much as Higgins was urging. The Navy had no intention of looking to a small-time Southerner to provide one. It was used to dealing with the big, patrician shipyards of the northeast, and to getting designs from the BCR, its own Bureau of Construction and Repair. Its senior officers, too, saw little need for landing craft. In the First World War, a million-plus American troops had been landed through the major ports held by their British and French allies. The top brass expected to repeat this if the European conflict resumed.

In 1936, under prompting from the Marines, the Navy did hold competitive trials for a landing craft at Cape May, New Jersey. This was after five boats developed from standard Navy launches foundered in a 4-foot surf in trials in San Clemente. "Navy standard boats are totally unsuited for landing troops, even under moderate surf conditions," the 5th Marines commanding officer complained. "They are in no sense tactical vehicles, lacking in speed and manoeuvrability and are extremely difficult to handle in surf. They do not permit rapid disembarkation of troops at the water's edge ..."

Higgins was not told that the Cape May test was taking place. The entrants, all from the eastern seaboard, included high-speed launches unsuitable for beach landings. Others were modified fishing skiffs, which needed good boat-handling skills to beach in surf, and were normally dragged ashore and turned before being relaunched bows-on into the sea. They were so high forward that

Marines had to drop 10 feet to the beach, and their exposed propellers and rudders tended to dig in when retracting off the beach. In any sort of swell, they had to kedge off, dropping an anchor as they approached the beach, and pulling back on the anchor warp and chain. The BCR produced its own boat. It also had grave defects.

Only Higgins's boat did not, but it was not until May 1938 that the Navy reluctantly contracted him to build a prototype 30-foot landing craft, which he based on the Eureka design. It paid him only US$5,200. The boat cost Higgins US$12,000, and he had to ship it to the Navy yard in Norfolk, Virginia, at further expense to his own near-empty pockets: his net earnings for 1937 were US$241.42. The boat did Higgins proud in testing conditions at Virginia Beach, with a stiff onshore breeze blowing. The observers watched the boat beach without difficulty and without dropping an anchor. Then, to their astonishment, it turned as it withdrew from the beach, and headed back to sea bow-first. For good measure, it also drove over a raft of logs, without damage.

"The Higgins boat gave the best performance under all conditions," the Marine observer reported. "It also has greater power in backing off the beach. Not once was the boat observed having difficulty in retracting."

The Navy still would not have it. "The Higgins boat is too heavy, the speed is too slow," the BCR's representative said. "All Higgins boats have 250 horsepower with accompanying excessive gasoline consumption for the speed obtained." The Navy preferred a modified Bureau boat.

Another contest was held in 1939. Again, the Marines insisted that the Eureka was "the best so far designed". The Navy's Atlantic Squadron was forced to admit that the Higgins was "the best all-around boat for the purpose intended", but added that "the Bureau boat was almost as good".

It took the outbreak of war in Europe to concentrate minds

313

on the frightening absence of American landing craft. In 1940 the Navy ordered the first 64 landing craft, though, reluctant as ever to endorse Higgins, it split the contracts 50:50 between Higgins and the Bureau boats.

Higgins dashed headlong into expansion, on the basis of British and Finnish interest. Luck intervened to sidestep his shortage of capital. He built PT (patrol torpedo) boats for Finland, but Washington refused to allow them to be delivered. So Higgins sold them to the British, and retained the Finns' payment for the time, giving him a half million dollars to work with.

In July 1940 Higgins started building his City Park plant in New Orleans. He was sure that the US would enter the war, and he was confident that when they did they would need his boats by the thousand. His existing plant was already too small, so he bought a marble and granite works, and took over an unused part of a neighbouring cemetery, without any title to do so.

Here he set about creating the world's largest covered boat-building plant, and the first to use mass-production techniques, in which boats were built on a line on the second floor, and then lowered on lifts to railway flatcars below. The plant was not on or near the water. The boats were taken by freight car to the Bayou St John, where they were launched and underwent trials.

Higgins was ferociously, almost foolishly honest about his boats. He was convinced that, though 30 feet was an ideal length for a workboat, 36 feet was much better for a landing craft, giving almost double the capacity at no loss in performance. Despite his need of contracts to fill his new plant, he urged the British not to buy his 30-foot boat. "We would like to have you lose your interest," he wrote to them, with impatient underlinings. "We *do not like this boat* for the reason that the length is too short for the beam." He pointed out that the 36-footer was faster than the smaller boat, though it had the same engine, and suggested the British use it for raiding parties.

The US Navy was by now converting large merchant ships into troop transports. A decision on the landing craft to be carried aboard them could be postponed no longer. The davits on the merchantmen handled 36-foot craft. The Navy adopted the 36-foot Higgins boat as standard in September 1940. After five years' hard lobbying, the Marines had the boat they needed. A lifetime had prepared Higgins for this moment.

He built two boats at his own expense to ensure the best possible hull design. One boat had a V-shaped hull like the classic Eureka. The other had a flatter forward section. Trials at Virginia Beach in October 1940 showed that the V-shape had greater speed, but the flatter bottom was easier to retract off the beach. Handling was more important. An order for 335 of the 36-footers came in November. Higgins built them to the flatter design.

One final refinement was added. An American invasion of the French Caribbean island of Martinique seemed possible in March 1941. It was feared that the Vichy government in German-controlled France would allow it to be used as a German base. Plans for an amphibious assault were mooted.

The Higgins troop landing craft had the same fixed spoon-bill bow as the work-boats. This meant that everything in it – troops, supplies, equipment – had to be unloaded over its relatively high sides. To get jeeps and guns ashore meant replacing the bow with a ramp, and a mechanism to raise and lower it. Disembarking men and materiel would also be made easier. The Marines sent two officers to New Orleans to discuss a vehicle landing craft. One of them, Captain Victor H. Krulak, had been a US Marine Corps observer of the long war the Japanese were fighting in China. In 1937 Krulak had seen and photographed wooden boats with crude ramps being used by the Japanese to land trucks and guns during an attack on the River Yangtze. He sent a file of his observations to the Bureau of Ships. Krulak dug out the file on his return – he found it with a note in the margin that said it had been written by "some nut out in China" – and he brought it to New Orleans with him.

Higgins converted a standard 36-footer into a ramp-bow boat, at his own expense and within a fortnight. It was tested on Lake Pontchartrain on 26 May 1941, with a truck loaded aboard, and then with 36 of his employees embarking and disembarking in the role of assault troops.

Thus was finalized the classic LCVP. The hull was built of oak, pine and mahogany, with a metal ramp, and a beam of 10 feet 10 inches on a length of 36 feet 3 inches. It had a shallow draft, 3 feet at the stern and 2 feet 2 inches forward, so that it could it could power its way to the shoreline with its 225hp diesel. It carried 36 assault troops with their gear and equipment, or a jeep and a dozen men, or 3.6 tons of cargo. It had two .30 calibre machine-guns and a crew of three: a coxswain, an engineer and a crewman. The ramp tilted outwards to open.

The design retained all the virtues of the earlier craft. It could get a platoon ashore from the troopship, extract itself from the beach, leaving it clear for following boats, turn swiftly without broaching, and repeat the trip with more troops or supplies all day.

The Navy also wanted a larger landing craft capable of carrying a tank. In May 1941, in a period of 61 hours, Higgins designed, built and launched a completed 45-foot tank craft. He had an unfinished prototype of a dredge tender that was adapted for the hull, so cross-stitched with welded panels that it was called "Patches". It was the ramp that was challenging. Higgins assembled his key engineers, his draftsmen and his son Ed, and said that nobody was leaving the room until they had settled on an effective ramp and operating system. He kept them there until Graham Haddock, a draftsman of genius, recollected that he had made a model of a tank craft from a cigar box. It had an inward tilting ramp. The problem was solved. Higgins had created the LCM, the landing craft mechanized. The first order, for 50, was placed in June 1941, less than a month after he had begun work on the design.

A big order from the British in the autumn of 1941 convinced Higgins that he needed to build a new plant. The Bureau of Ships thought him reckless. The Navy captain who was head of its shipbuilding division "shook his finger" at Higgins in warning. Higgins ignored him. He was looking at a swampy tract of land on the Industrial Canal as a potential site for the new plant when he heard the news of the attack on Pearl Harbor over his car radio.

Now he was truly in business.

A BRIEF GLANCE AT GENERAL EISENHOWER'S original Victory Plan, sketched out in March 1942, shows the scale of Higgins's production genius. It called for an eventual invasion of France by 30 American and 18 British divisions, almost 1.5 million men, who were to be put ashore between Le Havre and Boulogne by 7,000 landing craft. These had yet to be built, and landing craft were tenth on the US Navy's list of building priorities. No Higgins, no boats.

Higgins ignored obstacles, or knocked them flat. He reacted furiously to criticism. "I don't give a tinker's god damn, except to do something to help win this war," he wrote of Congressional hearings into contracts. "I am no politician. I am awfully busy [with] companies and plants that I built at my own risk and expense with such money that I had or could borrow or go in debt for ..."

The Navy and bureaucrats disliked and mistrusted him. He had a final battle with the Navy in April 1942. The US Army needed a landing craft for its new 30-ton medium tank, urgently, for the coming landings in North Africa. The Bureau of Ships designed its own craft, and ordered 1,100 of them from other yards. Higgins produced his own 50-foot design. The Army demanded a competition, since the order was for its own amphibious operation. It was held off Norfolk, Virginia, on 25 May.

A stiff 20-knot breeze was blowing, with whitecaps and moderate seas, as the rivals headed out past the Cape Henry light, each with a 30-ton tank aboard. As they entered the ocean swell, the Bureau boat was immediately in trouble, down by the bow, and taking on water. Some of the crew bailed furiously. Others re-lashed the tank as the boat began to list. Sailors in lifejackets straddled the weather rail, fearing a capsize. The coxswain saw that he had no hope of making the landing beach. He headed back for the shelter of the harbour.

"The Bureau lighter almost capsized," admitted its observer, Commander Roth. "They couldn't steer it. They just drifted around. Almost lost everybody on board, almost lost the tank."

Only a little spray got aboard the Higgins boat as it made sharp turns through the wave troughs. "Performance was excellent in all respects," the Army observer aboard reported. "The lighter was beached in the surf and the tank ran off onto the beach ... As far as comparisons are concerned, it may be stated that there was no comparison." Roth was forced to agree: "Higgins's lighter came through fine and made the beach ..."

On 26 May, swallowing its pride, the Bureau instructed all the yards it had contracted to build its tank craft to switch to the Higgins design. The Higgins 50-foot LCM thus became the standard tank lighter of the war.

The nation warmed to the "boatbuilder from the bayous" and already saw him as a man of global significance. Higgins, the syndicated columnist Drew Pearson wrote, "is very disagreeable, likes to write insulting letters to admirals, gets on almost everyone's nerves, but is a genius when it comes to small-boat design". He was rebuffed, Pearson said, "because he got on the Navy's nerves" and as a result the "positions of Russia, Great Britain and the United States today have all suffered".

Body and soul went into production. "Bull gangs" of men carried steel plates of up to a ton apiece on their shoulders in a part of the plant too low to use cranes. Even before Pearl Harbor, Higgins had called a steelmaker off the golf course on a Sunday afternoon in peacetime Birmingham, Alabama, to demand steel supplies, which he then bullied the president of the Southern Railway to haul to New Orleans on flatcars at the back of passenger trains. Short of bronze shafting, he had his men plunder it from storage depots in Texas. The boats were built round the engines. When he ran out of supplies, he faced having to shut down the production line, and lay off workers. So he mocked up engines from pieces of pipe, and kept the line running by assembling the boats round them, installing the real engines when they arrived.

Louisiana had little large-scale industry. Thousands of untrained workers were turned into skilled shipbuilders. Higgins paid well, on Henry Ford lines. "I am paying the highest schedule of wages in the United States," he said proudly. "Every time I raise wages, the cost of the finished article goes down, because I have a bunch of men working for me who are Americans." He expected hard work in return. He had doctors, dentists and nurses on duty so that workers could be treated in the plants. Big signs festooned the workshops: "The Guy who Relaxes is Helping the Axis." He put posters of Hitler, Mussolini and Emperor Hirohito in the bathrooms. "Come on in, brother," they said. "Every minute you loaf here helps us plenty." When President Roosevelt visited the plant, Higgins gave him three cheers – after the 125-piece factory band had played "The Higgins Victory March" – and then turned to the workers. "And now," he said, "the president would like to see how quickly you can get back to work."

The sheer speed of manufacture threatened to overwhelm the Navy inspectors. No boat could be signed off to the Navy until it had been accepted by a specialist after a four-hour trial run. When production hit 54 boats a day, there were not enough inspectors to go round. Higgins had each inspector go out with a little fleet of four or five new boats, and hop between them over the four hours.

He wanted, too, to be sure that the crews knew how to use them. A sailor's natural instinct on approaching a shore is to kill boat speed. The coxswain of a landing craft, though, needs to keep his speed up so that the boat rides through the surf and onto the beach. He must keep the engine at full throttle even when the troops are disembarking, to keep square on to the beach, and then go hard astern.

Instinct being best overcome by training, Higgins ran 10-day courses in boat handling, beaching and maintenance. Another course covered loading and unloading tanks and trucks from the bigger ramped craft. Tough exams were held, with each man's grades sent to his commanding officer. Higgins gave graduates a Farewell-to-New-Orleans party at the Roosevelt Hotel's swanky Blue Room.

D-DAY WAS ONE OF SCORES OF LANDINGS made possible by Higgins boats. It was, of course, the largest, and made poignant by memories of Dieppe; those who went ashore in Normandy owed a debt to the dead Canadians, whose sacrifice had convinced the planners to use the immense flexibility the Higgins boats gave them to land on open and more thinly defended beaches.

Higgins was in Chicago, but sent a message to his employees in New Orleans. "This is the day for which we waited," he said. "Now the work of our hands, our hearts and our heads is going to be put to the test ... We may all be inspired by the news that the first landings on the Continent were made by the Allies in our boats."

A celebration was held on Lake Pontchartrain on 23 July 1944, to mark the delivery of the 10,000th boat built by Higgins for the US Navy, a 56-foot tank lighter completed the night before. He had built another 3,000 boats for other services, and for Allied navies, and 25 other American companies were building to his designs, royalty-free.

Guests watched assault craft landing troops a few feet from the viewing platforms, whilst aircraft howled over low, converting the ceremony into a major amphibious exercise. The rugged man thus honoured was now an industrial titan, his payroll worth more to Louisiana than its two great crops, rice and sugar, combined, his plants and yards and depots covering a hundred million square feet of space. Adolf Hitler knew of him: he had been told about Higgins when he asked how the Allies had landed so many men on the beaches. "Truly," he said, "this man is the new Noah."

The exercise was described as a re-enactment of D-Day, but it might as easily have been a Mediterranean or Pacific campaign. The characteristics of amphibious assault were familiar to hundreds of thousands of troops.

Typically, attack transports, APAs, carried 28 Higgins boats apiece and almost 2,000 troops to a position 6,000 yards or so offshore from the landing beaches. The boats were lowered into the sea by the transports' derricks and moored alongside. Nets were lowered for the troops to scramble down into the boats. This was tricky and dangerous if a sea was running. It was essential to be directly over the boat when the end of the net was reached, and not over the water.

"Higgins boats were bobbing up and down alongside the mothership," said Horace T. Jerald, a Marine. "Climbing down the nets was difficult and I kept bouncing off the side of the ship as it swayed side to side." It was important that the men already in the boat kept the net taut. "The weight I was carrying, the equipment and weapon, would drag me to the bottom, very quickly, if I fell into the water. There were men above and below you, all trying to navigate the nets ... There really was no room for mistakes."

The coxswain steered from the port side of the boat, while to starboard, on the other side of the engine, was a cockpit for the .30 calibre machine-gunner. Once they had the troops on board, with their mortars, BARs, bangalore torpedoes and rifles, the coxswain cast off. The controls were easy to use. "The wheel wasn't tilted, like a car's," said a coxswain, John Elsman. "It was flat, and had handles on it, so you could steer more easily. The throttle was a handle like a snow shovel. You'd push it forward to drive the boat ahead, and pull it back for reverse. The further you twisted the handle, the faster the boat went."

The boats then made for a staging area before starting their run in to the beach. By now, the tensions in the boat – "the rocking and pitching, the acrid smell of diesel fumes, and the battle close at hand" – had made many sick. The spray from the ramp-bow was so constant that it soaked cigarettes, and Higgins crewmen were known as tobacco-chewers. Colossal noise and concussions surrounded them. Rocket-firing landing craft poured fire at the enemy, and heavy naval salvoes crashed in from the fleet offshore. "You wouldn't believe it, but we could see a lot of those shells," said Milton Cooper, a coxswain at Guadalcanal. "If you're at a certain angle, you can see them – like tracer bullets – in broad daylight."

When the boat headed in for the landing, the coxswain kept the speed up whilst the crewman looked for sandbars or coral heads. As it hit the beach, the ramp went down. The coxswain kept gunning the engine as the troops dashed out. "You never shut her off," said Cooper. "Just put her in reverse."

The invasion force had now to be serviced with all its needs: fresh troops in, the wounded and shell-shocked out, rations, ammunition. Movements were often after dark. "One night, we got stuck on a coral reef for a while," Cooper said. "Our decks were stacked with boxes of canned food. The Japanese started shooting at us. I'll never forget the sound of those cans exploding, while I kept working the boat, back and forth, to get us off that reef."

An element of surprise was often preserved, as in Normandy. Not always, however, did the Higgins boats succeed in avoiding the sort of dug-in and expectant enemy who had awaited the Canadians at Dieppe. The Japanese sometimes guessed which island the Americans would invade next with enough time to make thorough preparations. They did so to greatest effect at Iwo Jima. This had its irony, for the Americans in fact had no compelling reason to bother with the sulphurous, black-sand island. They could have bypassed it, leaving its garrison to rot, too distant for the weakened Japanese to succour by air or sea.

Invade it they did, though, and the Japanese had started preparing for them in the summer of 1944. Much of the work was underground. This was doubly dangerous, because it negated the prodigious American strength in bombers and heavy naval guns, and, as the defences were unseen, tempted the Americans to underestimate the Japanese strength. Mining engineers cut more than 11 miles of deep tunnels in the black volcanic rock to link strongpoints and subterranean chambers capable of holding 300 men safe from surface attack. A vast cavern 50 yards long and 20 yards wide was excavated 65 feet below the surface for the main communications centre. The island's dark volcanic ash made a tough concrete when mixed with cement, for pillboxes, blockhouses and blast walls for dug-in tanks.

The civilians on the island were evacuated, replaced by a garrison of more than 20,000 men, with a wealth of large-calibre guns concealed in the high ground above the beaches and in the honeycombed tunnels of Mount Suribachi, the sulphurous, brooding centre of a submerged volcanic caldera whose dry slopes of ash and clinker looked far out to sea.

A Japanese naval aircraft spotted an invasion fleet of 170 ships steaming northwest from Saipan on 13 February 1945. The

Japanese awaited, in a strength and a state of readiness of which the Americans were completely unaware. They expected the fighting to be over in five days, with light casualties. Three of the Marine divisions assigned for Iwo Jima were scheduled in an early plan to be ready to be used again 40 days later to attack Okinawa.

At 02:00 on 19 February, American battleships began pounding Iwo Jima with salvo after salvo. A hundred bombers joined in the softening up at dawn. At 08:30, the first Higgins boats hit the black beach line. The Japanese let them get 500 yards from the sea before hitting them with their concealed arsenal. They had 361 guns of 75mm and larger, 33 naval guns, a dozen 320mm mortars, and scores of medium and light mortars. There were 70 rocket guns with their crews on the island, one of them a giant that hurled a 250kg warhead for over 4 miles.

Thirty thousand Marines went ashore in the first waves. The killing by the shore was continuing when Horace Jerald went in on his Higgins boat on the fourth day of the landings. "Mount Suribachi towered above us," he said. "The battleships fired salvo after salvo at the Japanese dug in on it. The crescendo of the battle increased as we shortened the distance to the beach." Men and equipment, supplies, ammunition, guns were piled up everywhere, as the beach master frantically flagged the Higgins boats where to beach. Mortar rounds hit the black sand terraces above the beach.

The surf lapped at their legs, and their feet sank into the black sand. Jerald came across his first dead Marine. The man had taken a direct hit, and was scattered in a radius of several feet, the upper torso separated from the lower body, the head still securely fastened within the helmet, the eyes wide open in surprise and horror. Jerald had seen mutilations before, but nothing like this. He stood staring. "When reality took over, I started to run," he said. "I ran faster, changing my course as I ran. I ran headlong into battle, my lungs on fire as I took long, deep breaths. I made every attempt to keep going, but finally I fell to my knees. There was an uncontrollable fear rising up in me ..."

When he looked along the beach, he saw his Higgins boat and the dead in the strong surf. The guns on Mount Suribachi were pounding the landings. "I could see men stumbling, falling, rising again, then fall and remain still," he said. "Others hobbled for cover. The beach was littered with the dead and dying. Equipment lay swamped, boats were capsized. The beach was a mess, an absolute mess. I rolled over again, dug my feet into the loose, black volcanic sand and slid back another foot."

A post was stuck in the beach above him. It had a sign on it printed in Japanese and English, vowing that the Japanese would kill ten Marines for each of them before they died. "As I looked around me," he said, "I began to wonder if the sign was right ..."

IT WAS THE RARITY OF SUCH SIGNS, indications that the defenders had had advance warning, that give Higgins his status. The enemy, Japanese or German, very seldom knew where these huge quantities of men and supplies were going to come ashore, such was the flexibility that the landing craft gave to Allied planners.

In 1939 the man himself had been, in military terms, at most a corporal amid the generals of industry, a small-timer who catered for fur trappers and oil prospectors, and, for a time, rum runners.

In his Thanksgiving talk to the nation in 1944, referring to this same person, General Eisenhower exhorted Americans: "Let us thank God for Higgins Industries, management and labour, which gave us the landing boats with which to conduct our campaigns." By the time the war was over, Higgins had delivered 20,094 boats.

The battle honours of the Higgins boats include North Africa, Sicily, Italy, Normandy, the Philippines, and islands from the Solomons, the Gilberts, the Marshals, the Marianas ... Guadalcanal, Vella Lavella, Bougainville, Tarawa, Kwajalein, Eniwetok,

Saipan, Iwo Jima, Okinawa ... ever closer to Japan. These battles could not have taken place where they did without Higgins. That is the measure of the man and his boat.

PEACE WAS NOT KIND TO HIGGINS. To keep his plants going, he came up with products for the leisure market. They included ingenious tent-trailers that were towed behind cars, like substitute caravans, and a range of volume-built cabin cruisers and sports boats, elegant and well-made, that might have sold in large quantities in the more affluent 1950s, but were ahead of their time in 1947.

Higgins also made shallow-draft freighters, specially designed for a steamship service he wanted to run from the Gulf Coast to Central and South America. He had plans to develop a Higgins helicopter. But a hurricane in September 1947 caused millions of dollars in structural damage and wrecked pleasure boats at his plants. Money haemorrhaged out of the business. By the end of 1948, the business was down to 75 men. The Korean War saw a pick-up in naval orders, but Higgins died in 1952. By then he was almost a forgotten man, and so – a fine biography by Jerry E. Strahan apart – he has remained.

14 · KONFRONTASI

The sergeant major who defied a president

The counterattack is an essential part of defence –
"a swift and vigorous assumption of the offensive ...
is the most brilliant point in the defensive"
(BOOK VI, CHAPTER V). This "flashing sword of vengeance"
is wielded here by a man who, severely wounded in
the head and half-blinded, was himself *in extremis*.

THE BORNEO JUNGLE ✳ 0° 55′ N 110° 28′ E ✳ 27 APRIL 1965

BEFORE THE BATTLE, HIS FELLOW paratroopers called John Williams "Drummie", because he had enlisted as a boy bandsman when he was 15. After it, because a black swatch of cloth now covered his eye socket, they called him "Patch".

Williams had never been a drummer – he was taught the French horn at the Army School of Music – but he picked up the nickname after he transferred from the regimental band to the infantry service. He was a natural soldier, and soon a sergeant.

By the late spring of 1965, he was a company sergeant major in the 2nd Battalion of the Parachute Regiment. The seasons meant little where he was posted, though. He was almost astride the equator, on the vast and still wild island of Borneo. Had he been a few miles further south, over the border that separates the East Malaysian state of Sarawak from Indonesian Kalimantan, he would have changed hemispheres, and it would have been autumn.

Williams was serving at a base camp in thick jungle near a kampong – a village of thatched longhouses – called Plaman Mapu. It was about 50 miles southeast of Sarawak's sleepy capital, Kuching: a few minutes by helicopter, or a three-day journey by foot and dugout.

An undeclared war was taking place along the border with Kalimantan. President Sukarno of Indonesia called it *konfrontasi*. He had inherited the Dutch East Indies, including the main island of Java and the Dutch slice of Borneo, on independence from Holland. The old British-administered territories – the federated states of mainland Malaya, plus Sarawak and Sabah in North Borneo – had joined together to form the new Federation of Malaysia.

Sukarno saw Malaysia as a conspiracy by the *Neokolim* – the British neocolonialists – to preserve their power. He vowed *konfrontasi*, armed confrontation, with the new nation. In a ranting speech in May 1964, he had sworn to crush Malaysia "before the sun rises on 1 January".

His attempts to infiltrate troops over the Malacca Straits into mainland Malaysia collapsed in farce and disaster. In the east, in Borneo, he sent guerrilla forces over the long and ill-defined jungle border with Sarawak and Sabah to foment rebellion among the tribesmen. They had no love for Sukarno, however, and a Commonwealth force of divisional strength, with British, Australian, Ghurkha, Malaysian and New Zealand units, played havoc with his attempts at sowing *konfrontasi* with irregulars.

Humiliated, Sukarno began to attack positions and mount ambushes along the border with crack troops from the TNI, the Indonesian regular army. British paratroops began their tour in Sarawak in February 1965. They established a headquarters at

Balai Ringin 60 miles from Kuching. Rifle companies in forward positions hacked out the virgin jungle to make heavily fortified static bases. The surrounding trees were cleared to give open fields of fire. The approaches were sown with wire, mines and panjis, sticks sharpened to such a point that they could penetrate a boot.

The only communication was by air drop or helicopter. Each base had a landing zone and a drop zone. There were also roping areas in the surrounding jungle, where troops could rope down from helicopters in an emergency. The camps were all within 2,000 yards of the Indonesian border – which British troops were covertly crossing, in the secret Operation Claret. Patrols of paratroops went out from the bases for three to ten days at a time, seeking to break up and ambush the Indonesian groups before they got into the tribal areas and kampongs.

B Company of 2 Para had only been in the Plaman Mapu base for a few days when signs of increasing enemy activity were noticed. Groups of 50 to 60 men were making incursions. Large numbers of Indonesians were seen in kampongs on their side of the border. Discarded ammunition wrappers revealed that the Indonesians were armed with Yugoslav-made 44mm rocket launchers. The paratroops found positions cut out of the jungle on the slopes above the camp, sites for rocket launchers or machine-guns. Fresh pony tracks were found, their depth showing that heavy loads were being carried.

A battalion of Indonesian RPKAD para-commandos moved up on 26 April. At 18:30, tribesmen later confirmed, two companies passed through Tembawang, a kampong just to the west of Plaman Mapu. A third company was holding a base just over the border, whilst a fourth was in ambush positions to catch any British troops who might advance.

The British position was vulnerable. It was overlooked by high hills, thick with jungle. Most of the company and the officers were out on patrols, too distant to offer support. The base was manned by an understrength platoon of 15 young soldiers, who had just completed jungle warfare training in Malaya. With them were Captain Nick Thompson, "Drummie" Williams, a mortar section, and some "cooks and bottle washers" from HQ staff.

During the early part of the night, two companies of Indonesian para-commandos made a close approach to the camp. Outnumbering the defenders by more than ten to one, they formed up in a deep gully close to the southwest perimeter. Two Very lights burst out of the rain-swept darkness at 04:45 on 27 April. An all-out assault broke on the camp, rifle grenades and machine-guns firing while 44mm rockets and 50mm mortar bombs exploded with flashes and bursts of earth. The noise echoed round the trees, and shrill bird calls began to mingle with the shouts of the men.

The defenders were barely getting into position when an incoming rocket hit the mortar pit. It killed one of the section, and badly wounded another. Williams was pulling his webbing on as he dashed for the command post, getting the wounded man to the aid post on the way. The Indonesians penetrated the perimeter wire, and took the mortar pit. They concentrated their fire on the British machine-guns, and succeeded in silencing one of them. At this critical moment, Williams realized that the camp would be overrun unless there was a counterattack to retake the lost mortar position. Williams led the counterattack, with Captain Thompson and a section following. A mortar bomb exploded among them, and Thompson and half the section were badly wounded. Williams was left with only two men – one of the them a cook-corporal – to dislodge at least 30 Indonesians.

Williams detailed Corporal Baughan, the acting platoon sergeant, to form a section counterattack. A sharp fight developed at close range. Baughan's paratroops were pinned down, three of them wounded. Williams now ran across open ground under heavy fire to man the silenced machine-gun. This brought the full weight of the Indonesian automatic and rocket fire onto him.

He was hit by splinters, suffering serious head wounds. One splinter tore into his left eye, half-removing it from its socket.

The Indonesians attacked the machine-gun bunker in platoon strength, coming close enough to throw grenades. Williams fought them off, though one fell two yards in front of him, and incoming fire smashed a radio set next to him, and twice ricocheted off his machine-gun. Despite this, and the loss of his eye, he fired steadily and accurately into the mortar pit, pinning down the Indonesians so that Baughan was able to continue his counterattack and clear the position.

A lull followed as the Indonesians regrouped in some dead ground 40 yards down the slope. Williams refused to have his wounds attended to. He helped to drag boxes of hand grenades to the perimeter. Only 15 British defenders were still on their feet. As the second assault began, the Indonesians were met by mortar fire and a stream of grenades. There was a desperate edge to their efforts. They knew that British aircraft and helicopters would arrive at first light. One of them, badly wounded in the leg, tied a rough tourniquet and continued to advance with a heavy rocket launcher.

As dawn broke, the attacks died away. The paratroopers heard the Indonesians moving away down the slope, firing mortar rounds from time to time to cover their retreat. Williams called for a clearing patrol to check that the jungle round the base was secured for helicopter landings. The teenagers from the training platoon volunteered to a man.

The medical officer aboard the first helicopter in was shocked to see Williams still on his feet, still dressed in just his trousers and webbing, with his head covered in blood, and his eye resting on his cheekbone. He finally allowed himself to be evacuated from the camp.

The paths the Indonesians took back across the border were marked by abandoned equipment and trails of blood. Villagers in the kampongs reported seeing long columns carrying dead and wounded. It was found later that the Indonesians had suffered 300 casualties. The British found few bodies because the dead and severely wounded had been thrown into a nearby river that flowed across the border.

Major General George Lea, the director of operations in Borneo, flew in within a few hours. He ordered all jungle bases to be moved to higher ground immediately, to improve their security. He realized how close a thing the battle had been. "Had we been turned out of Plaman Mapu," he said, "our little faces would have been very, very red."

In fact, though the paratroops went on to defeat a minor infiltration at Mongkus in May, Plaman Mapu was the critical *konfrontasi* battle. Never again were the Indonesians to cross the border in strength. Through his decisive leadership, and courage, Williams effectively brought Sukarno's campaign to a close. The threat to the integrity of Malaysia was ended, by a company sergeant major.

Williams recovered from his wounds, and was awarded the Distinguished Conduct Medal. The citation said that he "inspired his men with unbreakable fortitude though blinded in one eye during the fight". "Patch" Williams later served as regimental sergeant major, and as a lieutenant colonel staff quartermaster. He died in 2002.

15 · PETALS OF RARE BEAUTY

A sublieutenant outwits
Admiral Dönitz

The ability to think clearly under stress is an
important quality, for: "Presence of mind in a region of
the unexpected like war must act a great part ..."
(BOOK I, CHAPTER II).

THE NORTH ATLANTIC * 60° N 33° W * 9 MAY 1941

THE 43 SHIPS IN OUTBOUND CONVOY 318 were about 400 miles
south of Iceland on 7 May 1941 when they were sighted by a
U-boat. The captain, Herbert Kuppisch, sent a contact report, and
six other U-boats were sent to the scene. Kuppisch himself attacked
the convoy before the others arrived. He sank two ships, but his
submarine was itself badly damaged by the convoy escorts.

Adalbert Schnee in U-201 and Fritz-Julius Lemp in U-110 joined
the hunt. On the morning of 9 May they were waiting, ahead and
submerged, for the convoy. At 28, Lemp was already a veteran
Kapitänleutnant, with a Knight's Cross and ten war patrols and
19 ships totalling 96,314 tons to his credit. He had a devil-may-care
streak. He had claimed the first U-boat victim of the war, when, less
than twelve hours after war was declared, he had seen a large
blacked-out ship ziz-zagging at speed, which he said he thought

was an armed merchant cruiser. After he had sunk her, it turned out she had been the *Athenia*, a passenger liner, with many Americans on board, and 112 passengers were drowned.

Now, as they waited for the convoy, he and Schnee discussed tactics. Lemp wanted to attack that evening, hoping the convoy escorts would have left for Iceland, leaving the convoy to sail on its own for North American ports. Schnee feared that they might lose it and wanted to attack at once. The convoy had already made a sharp change in course, after an Admiralty warning. The British could not yet read German naval code, but they got a rough direction-finding fix on the U-boats' radios.

They agreed to attack in the morning. Lemp would move in first, with Schnee exploiting the confusion he caused. By noon, U-110 was at periscope depth on the convoy's right flank. Lemp selected his victims and began the ritual: *"Rohe eins, fertig?" "Rohe eins fertig." "Los!"* "Tube one, ready?" "Ready." "Fire!" He fired three torpedoes and heard an explosion. It was a hit. The leading merchantman, the *Esmond*, took the torpedo and sank bow down. A second ship was also hit. The fourth torpedo never left its tube. Despite that, seawater was still pumped into tanks in the bow to rebalance the boat's trim. The crew concentrated on the problem, rather than evasive action.

The British destroyers *Bulldog* and *Broadway*, and the corvette *Aubrietia*, were hunting for Lemp. They all got firm sonar contacts and started their attacks. *Aubrietia* spotted U-110's periscope. Lemp's crew heard the noise of her propellers coming in, and then the splashes from a pattern of depth charges, and then great explosions that shook the submarine violently. The diving gauges were smashed, the electric motors damaged, as were the diving planes and the rudder. The batteries gave off chlorine. A loud hissing indicated a compressed-air leak, a terrifying noise, for the air was used to blow water out of the tanks, and if it was gone the submarine would never surface again. With the depth gauges out, Lemp could not tell whether the submarine was in danger of surfacing, or was sinking further.

She suddenly surfaced. Ruptured valves may have blown the tanks. "Last stop. All out!" Lemp said, as casually as a bus conductor at the end of his route. Lemp was first on to the bridge to see three British warships bearing down and firing at him. He ordered "Abandon ship." A radio operator asked the captain if he should destroy the encoding machine and the code books. Lemp told him the boat was sinking. The 47-man crew struggled to get off. The engineer opened the vents so that the tanks would flood. Then he and Lemp jumped into the water. They assumed U-110 would soon slip away. When she did not, Lemp called out that he was going to swim back to do what he could to scuttle her. No one saw him again.

The escort commander, Joe Baker-Cresswell on *Bulldog*, had intended ramming U-110 to sink her. He realized she was more valuable afloat, and put his engines full astern to stop 100 yards short of her. U-110's crew were rescued by *Aubrietia*. Baker-Cresswell chose a young sublieutenant, David Balme, to take a boarding party to the submarine, to collect her signals books and "anything useful".

Balme had joined the Navy as a 13-year-old cadet at Dartmouth. He was now 20. He left *Bulldog* at 12:45. He had a crew of eight in the whaler. *Bulldog* was lying to windward of the U-boat and there was a heavy swell running. To save time, he made for the weather side of the submarine, though this slammed the whaler against the hull on the swell. "A submarine in a calm sea is difficult to board as it is so bulbous," he wrote later. "In a rough sea it's even more difficult. My bowman jumped onto the U-boat and I walked up to the bow over the oarsmen and so aboard and then I got my revolver out of its holster." He found numerous holes in the conning tower from *Bulldog*'s 3-inch gun and Pom-Pom anti-aircraft gun.

"I was duty bound to climb that conning tower, and descend into – what?" he said. "Remains of the German crew to greet me? Or scuttling charges rigged to explode as I opened the hatch? … 'Stop thinking. Do it,' I told myself." Still holding his Webley revolver, he put on his gas mask, in case of leaking chlorine.

The hatch at the top of the conning tower was closed. He put his revolver back into its holster. He needed both hands to climb 15 feet down the ladder, and the hatch was only 2 feet wide. "I felt there must be someone below trying to open the seacocks, or setting the detonating charges," he said. "But no one was there."

The control room was deserted. All the lighting was on. A large splinter from the conning tower lay on the deck. "The most eerie feeling was the complete silence except for an ominous hissing sound which was either from the batteries or a leak in the hull," Balme recalled. "The secondary lighting gave a rather dim, ghostly effect." There was no sign of chlorine, so he discarded his gas mask. He also put his revolver down. It "seemed now more of a danger than an asset".

She was new and a fine ship, he found, spotlessly clean throughout. The ward room was finished in light wood. U-110 had plenty of tinned ham, corned beef, cigars and cigarettes. The galley, forward of the wireless room, was "magnificent". He noticed a plate of shrimps in the wireless room, and a plate of mashed potatoes in the engine room, as if action stations had been sounded suddenly whilst dinner was being taken from the galley to the crew's space.

He rifled through the officers' clothes drawers. He found a sub-machine-gun in one drawer, and an armour-piercing rifle in another, together with very good clothing and well-designed foul-weather gear.

Gear and books were strewn all over the place. Balme got the boarding party down the ladders and formed a chain of men to pass up all the books and charts he found. Speed was "essential due to the possibility of the submarine sinking". The U-110 was low in the water at the stern, with the bow now sticking out of the water. It was still dry throughout, but Balme knew that would change in an instant if scuttling charges had been fixed. Large bangs echoed through the submarine as the *Bulldog*'s whaler was thumped against the hull by the waves. The whaler began to break up with the violence of the blows, then filled with water and sank.

There were reports of periscope sightings in the vicinity, and *Bulldog* took off after the suspected submarine. "Throughout, our escort vessels were attacking U-boats with depth charges, and my fear was that their explosions, which felt very close, would set off the detonating charges," Balme wrote. He sent all books up to the conning tower, "except obvious reading books", thus rescuing many comparatively useless navigation books. All the charts from the chart table were passed up the chain, along with signals books and log books. Balme had a telegraphist, Alan Osborne Long, with him. He sent Long to the wireless room, just forward of the control room on the starboard side.

Long was soon back. He asked Balme to come with him. "There's something rather interesting I want to show you," he said. The wireless room was in perfect condition, Balme said: "No one had so much as tried to destroy books or apparatus. Codebooks, signal logs, pay books and general correspondence were all intact." He found it impressive, "far less complicated than our own". The sets were more compact and did not have the usual excess of switches, plug holes and knobs.

What had caught Long's eye was an odd-looking machine, "plugged in and as though in actual use when abandoned". It looked like a typewriter, but it had no roller or sheet feed for paper. When Long pressed a key, a light would illuminate a letter on a display panel, but a different letter from the one that Long was pressing. The machine was fastened to a table by four screws. Long and Balme unscrewed it, and sent it up through the hatch.

Bulldog returned from U-boat chasing, and sent over her motor-boat, with some sandwiches. The men starting loading the papers. Baker-Cresswell looked on in horror as a wave caught one man with an armful of papers as he walked along the submarine's deck. When the wave passed, the man was still there, hanging on to the papers for grim death. Balme ate a sandwich sitting at Lemp's roll-top desk on the submarine. In the desk he found an Iron Cross, some photographs of Lemp's family, and a sealed envelope. Balme carefully put them in his pocket.

Attempts were made to get U-110 moving under her own power, but these failed. Balme tried to rig a towline on board, but *Bulldog* was drifting to leeward faster in the stiff wind than the submarine, and the line kept parting. *Bulldog* then sighted a periscope and went off on another anti-submarine sweep. Balme had been on board the submarine for five hours now. She was going down very slowly by the stern, and had taken on a list to port. He thought the port ballast tank might be flooding.

Bulldog returned, and with extra hands and shackles a towline was successfully secured. Balme, and his boarding party and their spoil, returned to the destroyer.

At about 18:30, *Bulldog* began towing U-110 towards Iceland. When Baker-Cresswell informed the Admiralty of events, he was told to refer to "Operation Primrose" in all future signals. References were to be prefaced "Top Secret" and signals made only in cipher. All ships at the scene were instructed that "Operation Primrose is to be treated with the greatest secrecy and as few people allowed to know as possible." A submarine expert was being sent out immediately by Sunderland flying boat.

IN THE EVENT, A GALE BLEW UP NEXT morning. U-110's stern was noticeably lower in the water. At 11:00, her bow reared suddenly until it was near vertical. Then she slid down stern-first beneath the grey Atlantic. The tow rope was cut. Baker-Cresswell thought it a tragedy, "one of the worst moments of my life". The Admiralty was more phlegmatic. "Primrose having sunk makes it no Repeat no less important that the fact of having had her in our hands should remain secret. This fact to be rigorously impressed on all who have any knowledge of the facts …"

Bulldog arrived in Iceland before dawn on 11 May. She refuelled and sailed on for Scapa Flow, arriving the following evening. Two naval intelligence officers boarded her. Baker-Cresswell showed them boxes of documents and the strange machine. "Oh surely not this!" one of them exclaimed. "We have waited the whole war for one of these." They told the captain that it was probably as well that he had lost the U-110. It would help keep the incident secret.

The intelligence officers left for Bletchley Park, the top-secret centre for British cryptologists, including those cracking the codes of Enigma cipher machines. They worked in huts in the grounds of the shabby Victorian mansion in Buckinghamshire. The Enigma machines were the backbone of German military and naval communications. The Enigma naval code was of piercing importance to the U-boat war.

Admiral Karl Dönitz had evolved *Rudeltaktik* or wolf-pack tactics for his U-boats. Instead of operating as lone wolves, as submarines always had before, he put them in packs so that they could overwhelm even heavily escorted convoys. In 1940 and the first part of 1941, known as the "happy time" to the U-boat aces, the campaign seemed on the way to meeting Dönitz's aim of knocking the British out of the war. Between July and October 1940, over 220 ships were sunk. On 1 December, convoy HX-90 lost ten ships. A month before U-110 was sunk, convoy SC-26 had also had ten ships destroyed.

Communications were essential to the wolf packs. They would lie in a line across the convoy routes. Once a captain spotted a convoy, the position was radioed to the other waiting U-boats, and the pack converged on its victims. The British were picking up the radio transmissions, but they could not break the code, encrypted by Enigma machines, which used three or four wheels whose settings were changed daily to create the cipher.

Balme's haul was of immense value. He brought back an intact Enigma machine. He provided the key to *Offizier* messages, important messages, enciphered on the Enigma machine using the U-boat officer's settings, and then enciphered again on the settings used by the Enigma operators. The envelope he found in Lemp's desk included the special settings for June 1941. He had found the short signal codebook used by U-boats, and the short weather-report codebook used by U-boat crews to send weather reports back to base. These were later also of great use in breaking the naval Enigma code.

King George VI personally decorated Balme later that summer, referring to the taking of U-110 as "the most significant event of the war at sea". It was not quite that. The breaking of Enigma was a continuous process, upon which the outcome of the Battle of the Atlantic depended, and that outcome would in turn dictate the degree to which the Canadians and the Americans were able to aid the Allied cause in Europe. No single mind, even one as filled with genius as the cryptographer, mathematician and computer pioneer Alan Turing, can be credited with so vast an enterprise. Nor can any single event. It was an ongoing process. The capture of German weather ships proved equally vital as the capture of U-boats. But David Balme's action most certainly deserved the congratulations on Operation Primrose that the First Sea Lord sent to *Bulldog* as she sailed back to Iceland: "The petals of your flower are of rare beauty."

Balme survived the war, and retired from the Royal Navy as a lieutenant commander.

Bibliography

1· THE STURMPIONIER

For a detailed account of the whole campaign with excellent maps see:

Karl-Heinz Frieser, *The Blitzkrieg Legend* (Annapolis MD 2005)

A classic French account is:

Paul Beren and Bernard Isselin, *Les panzers passent la Meuse* (Paris 1967)

ALSO:

André Beaufre, *The Fall of France* (New York 1968)

Jacques Benoist-Mechin, *Sixty Days that Shook the West* (New York 1963)

Marc Bloch, *Strange Defeat* (London 1999)

Len Deighton, *Blitzkrieg* (London 1980)

Robert Allan Doughty, *The Breaking Point: Sedan & the Fall of France* (Hamden CN 1990)

Jacques Enfer, *10 mai–25 juin: France 1940* (Paris 1990)

Heinz Guderian, *Panzer Leader* (London 1952)

Alistair Horne, *To Lose a Battle: France 1940* (London 1969)

2· ACTION, ACTION, ACTION! PROMPTITUDE!

For Edwardes's own detailed account see:

Herbert Edwardes, *A Year on the Punjab Frontier* (London 1851)

ALSO:

Charles Allen, *Soldier Sahibs* (London 2000)

Saul David, *Victoria's Wars* (London 2007)

Lady Edwardes, *Memorials of the Life and Letters of Maj Gen Sir Herbert Edwardes by his wife* (London 1886)

Roger Hudson, ed., *Raj: An Eyewitness History of the British in India* (London 1999)

James Lawrence, *Raj: The Making and Unmaking of British India* (London 1999)

3· PAVLOV'S HOUSE

Antony Beevor, *Stalingrad* (London 1999)

Seweryn Bialer, *Stalin and his Generals* (London 1970)

V. I. Chuikov, *The Beginning of the Road* (London 1963)

Alan Clark, *Barbarossa* (London 1965)

William Craig, *Enemy at the Gates* (New York 1973)

John Erickson, *The Road to Stalingrad* (London 1983)

John Erickson, *The Road to Berlin* (London 1983)

Curzio Malaparte, *The Volga Rises in Europe* (London 1958)

Brian Moynahan, *The Claws of the Bear* (Boston 1989)

Alexander Werth, *Russia at War* (London 1964)

4 · THE FIELD MARSHAL, THE PRIME MINISTER AND THE SERGEANT

Pierre Gioliotto, *Histoire de la Milice* (Paris 2002)

John Keegan, *The First World War* (London 1999)

Erich Ludendorff, *My War Memories* (Uckfield 2005)

Brian Moynahan, *The French Century* (Paris 2007)

Hugues Viel, *Darnand: La Mort en chantant* (Paris 1996)

David T. Zabecki, *The German 1918 Offensives* (Oxford 2005)

5 · THE BIPLANE AND THE BATTLESHIP

Robert Ballard, *The Discovery of the Bismarck* (Toronto 1990)

C.S. Forester, *Hunting the Bismarck* (London 1959)

Ludovic Kennedy, *Pursuit: The Sinking of the Bismarck* (London 1974)

John Godley Kilbracken, *Bring Back my Stringbag* (London 1996)

Charles Lamb, *War in a Stringbag* (London 1977)

Burkhard Baron von Mullenheim-Rechberg, *Battleship Bismarck, A Survivor's Story* (Annapolis 1980)

Graham Rhys-Jones, *The Loss of the Bismarck: an Avoidable Disaster* (London 1999)

Stephen Roskill, *The War at Sea* (London 1954–61)

6 · CAST NET – THROW SPEAR

Bernard Fall, *Street Without Joy* (Harrisburg PA 1963)

David Halberstam, *The Making of a Quagmire* (New York 1965)

Stanley Karnow, *Vietnam: A History* (New York 1983)

Philip Knightley, *The First Casualty* (London 1975)

Le Hong Linh, *Ap Bac: Major Victories of the South Vietnamese Patriotic Forces* (Hanoi 1965)

Charlie Ostick's account of the battle is on the Vietnam Helicopter Pilots' Association website, www.vhpa.org

Neil Sheehan, *A Bright Shining Lie* (London 1989)

David M. Toczek, *The Battle of Ap Bac: They Did Everything but Learn from It* (Westport CN 2001)

7 · THE ONE-SHOT WONDER

Stephen E. Ambrose, *Pegasus Bridge* (London 2003)

Richard Gale, *With the 6th Airborne Division in Normandy* (London 1948)

Max Hastings, *Overlord: D-Day and the Battle for Normandy* (London 1999)

David Howarth, *Dawn of D-Day* (London 1959)

John Keegan, *Six Armies in Normandy* (London 2004)

Cornelius Ryan, *The Longest Day* (London 1959)

8 · THE BEARER OF THE EAGLE

Julius Caesar, *The Gallic War* (London 1984)

Stephen Dando-Collins, *Caesar's Legion: Julius Caesar's Elite Tenth Legion* (Hoboken NJ 2004)

Adrian Goldsworthy, *Caesar: The Life of a Colossus* (London 2006)

John Peddie, *Conquest: The Roman Invasion of Britain* (Stroud 2005)

9 · THE BICYCLE BLITZKRIEG

Noel Barber, *The Fall of Singapore* (London 1968)

Stanley Falk, *Seventy Days to Singapore: The Malayan Campaign* (London 1975)

Jim Fitzpatrick, *The Bicycle in Wartime* (Washington D.C. 1998)

Colin Smith, *Singapore Burning* (London 2005)

Manosubu Tsuji, *Japan's Greatest Victory, Britain's Worst Defeat* (New York 1997)

10 · THE LOOSE CANNON OF YOM KIPPUR

Jerry Asher, *Duel for the Golan* (Pacifica CA 1987)

Simon Dunstan and Kevin Lyles, *The Yom Kippur War: Golan Heights* (London 2003)

Chaim Herzog, *The War of Atonement* (Tel Aviv 1975)

Insight Team of *The Sunday Times*, *Insight on the Middle East* (London 1974)

Walter Laquer, ed., *The Israel-Arab Reader* (London 2001)

Abraham Rabinovich, *The Yom Kippur War* (New York 2004)

Patrick Seale, *Assad: The Struggle for the Middle East* (Berkeley 1988)

11 · BLOOD FOR ELEANOR!

James Bradley, *Flags of our Fathers* (New York 2000)

Richard B. Frank, *Guadalcanal: the Landmark Battle* (London 1992)

Robert Leckie, *Challenge of the Pacific* (New York 1999)

Samuel Eliot Morison, *The Struggle For Guadalcanal, History of US Naval Operations In World War II*, Vol. 5 (Chicago IL 1960)

Jim Prosser, *I'm Staying With My Boys: The Heroic Life of Sgt John Basilone* (USMC Hilton Head 2004)

Don Richter, *Where the Sun Stood Still* (Agoura Hills CA 1992)

12 · KILLED COLD-DEDE AND CASTEN OVER-BORDES

Jean Froissart, *The Chronicles of Froissart* (London 1904)

13 · "TRULY, THIS MAN IS THE NEW NOAH"

Jerry E. Strahan, *Andrew Jackson Higgins and the Boats that Won World War II* (Baton Rouge LA 1998)

Anne Cipriano Venzon, *From Whaleboats to Amphibious Warfare* (Westport CT 2003)

14 · KONFRONTASI

Nick van der Bijl, *Confrontation: The War with Indonesia* (London 2007)

Peter Harclerode, *Para!: Fifty Years of the Parachute Regiment* (London 1996)

Will Fowler and Kevin Lyles, *Britain's Secret War: The Indonesian Confrontation 1962–66* (Oxford 2006)

Harold James and Denis Sheil-Small, *The Undeclared War* (Towota NJ 1971)

15 · PETALS OF RARE BEAUTY

David Balme, 'Operation Primrose: the Story of the Capture of the Enigma Cipher Machine from U-110', in *Military History Journal* Vol. 9 No. 3

Stephen Roskill, *The Secret Capture* (London 1959)

Hugh Sebag-Montefiore, *Enigma: The Battle for the Code* (London 2001)

David Fairbank White, *Bitter Ocean: The History of the Battle of the Atlantic* (New York 2006)

Frederick Winterbotham, *The Ultra Secret* (London 1974)

John Winton, *Ultra at Sea* (London 1988)

Index